Anarchism and Workers' Self-Management in Revolutionary Spain

Anarchism and Workers' Self-Management in Revolutionary Spain

FRANK MINTZ
Translated by Paul Sharkey

Anarchism and Workers' Self-Management in Revolutionary Spain

© 2013 Frank Mintz. This edition © 2013 AK Press (Oakland, Edinburgh, Baltimore). Prologue © 2010 Chris Ealham.

ISBN: 978-1-84935-078-5 | eBook ISBN: 978-1-84935-079-2
Library of Congress Control Number: 2011936251

AK Press
674-A 23rd Street
Oakland, CA 94612
USA
www.akpress.org
akpress@akpress.org

AK Press
PO Box 12766
Edinburgh EH8 9YE
Scotland
www.akuk.com
ak@akedin.demon.co.uk

The above addresses would be delighted to provide you with the latest AK Press distribution catalog, which features the several thousand books, pamphlets, zines, audio and video products, and stylish apparel published and/or distributed by AK Press. Alternatively, visit our websites for the complete catalog, latest news, and secure ordering.

Visit us at:
www.akpress.org
www.akuk.com
www.revolutionbythebook.akpress.org

The production of this book was made possible in part by a generous donation from the Anarchist Archives Project.

Contents

Prologue, by Chris Ealham 1

Introduction
Self-Management and Anarcho-Syndicalism 9

Chapter One
Introducing the Anarcho-Syndicalist Movement, the CNT 19

Chapter Two
Catalonia as a Model: Self-Management Arrives in Barcelona; the First Contradictions 63

Chapter Three
A Brief Survey of Self-Management in Other Regions of Spain 79

Chapter Four
Organising Self-Management across the Nation........................... 101

Chapter Five
Self-Management under Attack 131

Chapter Six
Self-Management's Outcomes: Overall Conclusions and Estimates...137

Chapter Seven
Conclusions about Self-Management in 1936–1939, and Broad Reflections..141

Appendices
Introduction to Appendices 155

I: Notes on the Spanish People's Superficial Catholicism 157

II: Revolutionary Uprisings in Spain, 1932–1934......................... 162

III: One Example of Monetary Reform and Scheme for Currency Circulation in a Social Economy.....................................174

IV: The CNT and the FAI: Pressure Groups 179

V: The Two Libertarian Communisms, or The Libertarian Party versus Anarcho-Syndicalism 191

VI: Notes on Governmental Collaboration 209

VII: Making Sense of the Plenum of Confederal Militias and Columns 215

VIII: Evidence about the Collectives of Ascó, and Flix (Tarragona) and the Barcelona Barbers' Collective 235

IX: The Madrid Peasants' Collective 247

X: The Adra Fishermen's Collective 249

XI: The Artesa de Lérida Collective 252

XII: The Barbastro Comarcal Federation of Collectives 262

XIII: UGT CNT CLUEA. Citrus Fruit Exports from Revolutionary Spain, 1936–1937 273

XIV: The Establishment, Growth and Operation of the Barcelona and District Locksmiths' and Corrugated Shutters Collective 279

XV: Marx, Engels, the CP, Councilism, Historians and Revolutionary Spain 286

XVI: Francoism, Transition to Democracy and Thoughts on Collective Management 305

Glossary of Terms and Initials Used in the Text 313

Index 317

Prologue

Frank Mintz's classic study of the Spanish revolutionary collectives—now revised and available here in English for the first time—is a penetrating analysis of the most extensive and deeply rooted experiment in workers' self-management since the advent of capitalism. It is also a book with a mission. If E. P. Thompson's famous motivation was to rescue the history of the British working class from the 'condescension of posterity', Mintz was inspired by a far more overarching objective: to penetrate the wall of silence erected around Spain's revolution of 1936. Spain's revolutionary experience, the great beacon of hope in the prevailing darkness of what Victor Serge dubbed the midnight of last century, was devoured by a civil war that was almost immediately eclipsed by the horrors and Holocaust of World War II. As the first chill winds of the Cold War scattered dust and fog across the rubble of post-war Europe, from Madrid to Moscow, the grand narratives of the victors' versions of history—be it Stalinist, liberal-left or Francoist—all ensured that the Spanish revolution became shrouded in silence, or, at a minimum, distorted beyond recognition.

For decades, the historiography of 1930s Spain confirmed the maxim that the history of 'failed' revolutions tends to be ignored. During the long winter of Francoist dictatorship, the apologists of the regime imposed an official bi-polarity on the history of the 1930s, constructing a division between the forces of 'good' and 'evil', of 'Spain' and 'Anti-Spain'. Prominent here was policeman-Historian Eduardo Comín Colomer, who used police archives as the basis of his calumnies against the anarchists, who were depicted as having imposed themselves on an otherwise law-abiding working class. Yet the exigencies of the Cold War, so adroitly exploited by the dictatorship for its self-preservation, led to an even greater distortion: in its readiness to highlight the 'red menace', Francoist historiography downplayed the role of revolutionary anarchist masses in the 1930s, prioritising instead organised Stalinism, a force that, prior to the civil war, was largely insignificant on the Spanish left. Thus, the red-and-black that heavily inflected the collectivisations was recast as a 'red revolution', a legend that was extremely flattering for the official communist movement.

Perforce, Stalinist interpretations downplayed the role of the anarchists in the Spanish revolution. The internal culture of the Spanish communist party hinged on the axiom that it was the 'party of revolution', so it was historically absurd to conceive of a revolution occurring outside of its control. Yet the bureaucratic camarilla at the head of the 'socialist motherland' had no desire to see a revolution in Spain in 1936. By 1934, with the triumph of fascism in Italy, Germany and Austria, the Soviet leadership felt internationally isolated and threatened by right-wing dictatorships. Stalin's foreign policy, therefore, became committed to the objective of forging an international alliance between the Soviet Union and the liberal democracies, especially Britain and France. To this end, Stalin, via the Communist International, instructed the various national communist parties to shelve any revolutionary ambitions in order to form Popular Front alliances with those democratic parties prepared to resist fascism.

Given all this, the Spanish revolution of 1936 presented Stalin with a grave dilemma: not only was it beyond his control, it also carried the danger of driving the western democracies into an alliance with Italo-German fascism. The Spanish communist movement therefore recast the issues at stake in the civil war: far from being a revolutionary war, the Stalinists defined the conflict as an armed clash between democracy, in the form of the Republic, and fascism, in the guise of General Franco and his Italian and German allies.

The nature of the Spanish revolution was now also deformed beyond recognition. Rather than a social revolution, this was instead a new phase in Spain's 'democratic revolution', thus, the official party history of the civil war defines the Spanish revolution as "a popular, democratic, anti-Fascist movement, the principal aim of which was to defend the Republic, freedom and national sovereignty against the Fascist rebellion".[1] Social revolution, in the eyes of the Stalinists, was dangerously premature: it would break the 'anti-fascist unity' between the working and middle classes that they claimed was crucial to winning the war and, moreover, alienate the western democracies from supporting the anti-fascist struggle against Franco, Hitler and Mussolini. (Of course, when it came to confronting the social revolution, the Stalinists had no qualms about breaking 'anti-fascist unity', while the western democratic governments, principally that of Britain, wanted Franco to win the war come what may.)

In a very real sense, therefore, Francoist and Stalinist versions of history fed into one another, their shared set of assumptions serving to inflate the role of the communist movement and distorting, or simply ignoring, the history of the revolution. Curiously, the same was also true of much liberal historiography, which tended to advance the Manichean vision of the civil war as a conflict of 'democracy versus fascism', as little more than a prelude or a warm-up to the global conflict between democracy and fascism during World War Two. Again, such a reading of the civil war left little or no room whatsoever for the Spanish revolution.

The 1960s saw the first attacks on the unlikely bedfellows that preserved a conspiracy of silence about the Spanish revolution. In the Anglo-Saxon world, liberal historiography received a major blow with the publication of Noam Chomsky's celebrated essay "Objectivity and Liberal Scholarship" in 1969, in which he criticised those historians

---

[1] Dolores Ibárruri et. al., *Guerra y revolución en España, 1936– 1939*, Moscow, Progreso, 1966–1971, 4 vols. (vol. 1, p. 256).

marked by their "antipathy towards the forces of popular revolution in Spain, or their goals".[2] By then, Frank Mintz, a young Franco-Bulgarian activist-historian, had already devoted several years to researching the book you now have in your hands. Fascinated by the historical experience of the Spanish revolutionary collectives since his early twenties, when he was inspired by his conversations with Spanish anarchist exiles in Paris, Frank is in the tradition of the other great French activist-historian and eye-witness Gaston Leval (Pierre Robert Piller).[3] Mintz has built on Leval's eye witness account of the collectives by subjecting the revolutionary process to a deeper analysis in order to provide a series of historical reflections. From the outset, he battled against the obstruction of those with an interest in preserving the silence on the Spanish revolution—Soviet archivists didn't trouble to reply to his written requests for access to their holdings. Undeterred, Frank's book appeared first in French as *L'autogestion dans l'Espagne révolutionnaire*, in 1970,[4] and in Spanish, shortly after Franco's death.[5]

By foregrounding the role of revolutionary collectives, this book was at loggerheads with the Francoist-Stalinist-Liberal, an important work that recuperated the experience of the struggle of thousands of anonymous workers for social and economic justice. It is concerned with questions such as why did self-management assume the proportions it took in Spain? How did it develop? Who organised the collectives? Were they spontaneous or forced? What motivated the collectivisers? What were their consequences and achievements? If compared with other attempts at

---

2 Noam Chomsky, *American Power and the New Mandarins*, Harmondsworth, Penguin, 1969, p. 64.

3 Gaston Leval, *Collectives in the Spanish Revolution*, London, Freedom Press, 1975.

4 *L'autogestion dans l'Espagne révolutionnaire*, Paris, Bélibaste, 1970.

5 *La autogestión en la España revolucionaria*, Madrid, La Piqueta, 1977.

collectivisation, did the Spanish case possess any unique characteristics?

When it comes to addressing why this movement emerged, the book starts by locating the collectivisations in terms of the local context and in relation to the CNT's culture of self-organisation and self-expression. Accordingly, when the fascist-military coup of July 1936 was put down by a combination of armed workers' militia and the police and military units that remained loyal to the republican government, profound revolutionary tensions within the heart of Spanish society exploded. The failed coup fractured the authority of the republican state, which now lost its monopoly of armed power and it was in these circumstances that agrarian and urban workers took over the means of production. None of the leaders of the leftist or trade union organisations called for the revolution: the collectivisations were the spontaneous remarkable response of legions of anonymous labourers to the practical issue of getting production on the land and in the factories up and running again.

Certainly many thousands of these workers were immersed in revolutionary syndicalist and anarchist ideas. But perhaps most remarkable of all, as you will read ahead, was that there were collectives organised by labourers who we might label 'spontaneous anarchists', who had no idea that they were organising along anarchist lines. This was most evident in rural Castile and Extremadura, where the anarchist tradition was weaker and where the dominant agrarian unions were mainly socialist in inspiration. This is all testimony to the profound autonomy of Spanish workers who embarked on a collective experiment that developed independently of the leaders of the union organisations. Reflecting the importance of workers' economic organisations over political parties, the collectivisations were, for the most part, impelled by grassroots anarchist and socialist trade unionists. But this was a genuinely popular revolution that drew in many non-affiliated workers. We must also recognise the important contribution of members of the dissident, anti-Stalinist communist party, the POUM, and, in some cases, of rank-and-file activists from the Stalinist PCE, even though its leaders were formally hostile to the revolution. In short, this was a revolution that occurred beyond the control of the leadership of the Spanish workers' and left-wing organisations, including those of anarchist tradition; it was a leaderless revolution, characterised by a high level of direct democracy.

This book is essential reading for anyone interested in either the Spanish revolution or the history of workers' self-management. It provides a global survey of the collectivisation process across Spain, revealing the scope and achievements of this far-reaching revolution, that was nothing less than the material expression of the will of hundreds of thousands of workers to seize control of their destiny and eliminate capitalism. In response to those who cling to the view that private property offers the only effective economic model, here we have eloquent proof of the creative energies of downtrodden, sometimes illiterate, pariahs of their capacity to run a complex economy while reconstituting everyday life in a non-hierarchical manner; of their readiness to confront historic problems, such as the problems of coordination between urban and rural economies; and the quest to raise the productivity of a backward agricultural system. Interestingly, the published testimonies of several landowners and industrialists who later regained their land and factories, thanks to Franco's victory in the civil war, pointed to the vast economic improvements introduced by the collectivisers. And all this was the more audacious since it occurred in the context of a violent civil war that ultimately devoured the revolution.

We also see here the forces allied against the collectives, both inside and outside the anarchist movement. In this respect, the author had unrivalled access to anarchist exiles in France, whose oral testimony constitutes a precious historical resource, especially vital when it comes to giving a voice to the truncated fight for justice of the defeated and compiling the fragments of their broken and unfulfilled hopes. Inevitably, these themes presuppose some discussion of the bureaucratisation of the CNT, how its leaders prioritised the civil war over the revolution and embraced the ideology of 'circumstantialism' to justify the entrance of anarchist ministers in government.

When we look back at how the anarchist ministers conspired in the destruction of the revolution, ensuring the militarisation of the militias and the extension of state control over the collectives, it seems a bitter irony that the likes of Juan García Oliver and Federica Montseny defended joining the republican government as a means of strengthening the revolution from a position of power—justifications that seem nothing short of delusional and vain today. Certainly, we cannot dispute Montseny's judgement that for her, antifascism had become 'something more important than the realisation of our own ideals'.[6] As well as turning their backs on ideals, the collaborationist sector of the CNT distanced itself from the movement's traditions of internal democracy: the decision to join the government was never ratified by the organisation in an open assembly or congress. The same bureaucratic sleight of hand also ensured that the rebellion of the anarchist opposition to 'governmentalism' was contained, isolated and then defeated.

Attacked by their natural enemies and by those leading what they had come to identify as *their* organisations, the defeat of the revolutionaries of 1936 was doubly bitter. In 1999 Dolors Marín asked Concha Liaño, a founder of Mujeres Libres, if all the defeat and betrayal that served as a prelude to the hardships of exile had been worthwhile. With tears in her eyes Liaño replied: "Yes. We gave a lesson to the world. We showed that you can live communally, sharing everything there is. That you can educate people in freedom and without

---

6 Federica Montseny, *Mi experiencia en el Ministerio de Sanidad y Asistencia Social*, Valencia, Sección de Información y propaganda de la CNT, 1937, p. 6.

punishing our children, that it is possible to appreciate nature and acquire culture. Yes, we did all this for a very short while, but we gave a lesson to the world".[7] This book, so pregnant with observations about how socio-economic transformation occurs, presents this same lesson for a new generation.

Chris Ealham, Madrid, July 2010

---

[7] Dolors Marín, *Ministros anarquistas: la CNT en el gobierno de la II República (1936–1939)*, Barcelona, Random House, 2005, pp. 245–246.

Introduction
Self-Management and Anarcho-Syndicalism

An army revolt erupted in the Spanish protectorate in Morocco and in the Canaries on 17 July 1936 as a backlash against the Popular Front's victory in the elections that February. The united right—including Gil Robles's very proper CEDA party; the Falange with the laughable vote scored by its leader José Antonio Primo de Rivera in those elections and its prolific record of violent attacks; the Don Juan de Borbón-supporting monarchists and the dissident monarchists of the Carlist stripe with their *requeté* paramilitary groups in Navarra; most of the latifundists of Old and New Castile, Extremadura and Andalusia and virtually the entire upper echelons of the Catholic Church (except in the Basque Country and Catalonia)—fell into line behind the coup-makers (*golpistas*) who were led by generals Mola, Sanjurjo, Franco and the like.

> It is to be borne in mind that the action must be violent in the extreme so as to shatter (as quickly as possible) the will of an enemy who is strong and well organized. Naturally, all leading lights of the political parties, societies or trade unions not committed to the Movimiento are to be jailed and exemplary punishment inflicted upon said individuals in order to snuff out acts of defiance or strikes... we must spread a climate of terror. [Secret Order No 1, signed by Mola in Madrid on 25 May 1936, the originally planned date for the coup.]

What lay behind such violence? General Gallifet set the example with his repression of the Paris Commune, where upwards of 30,000 children, women and men were shot down: capitalism needs its workforce terror-stricken, domesticated and decapitated.

The republican government, made up of the centre left parties and PSOE (*Partido Socialista Obrero Español*/Spanish Socialist Workers' Party), had been very naive about the right back in 1931, and failed to purge the previous regime's forces of repression or to implement immediate social reforms in the countryside and in industry (as they had been promising they would just before they came to power). In the face of a right that made no bones about its admiration for Mussolini's fascism and its sympathies for Hitler's Germany, the republican government of 1936 proved incapable of devising an effective defensive strategy or of taking self-preservation measures.

Trade union militants and a few leftist groups were the galvanising factors driving the resistance of masses of workers and the odd segment of the republican forces of repression. And, paradoxically, the workers saw off the *golpistas* across more than half the country, which is why Mussolini and Hitler (and, to a lesser extent, Portugal's Salazar) rushed in thousands of soldiers and impressive heavy military equipment.

Hitler, Mussolini and Salazar's well-known contempt and disrespect for constitutional or international law, the grotesque 'Non-Intervention' policy adopted by France and Great Britain, the early leaks about genocidal slaughter of leftist militants throughout 'rebel' Spain and especially in Badajoz, triggered feelings of outrage and repugnance in workers who entrenched their gains and immediately converted the economy to meet the needs of those who had until so recently been overlooked.

Abroad, those same factors inspired many to assist the Spanish workers who were not only standing up to the right-wing, Catholic fascist crew but who had spontaneously taken over the means of production across much of republican Spain.

Hence the arrival in Spain of tens of thousands of genuine volunteers (as opposed to fascist mercenaries and Soviet 'advisors' and their cohorts from a number of communist parties in exile in France) from a range of nations, especially the Anglophone world. Among those front-line fighters, one of the most committed and thoughtful, albeit a man very modest and taciturn in the ranks of his Spanish comrades (because of the language difficulty no doubt), was George Orwell. Very many of these volunteers irrigated the soil of Spain with their blood (Orwell for one) or ended up buried there.

There are countless accounts in dozens of languages and particularly in English, emanating from both combatants and historians and researchers. I personally have drunk deeply of Burnett Bolloten's erudite technique of backing every claim up with data, and checking out most of the historians' quotations against the original sources. A reading of Vernon Richards's *Lessons of the Spanish Revolution*, Orwell's *Homage to Catalonia* and Gerald Brenan's *The Spanish Labyrinth* (a positive inspiration to anyone unfamiliar with Díaz del Moral's 1923 essay "Historia de las agitaciones campesinas andaluzas", not to mention that it is an interesting and honest book) has proved enlightening. I relished and continue to relish my friend Noam Chomsky's essay on the academic blindspots of bourgeois historians (taking as his example Gabriel Jackson's book on the Spanish Civil War) in *American Power and the New Mandarins* (1969) and his comment that "a deep bias against social revolution in Spain and a commitment to the values and social order of liberal bourgeois democracy has led the author to misrepresent crucial events and to overlook major historical currents". Equally laudable are his many references to the impromptu achievements of the Spanish workers during the Spanish Revolution.

> "A day will come when we will have to sum up the lessons of experience thrown up by our revolution", Abad de Santillán, *Por qué perdimos la guerra* (Madrid 1975), p. 78.

"The anarchists themselves, who were and are most concerned to propagandize the work of the collectives, have produced at best only very limited surveys of them. Eye-witness accounts have also a fragmentary quality which makes generalization from them difficult", Stephen John Brademas, *Revolution and Social Revolution: Contribution to the history of the Anarcho-syndicalist Movement in Spain 1930–1937* (Oxford, typewritten thesis, 1953), p. 313.

"In spite of sabotage from bourgeois republicans, some two million workers ran the factories and harvested the crops and tended the land, turning the capitalist consumer economy into a war economy. In the midst of revolution, and its contradictions and controversy, these were workers who knew that they were not prepared to suffer any longer, that they were trying to build a new life, having started on the basis of past experience by rejecting the assumption that their leaders might approve, because in such circumstances 'order and discipline' is simply a weapon in the armoury of the traitors who would disarm the people and reintroduce the police who will stand guard over their property. There is only one yardstick by which the Revolution can be judged: the workers' conditions, their standard of living and their power. And only in Spain had the workers sufficient clarity and strength thanks to their anarcho-syndicalist training to pursue their ideal of emancipation in the sphere of the economy", foreword to the French translation of Vernon Richards's *Lessons of the Spanish Revolution* (1973, revised 2009).

The three quotations above address a double reality: a dearth of information and deliberate misinformation. Caught up in a tunnel-visioned struggle against Francoism, teetering between hopes of evolution or revolution, Spanish anarcho-syndicalists—with the odd exception—forgot to publicise their ventures into self-management, just as their Russian brethren banished from the USSR twenty years previously had done.

The official reporters and historians—in the pay of the masters of capitalist bounty or the communist parties (Moscow once upon a time, and these days Beijing)—are not at liberty to publicise and heap praise upon periods in history when millions of inhabitants organised themselves from the ground up, free of 'upper echelons', free of parties and university- or central-committee-schooled leadership.

From the infancy of human organisation and the days of cave paintings, a hierarchical arrangement of society has been foisted upon us as the only possible and efficient model. It stands for the rule of the rich white man, with the odd and occasional female gate-crasher to ease and offer diversion from the toil of man. Self-management in Spain, imposed from below, was largely the handiwork of the women, the elderly, the young and the disabled (See Appendix VIII).

And their feats belong to one and all. From the epic of Spartacus through to the day-to-day rejection of capitalism across every continent, the class struggle is replayed on a small scale and, sometimes, on a larger one (as in Ecuador, Bolivia and Argentina since 2001). Such is the ongoing contribution that the battlers have to offer: a past to learn about and be inspired by with an eye to improvisation in today's world.

Not that the pressures of neo-liberalism and economic crises serve only to fragment the exploited and reduce them to despair and isolation in the face of poverty and police repression. A long way away from Spain, in Argentina, in Patagonia in the south and in the northern reaches close to the border with Bolivia, since 1996–1998, women have been heavily involved in agitation (though the feminists have been largely absent). The unemployed have cordoned off the highways, which, following the collapse of the rail system due to the privatisation policies of neo-liberal Peronista president Carlos Menem, are almost the only means of communication within the country. A national highway, sealed off, promptly creates a breakdown of stocks and the supply chain in every realm: from medicines and foodstuffs to spares in every sector of the economy.

Maybe this had to do with the trail blazed by the Mothers of the Plaza de Mayo during the Argentine military dictatorship between 1976 and 1983. Virtually alone in the midst of the raging repression, the Mothers mounted a week-in, week-out silent, unrelenting, peaceful demonstration right in the heart of the federal capital, demanding answers to their questions about the violent, unlawful kidnappings of their sons and husbands. They were and are still a source of inspiration, an approach to be aped, an improvised example to be imitated. Or maybe it was the pre-Columbian tradition of collective mutual aid seen among the Mapuches in southern Argentina or among the Guarani in the north. But the fact is that the picket-lines made up of class-conscious, jobless *piqueteros*, active alongside their wives and children, with solidarity forthcoming from small producers and businesses, blocked the traffic and eventually secured subsidies and a few jobs. As the tide of privatisation continued in Argentina and with the crisis of 19 and 20 December 2001, the *piquetero* phenomenon and the attitude of "a plague on all their [those responsible for the crisis] houses" swept the entire country.

In spite of all the pressures and politically motivated bribery, the *piquetero* movement continues to impact Argentine society. Naomi Klein and Avi Lewis's documentary *The Take*, about the collective resistance by the exploited, is a faithful reflection of this (albeit somewhat overtaken by events, given the pace at which Argentine social life moves). Self-management of struggles and a reorganisation of the fabric of society represent the response of the most oppressed to unbridled capitalism. Confronted with the capitalist cult of 'winning' and of success for success's sake—no matter how that success may be achieved and blessed by financial and legal rewards—in Argentina there are groups of individuals who, for their survival, look to the collective, creative daily practices of allotments, roadblocks, bakeries and even schools—eschewing all hierarchy.

Amid the usual blinkered outlook of the ruling class, this vision comes very close to something first spelled out a long time ago: "Our ideal for everybody...is freedom, morality, intelligence and well-being for each through the solidarity of all—the brotherhood of man".[1] The counsel and promises offered by a political leader to the workers and unemployed amount to a hoax: "if, when speaking to them about revolution or, if you prefer, social change, he tells them that political change must come before economic change: or if he denies that they should pursue both simultaneously, or even that the political revolution should be merely the short-term, direct implementation of the complete and utter liquidation of society, they should turn their backs on him, for he is either an out-and-out fool, or a hypocritical exploiter".[2] What we have is not so much short-sightedness on the part of the ruling classes as the mounting of an all-out, unrelenting genocide against the disinherited of the Third World, driven by the First World and with the connivance of Third World rulers. One has only to look at France's policies towards her erstwhile African possessions. The success of presidents Mitterrand, Chirac and Sarkozy is measured in terms of their implementation of a policy of terror and slow slaughter in those ex-colonies alongside a 'quiet fascism' in the metropolis and with *Le Monde diplomatique* rinsing First World imperialism in 'criticism-light'. Those who prattle about a different world cannot pretend to endow capitalism with a human face if its very mechanisms and postulates amount to a seed-bed of criminal inequality. The so-called 'nanny state' or periods of apparent prosperity for the First World's lower classes were always bought at the price of ongoing bloody

---

[1] Bakunin, *The Secret Statutes of the Alliance: The Programme and Purpose of the revolutionary organisation, the International Brotherhood*, 1868.

[2] Bakunin, "The Policy of the International" in *L'Égalité*, No 31, 21 August 1869.

exploitation and the looting of continents that are wide open to exploitation by the multi-nationals.

I was not trained on the basis of some vocation as a professional historian, but rather became one out of the need to clarify and criticise anarchist thought, in France and in Spain alike; I refer to the critical, anarcho-communist (and, later, anarcho-syndicalist) strain of anarchism that I picked up in the Noir et Rouge group. Then again, when I read descriptions of Russian *kolkhozes* and Chinese communes, I had the impression that I was reading naive texts, or that they were interweaving truth and lies and were bereft of critical capacity. But the same feeling stole over me when I came to read references to the Spanish libertarian collectives by authoritative writers such as Gaston Leval or José Peirats. Such was the depth of conviction of those comrades that they forgot to systematically rehearse the economic advances made.

In 1962, at the Sorbonne, I submitted a thesis in Spanish on collectivisation during the Spanish Civil War of 1936–1939, adopting a resolutely critical approach and shunning triumphalism in my statistical estimates and spelling out potential contradictions between the theory and the practice. A French translation saw publication in 1969. In 1976, further documentation was added and an expanded Spanish edition was published in Madrid in 1977 as *La autogestión en la España revolucionaria*. In 1999, I produced an overview in French, dispensing with the economic tables and devoting additional space to reflection. In 2006, an updated version was published in Madrid, and a more comprehensive edition in Buenos Aires in 2009.[3]

---

3 Ever since I first came to grips with the question of the Spanish Revolution, back in 1936, I have been indebted to the Noir et Rouge group, specially Christian Lagant and Todor Mitev; my colleagues Aristide Rumeau, Rafael Pujol Marigot, Josep Fornas; my anarchist or anarcho-syndicalism comrades Antonia Fontanillas,

At the same time I carried on publishing analysis that recognises no sacred cows by helping with the publication of a Spanish version of Vernon Richards's *Lessons of the Spanish Revolution*, by La Hormiga publishers in Paris.[4] I was able to carry on raising and publicising a number of writings and issues relating to the Spanish libertarian movement and other broader issues by means of essays, anthologies and translations (French editions of writings by Berneri, Malatesta, Kropotkin, Chomsky, Pano Vassilev, the *Noir et Rouge* review, Max Nettlau, Osvaldo Bayer's *Patagonia rebelde* and Bakunin, plus, in Spanish, works by Kropotkin, Bakunin and Anatol Gorelik), with or without recourse to pen names (such as Israël Renof or Martin Zemliak). Pen names were a necessary precaution due to monitoring by the Bulgarian counter-espionage agency (1965–1989), as I'd married a Bulgarian woman, the sister of an anarcho-communist comrade living in France as a political emigré, after fourteen months of (fruitless) search for 'connections'. Having seen Marxist-leninism and 'actually existing socialism' at close quarters,[5] as well as having an inside knowledge of European and Latin American capitalism, I was convinced of the economic and

---

Fernando Gómez Peláez, Gueorgui Balkanski, Rudolf de Jong, Renée Lamberet, José Llop, Valerio Mas and Liberto Sarrau. Subsequently joined by Simone Guittard, the comrades from the Paris-based ...editions CNT-RP, the team at the International Institute for Social History in Amsterdam, the friends and comrades from 'Traficantes de Sueños' in Madrid, the CGT of Spain and 'Anarres' in Buenos Aires.

4   The translation of this book by the Chilean comrade Laín Díez was rejected for publication in the 1960s by the Argentinean anarchist publishing house Proyección as unduly critical of the CNT.

5   I have known exceptional people, one-time Leninists or Leninist faithful who have been open-minded and 'sound' and who saw eye to eye with me in exposing oppression and the bourgeoisie in the light of their ideology. My criticisms are directed at the body of doctrine rather than at those who genuinely strive for a better world (and this goes also for the followers of any religion, as long as they are tolerant and 'sound').

social inanity of them both (having seen little improvement for the people between 1950 and 2009).

As a lecturer working on the outskirts of Paris and now in retirement, I have alternated between such work and trade union activity within France's home-grown CNT (since 1994). My own ideology is not the anarchism that customarily embraces differing tendencies within a single whole, with the inevitable frictions and impediments for one and all. I prefer to describe myself as an anarcho-syndicalist, in the knowledge that the practice of solidarity and direct action is more important than any label, as was seen in the Spain of 1936 and as can be found among critical *piquetero* sectors in today's Argentina.

Frank Mintz, February 2009

Chapter One
Introducing the Anarcho-Syndicalist Movement, the CNT

"The Russian revolution, which is the first historical experiment on the model of the mass strike, not merely does not afford a vindication of Anarchism but actually means *the historical liquidation of Anarchism*". [1905][1]

"The Spanish peasant is even more of an individualist than the French peasant: he is haughtier, prouder". [1927][2]

Subsequent historical events made nonsense of both of the above quotes, the first of which emanates from a Marxist and the second from a bourgeois advocate of cooperatives. They are enlightening as to the shortcomings of supposedly scientific or universal analyses that amount to nothing more than "cover" for subjective personal opinion (not to mention outright lies, as witness those 'scientific' studies justifying genetic modification or denying global warming, etc.).

Rather than delving into the facts and figures of Spanish anarcho-syndicalism, it might be wiser to explain how and why it came to be so strong.

From without and from within: the reasons behind the endurance of anarchist trade unionism (or, from the 1930s

---

[1] Rosa Luxembourg, *The Mass Strike, the Political Party and the Trade Unions*, (1906).
[2] Charles Gide, *La coopération dans les pays latins, 1926–1927* (Paris), p. 144.

onwards, anarcho-syndicalism) in Spain, seen through the eyes of outsiders and insiders.

One logical question that arises is: why was anarchism so strong in Spain from the late-nineteenth century through to 1936, when it had vanished elsewhere? The question becomes a lot clearer when we note that in the United States during the same period the workers' movement was anarchist as well—as witness the Haymarket Martyrs—and it would effectively remain such in the form of the IWW, which subscribed to no particular ideology and no political party, but championed direct action and working-class solidarity ("an injury to one is an injury to all").

In Spain, there was a labor, socially minded anarchism just as there was in the USA. This was not the anarchism of some Bohemian intellectuals or navel-gazing individualists. By the late-nineteenth and early-twentieth centuries, initially in France, and then in Russia with the soviets of 1905, labor used direct-action tactics and had a mistrust of the parties of the left. Such was the effect of this repudiation that, in April 1917, Lenin had to oppose his own party's central committee and push through the anarchist watchphrase of "All power to the soviets" in order to win power by means of manipulation (through trade union officials—paid officials—and self-styled workers' leaders like Trotsky) and through the creation in 1917 of the Cheka in order to end the notion of a horizontal revolution benefiting the workers themselves and establish instead a *nomenklatura* (a privileged class within or dependent upon the Party) along with the NEP,[3] and privileges for a new, Red class.

Anarcho-syndicalism and the Spartakists were on the rise in Germany between 1918 and the end of the 1920s, when they were swept aside by armed socialists and right-wingers, not to mention Nazi and capitalist pressures.

---

3   NEP (New Economic Policy) introduced by Lenin, freeing up individual trading, meaning the petite bourgeoisie, the Party's economy having proven itself ineffective.

And if this labor-based, socially minded anarchism petered out, or almost, within the proletarian movement in many countries such as the USA, France and the USSR, this was due to murder, heavy sentencing and huge fines, to the judges and the bosses, to corruption and gangsterish pressures brought to bear by reformist trade unions and the gulags of "actually existing" socialism.

In Spain, anarcho-syndicalism's sway can be explained first in terms of the make-up of the CNT, the political and social extraction of its membership and the determination and organisation without which nothing durable can be achieved. Whilst the goal of the CNT was libertarian communism as defined by Bakunin, Kropotkin and the like, the union was open to *all* workers, regardless of political or religious differences. It was notable that Spanish workers made their choice by espousing libertarian tactics against the oligarchy. In Spain, anarcho-syndicalism's sway over artists, writers and the petite bourgeoisie was less than was the case in France. Terrorism was also less of a factor in Spain than in France, Italy or Russia. Individualists and attempts to launch communes were less also, contrary to the experiences in France and Russia.

In order to gloss over the repression of anarchism in many countries, historians ask why anarchist influence was so strong in Spain (for the Marxists, see Appendix XV below, page 286).

On the subject of anarchism, Gerald Brenan, a fine English Hispanist, borrowed heavily from Díaz del Moral (whose ideas are set out here) and argued that anarchism reflected millenarianism, with a yearning for the egalitarianism of the Middle Ages. Hugh Thomas, James Joll, Eric Hobsbawm (who serves it up in a Marxist sauce) and Nazario González however have knowingly rehearsed the Díaz del Moral line without acknowledgment.

Not that the anarchists' own views of the reasons for their success should be immune from criticism. Alongside the rather accurate overall analysis from Renée Lamberet who highlighted the natural geographical barriers suited to federalist ideas, the oppressiveness of iniquitous exploitation in an industrial and agricultural setting or the *gravitas* of Spanish workers, we find far-fetched explanations invoking the "temperamental anarchism of Spaniards",[4] not to mention newspaper articles talking about the death-defying CNT, the phoenix risen from the ashes, etc.

With a degree of success, Brenan strove to delineate and separate the anarchists and the socialists geographically. And it looks as if some scholars have also been drawn to class divisions: "In Valencia and Castellón, well-to-do peasants belonged to the Catholic right or to the republican camp, just as those from fertile Granada belonged to the socialists".[5] But reality does not fit into such deterministic patterns: in Madrid, printing workers belonged to the UGT; in Barcelona, they belonged to the CNT. The Asturian miners were socialists, with a sizable CNT minority, whereas their counterparts in Aragon and Catalonia belonged to the CNT. Dockers in Barcelona and Gijón were in the CNT, but in Seville, were communists.[6] This list might be extended to take in poorer peasants who were with the CNT in Aragon, with the home rule republicans in Catalonia, with the UGT in Castile and split between the CNT and the UGT in Levante.

In our own view, there are two explanatory factors at work here. Direct action trade unionism was a tactic that met the workers' requirements. And that brand of trade unionism came first in Spain and left little opening for other movements to develop.

We need look no further than to a few of its opponents for an assessment of the pros and cons of the Bakuninist-style trade unionism that put down roots in the Iberian peninsula from 1868 onwards. Three witnesses, unconnected

---

4 José Peirats, *La CNT en la revolución española, Tomo 1*.
5 Fernanda Romeu, *Las clases trabajadoras en España* (Madrid 1970), p. 40.
6 According to Según Romero Maura, "The Spanish Case" in *Government and Opposition* (1970).

with trade unionism (one a republican free-mason, one a soviet Marxist and one a co-founder of the POUM—see note 20 below) have useful comments to make (given their particular outlook and the way they confound anarchism and anarcho-syndicalism) regarding the foothold gained by Spanish anarcho-syndicalism between the late-nineteenth century and the early years of the twentieth century.

> Anarchism has, very wrongly, been taken to task for its tremendous tactical errors. But apart from the terrorism and individual acts that represent the blot upon its escutcheon what else would have worked in Andalusia? What other school of social thought could, in such a short time, have mobilised the broad masses of wage-earners, that imaginative but uneducated breed, whose apathy yields to nothing except fits of enthusiasm? The socialists' dusty, cold message, a thousand leagues removed from the hearts of the workers, would have needed a century to rouse the slumberers. Republicanism quickly ran out of myths. Only a doctrine of the religious and utopian cast, with its many fervent apostles, its ardent, prolific preaching, its impulsive sectarianism, its dizzying enthusiasm, its naïve, primitive, simplistic teachings (which brought it all the closer to the sensibilities and understanding of the Andalusian masses and suited it to their psychic make-up and underlying yearnings) had virtue enough to bring off the miracle [...] Anarchism sees the social question as a matter of knowledge: in times of conflict and in average circles at any rate, the belief—shared by Socrates—is that one cannot be aware of what is good and then fail to practise it and that error is the source of evil: only out of ignorance of anarchist teaching could someone espouse a position indifferent or hostile towards it. Hence the drive to spread the word and the implicit confidence in the effectiveness of the spoken word. Neither the socialists nor the republicans nor any other party aspiring to win the

people's hearts can stand comparison with the anarchists in this regard. At the turn of the century virtually all of the most highly regarded inspirational works of this school of thought were published in Spanish: a tide of translated pamphlets or originals from the pens of native-born militants pushed the libertarian message everywhere; the anarchist press reached into the furthest-flung corners of Spain; armies of agitators, spurred on by a burning sectarianism, toured the cities, towns and villages preaching the good news [...] Besides, their teaching and propaganda were normally shot through with moralistic themes. Respect for womanhood and equality of the sexes in the home and in society, love of nature and of learning, the drive against alcohol abuse, tobacco and gambling are recurrent themes in their newspaper articles and rally speeches. Finally, the Iberian anarchist greedily gobbled up and harnessed to his creed all social trends marked with the cachet of novelty. [Apropos of a strike by Andalusian farm laborers in 1919] the masses were gripped by an ardent craving for knowledge as in 1903. Reading was unrelenting by night in their farmsteads; by day in the ploughed fields, during (smoking) breaks the spectacle was always the same: some worker reading and the rest listening very attentively. A newspaper was the most-welcomed gift that could be bestowed upon a working man who found himself at a loose end. Farm labourers carried some pamphlet or newspaper in their knapsacks along with their lunches. Any one of the trade unionist villages received hundreds of copies of the like-minded press, purchased even by those who could not read.[7]

---

7   Díaz del Moral, *Historia de las agitaciones campesinas andaluzas— Córdoba (antecedentes para una reforma agraria)* (Madrid, 1967 reprint) pp. 447–448, 170–171, 182 and 285–286. This study, which dates from 1923, was not published until 1928, due to the dictatorship of Miguel Primo de Rivera, father of the founder of the Spanish fascist party (Falange), José Primo de Rivera.

Another significant factor in the reinforcement and growth of the anarchist influence in Spain was its very own organisational approach: anarchist agitation was essentially flexible and akin to traditional native forms of organisation and struggle tailored to the needs of revolutionary consciousness and indeed of the less mature masses [...] Thus, in Spain, anarchism was not confined to the peddling of social utopianism and terrorist acts. It invited mass activity and scored a number of practical successes. After half a century of growth, that very tradition on the part of the anarchist movement became a serious material factor in the further strengthening of its influence.[8]

In the forty-one years between the anarchist-socialist split at the congress in The Hague and the Russian revolution, the anarchist movement was fighting a rearguard action in the face of the socialist advance on all fronts (except for Spain and Portugal where anarchists in the nineteenth century, and anarcho-syndicalists in the early twentieth, still outnumbered and outmatched the socialist movement). There are several reasons why the process in Spain was rather different from that elsewhere:

One— Spanish anarchists got the measure of the peasant question long before the socialists, and, right from the outset, anarchism took root in Andalusia, the heartland of the Spanish agrarian question.

Two—Anarchists established their main base in Barcelona, which was the industrial heart of the country, whereas the socialists were centered in Madrid.

Three—The anarchists were formidable and indefatigable propagandists. They published newspapers, reviews and pamphlets galore. At the turn of the century,

---

[8] K. L. Maidanik, *Ispanski proletariat v natsionalno-revoliutsionarioni voine* (The Spanish Proletariat in the National-Revolutionary War) (Moscow 1960), p. 35.

the *Tierra y Libertad* (published in Madrid) went from weekly publication to daily and, without question, became the world's very first anarchist daily newspaper. The Sempere-Prometeo publishing house, based in Valencia and run by Blasco Ibáñez, was offering the full gamut of the anarchist literature of the day at prices to suit every pocket. Socialists never placed any great stock in printed propaganda; they made do with publishing three or four weeklies around the country.

Four—Even though the number of intellectuals belonging to their organisations was very tiny, anarchists pursued an intelligent policy of wooing them, by inviting them to contribute to their reviews and newspapers. The so-called *'generation of '98'*, which ushered in a whole new era in Spain's intellectual life at the turn of the century, was intuitively anarchist. By contrast, up until the latter half of the twentieth century, socialists were suspicious of intellectuals, and shunned them.

Five—The anarchists were more 'up for a fight' than the socialists. Though, more often than not, crude and wrong-headed, the peasant uprisings in Andalusia ignited the flames of a yearning for liberation, the embers of which never quite died out even in the wake of failure. Humble peasants would gather around those smouldering embers to listen to readings from Malatesta's pamphlets or Kropotkin's *The Conquest of Bread*.

Six—Anarchists caught on to the importance of educating the young as a means of shaping the fighters of the future. They set up rationalist schools, the chief proponent of which—Francisco Ferrer—added a martyr of international repute to the anarchist pantheon when he was executed by firing squad in 1909.

Seven—Anarchists resorted to terrorism as a political weapon. Though in some instances this backfired, in other instances the outcome was positive, and at all times it was terrifying.

Eight—Relentlessly harassed, the anarchists acquired a practical grounding in subterranean activity, whereas the socialists were preoccupied with *not* infringing on the established law.

Nine—The Madrid-Barcelona or Castile-Catalonia divide proved of assistance to the anarchists whose opposition to Madrid was in line with the opposition coming from the Catalan middle class.

Ten—Being rather mystical, quixotic, adventurous and individualistic, anarchism was a closer fit to the psychological profile of the Spanish people than a socialism that was cold, schematic and all formality, discipline and regulation.

Eleven—The First World War triggered rapid industrial expansion in Catalonia with a resultant expansion of the workers' movement, which was marshalled and led by anarcho-syndicalists.

Twelve—Anarcho-syndicalists were quicker off the mark than the socialists when it came to appreciating the advantages of turning craft unions into industrial ones. The emergence of the *Sindicato Único* (one, all-embracing union) was a revolutionary event and proved such a boost to anarcho-syndicalism that the bulk of the Spanish working class was drawn into the orbit of the National Confederation of Labor (CNT).

Thirteen—Last, but not least, anarchists demonstrated an imagination lacking in the socialists.[9]

The effectiveness, adaptability and inventiveness of the CNT over time and space are apparent from the following quotes, quite apart from the remarks about the religiosity or utopianism applicable to just about any "-ism", starting with capitalism. The CNT outlook itself explains the impact.

---

9   Joaquín Maurín, 1964 afterword to *Revolución y contrarrevolución en España* (1935) (reissued, Paris 1966), pp. 242–244.

The ideological essence of syndicalism

In labor organisations whose members are not entirely driven by their bellies, there is, as in everything in life, a material part and a separate essential, spiritual or ideological part, call it what you will. If only the material part grows, to wit, the pursuit of more money and reduced hours, it will never be anything more than a sort of an aperitif or stomach-liner and an imitation of the miller's donkey or the 'carousel' pony. Meaning that after several centuries of dogged struggle, they will remain what they were the day they started out: a mass of exploited wage-slaves barely able to cover their most basic needs. And this must necessarily be the case: the worker is producer *and* consumer, and unless a radical attack is mounted upon the unjust right of private property, which allows some to lay hands upon what others produce, rendering economic equality—the foundation of harmony and human brotherhood and the fountain of all true freedom and justice—impossible, all the money he earns as a producer will promptly be wrested from him as a consumer. The more expensive the labor, the pricier the product. The upshot being that, when their time has run out, they will have frittered their time away on skirmishes and intestinal strife, only to finish up marooned in the vicious circle of the exploited wage-slave [...]

One cannot *preach brotherhood* and then be a splitter of hairs, a bearer of grudges, a moaner, a gangster, a slanderer or begrudger. One cannot claim to be enamoured of freedom and a fighter for emancipation and then dig in one's heels and be overbearing in company, at meetings and in one's social relations, and *at home with one's partner and children... a tyrant and inquisitor, not to say a wretched exploiter.*[10]

---

10 Galo Díez, *Esencia ideológica del anarcosindicalismo* (Gijón 1922), pp. 10, 38. The italics are mine.

Introducing the Anarcho-Syndicalist Movement

Direct-action syndicalism and Salvador Seguí (painter and decorator, Barcelona):

[*El Heraldo* newspaper] *But do other trade union leaders say the same? Or at any rate can they guarantee as much with the same determination with which you have answered me?*

[Salvador Seguí] Yes, of course. They guarantee it too. At least they point out that becoming a deputy means giving up the leadership of the union. I cannot answer for them because they are old enough to answer for themselves.

Not that we hate Parliament: it is simply that we have woken up to the fact that the parliamentary system is utterly useless. It needs to be jettisoned as something there is no point in our bothering with. Take it from me! We have resolved this matter and turned our backs on the matter.

Yes, but the tactics you adopt in your organisation have no need of parliament's assistance. [Seguí looks at me rather ironically, suggesting that the question should be put to him bluntly. This was no time to accede to the invitation. I carried on regardless.]
What are your tactics?

Very simple, actually. The organisations predating those presently in existence were not practical, or they were not entirely practical. The gains made on the worker's behalf were so slow in coming and so insignificant as to make the creation of new organisations imperative. We school the worker to a climate of confidence in his own determination and his own endeavours. That everybody is sufficient unto himself when it comes to carrying out his mission as a human being. We simply teach them to struggle against all who may be their enemies. People believe that we are only out for an extra peseta a day and, perhaps, an hour off the working day. They are mistaken. We seek our emancipation as workers and thereby the destruction of the law of wages. Let everybody work, *everybody*, all of us equals! We enter the fray with the Unions, yes, and that is the reason why we have organised them appropriately.

The organising is admirable. We all know that by now. But the tactics, what are the tactics?

Well, each is the outworking of the other. Don't go thinking that we prefer quantity over quality. At the outset what we were after was ten competent workers, worthwhile and alive to their duties and their rights, rather than ten thousand workers who might not be able to stand up to the harassment, the abuse, the hunger, imprisonment and the entire litany of dirty tricks deployed in efforts to intimidate us. For we knew that the example set by those ten would be enough to educate the masses in the pursuit of social improvement. So that it would be impossible to stand against us. Should that ten be rounded up, another ten will pop up and so on and so on until we number ten thousand. Terrifying and monstrous though it may be, high-handedness can never cope with such numbers. By looking out for quality alone we have achieved the numbers that have rocked governments and the bosses on their heels during the recent campaign in Catalonia. Many of the workers who came out on strike may well not have had a full grasp of the essential meaning of syndicalism. But hatred for the boss who exploits and niggles them, and the daily dose of high-handed treatment, as well as the example set by other workers—in terms of self-denial and disinterestedness—were enough. They knew just what needed doing should the strike carry on, and that did the trick.

Yes, Pestaña said the same thing only yesterday.

Well that's all there is to it. We teach them how to look out for themselves. Do you think it takes long to get the hang of it? And once learned, do you think there is any need to take the worker from here and plant him down somewhere else and tell him: Now, rebel at five o'clock tomorrow morning, back down at seven and rebel again at nine and back down at twelve, only to rebel again at nine and back off yet again at twelve? No. That would be an impossibility. The social question boils down to this: learning how to do for oneself. We do not have anything great to give the worker, nor do we promise him a rose garden. Rose gardens are within his reach, just as they are within the reach of bourgeois avarice. Within and without, we are all equal, or maybe you doubt that on the grounds that the ransacking of a Bank today brings the proletariat no benefit. And that it is still subject to the boss's exploitation the day after [...]

The oppression of the majority, the strait-jacket of authority, the persistence of bullying, the gobbling-up of worthwhile things created by other people... As long as this endures, we have no option but to plump for unionisation that will assume various forms: violent forms, every time, if violence is imposed upon them. With agencies for resistance up and running, these may well, by themselves, be equal to the attack. This is the education we offer the working man: we see to it that he acquires the habits of cohesiveness and discipline, so that, when the time comes, all syndicalists act as one man. And it seems to me that in Catalonia we have pulled it off.[11]

The malaise among the masses, generated by their wretched, enslaved conditions, prompts them blindly to embrace ideas offered to them like drink to a thirsty man,

---

11 *Artículos madrileños de Salvador Seguí*, (Madrid 1978), pp. 67–70 [Interview in *El Heraldo*, a bourgeois newspaper, Madrid, October 1919].

like a balm, like an antidote to the world as it is. But do the masses look any further than that? Are they aware of how they might set themselves free? We say no. At best, they know that they should set themselves free, but this is not enough. What is needed is a clearer picture, a sharper picture of the order to be established and, if any attempt is to be made to carry out an overhaul as far reaching as the one we would like to come to life, at the very least the chief principles upon which justice rests need to be planted in the minds of the masses in order to conjure up a new consciousness. That is the sort of education we reckon should come before any decisive action.

If we pause for a moment to reflect upon what our revolution ought to be, we will see that it cannot follow any other course. We do not want the people mounting all this effort just to effect a change in overseer, but rather to shrug off all oversight. Which is why we mean to strengthen the individual by educating him. The herd instinct must be banished from humanity. Unless we turn our thoughts to that, we should not describe ourselves as libertarians because the freedom we crave cannot exist wherever there are those determined—if it can be called determination—to offer unthinking obedience to the orders of a minority.

We cannot say how long it will take to educate the people. In our view this depends on how much effort we put into it. However, we can say that, without such education, there can be no talk of genuine emancipation for them, and that arguments to the contrary are self-delusion or the deception of others![12]

Anarchists inside the trade unions. Work to be done.

What is it that those anarchists, who do not believe that organisation should be along state lines, want? They will

---

12 Op. cit., pp 135–136 [See *Vida Nueva*, 12 June 1922].

say that they practice Anarchism so as to arrive at near perfection. Might it not be the case that the comrades back in '68 and '73, in their congresses and despite their sectarian practices, foresaw and understood that the economic side to Anarchism might be implemented immediately? I reckon the answer is yes.

Certain facets of the issues raised by Anarchism can be put into effect. Who but the workers were in a position to understand this new thinking? Who but the workers can carry out the overhaul?

But I doubt there is anybody who thinks he is watching the defeat of the bourgeois capitalist world's economic values; that he is witnessing the collapse of phony old ideas that are likewise bourgeois and being replaced by values and ideas such as the issues that Anarchism poses in the round. Let us say, for we owe it to the truth, that we are moving towards the posing of some of the problems raised by anarchism.

Anarchists have a mission to perform within the unions, watching over their survival and orientation. By not neglecting trade union activity, their influence will grow; the organisation will be that much more libertarian and will trigger the advent of a new society that much sooner. Anarchists should act out their anarchist ideals within the trade unions. It is suicide for anarchists to hold aloof from trades organisations. Everything should and can be done within the Unions.

Which is not to say that they should dissolve the groups already in existence. No, not at all. On the contrary, these can amalgamate with the Unions. The greater the influence they wield, the more Anarchism and the more anarchists. These days, Anarchism is not the bogeyman it once was, and this is because of the persuasive work carried out. It was thanks to anarchist influence that, at the regional congress in Catalonia and at the national congress in 1918 and 1919, respectively, the trade union organisation embraced the emphatic statement that our sights are set on achieving libertarian communism, something that might well have been rejected in 1914 since anarchists kept their distance from the organisations then.

The Russian state. The role of the unions.

Production should be organised and regulated, not by the anarchist groups nor by state organizations, but by the unions.

We are not Leninists, in that we do not believe that the State, no matter how revolutionary and socialist it may purport to be, should have the usufruct of the means of production.

[We believe] that the only ones equipped for that are the Unions, because, for one thing, they are more moral. And for another, because they are more competent.

It is not the calling of the Russian State, no matter how essentially socialist it may be, to distribute production. That would be like getting folk to believe in some supernatural agent. In Germany we have already seen a number of failures under a socialist State. And even though the situation there is not the same as in Russia, the State has proven itself markedly incompetent.[13]

Ángel Pestaña (watch-maker) was equally blunt:

Of all the issues raised in the Unions, this one, relating to officials or persons paid for handling administrative and secretarial business, may well be the one that provokes the gravest and most serious difficulties [...] Experiences elsewhere should caution us against using our hard-saved pennies on the upkeep of the harmful beast that would devour us: the bureaucrat.

---

13 Op. cit. p. 284–285 [A talk on "Anarchism and Trade Unionism" given in La Mola prison in Mahón, 31 December 1920].

How are we to get around this snag and break out of the vicious cycle in which necessity has us trapped? By switching away from the approach used in other countries. Elsewhere, the permanent official is still the general secretary of the Union who is in charge of the organisation and of leading it, until he turns into a bit of a lordling imposed on the Union.

The approach we should take, since we cannot get by without standing officials, is to ensure that the latter are mere employees, in the strictest sense of the term. They would have no vote and no voice at committee meetings and would attend those in order to take the minutes, offering an opinion only if asked. A functionary... a functionary and nothing more.

The general secretary, like the treasurer and like all the members of the committee, must work for a living and report to the workshop every day, lest they lose touch with the workers. They must also show that they are not living off the union dues. If anyone is to be paid out of those dues, it should not be the committee proper, and some comrade employed out of the union's necessity, but one who has no say in the union's decision-making.

This should apply also to the Local Federation and Regional Confederation.

This policy is harder to apply to the National Confederation. But on the other hand, the general secretaryship should be renewed at each congress, with the incumbent prohibited from being re-elected for more than two consecutive terms—although alternate terms may be acceptable. The danger here is much reduced, and anything representing a help in averting or reducing it—should it not prove possible to banish it altogether—should be welcomed.[14]

---

14 Ángel Pestaña, ¿*Sindicato único?* *(Orientaciones Sobre organización sindical)* (Madrid 1921), pp. 19–21.

The Sindicato único

This is one of the most interesting issues raised by the congress, which recognized the enormous implications, and two whole sittings were set aside for its discussion and approval. The unanimity by which the resolution was carried is clear proof of the proletariat's yearning for change, in respect to organisational matters related to workers' associations. It was an oddity that groups of workers, drawn not from a similar sector or industry, but from a given trade or profession, should have launched two, three or more unions for that trade or profession within the same locality. The drawbacks to such organisational arrangements were exposed time and time again when those bodies were defeated by the bourgeoisie, and on other occasions when, without quite failing, the success of our struggle was compromised for the want of unity among workers. It was because of this that the congress saw fit to render more compact and close-knit through its resolution on the *sindicato único*, which embraces an entire sector or industry.

There is no question that this amendment to organisational methods is very important, but it would be childish to argue that we can implement it fully in a very short period of time as some have suggested. Within some sectors and industries implementation is not going to be feasible until such time as genuine enthusiasm is consistently invested in efforts to achieve the desired end. So there is no question of eliminating the time factor from a matter of such overwhelming significance [...]

Furthermore, we hold that this mode of organisation is futuristic in that its very simplicity will, if necessary, make it feasible to compile complete figures for overall production, as well as to proceed with the distribution of said production.

It is, therefore, understandable if the *sindicatos únicos*

should be the most faithful expression of the constructive, offensive and defensive provision sought by us producers.

Its organisational make-up

A *sine qua non* of the establishment of sectoral and industrial unions is for at least half of the sections (still trade unions at present) to be in favor of their establishment. Let us imagine that in some locality there are six organised sections engaged in the same branch of activity. Three are all for amalgamation and three against it or, for the present, not disposed to follow the example set by the three amalgamating sections. The latter should proceed as quickly as they are able with the launching of a *sindicato único*. In any case, it is imperative that they not turn their backs on those sections that are not currently joining the newly created body. On the contrary, the former need to keep the latter briefed on all the business and activity they carry out; it is our belief that such ongoing and amicable liaison will better serve the purpose in mind. Keeping to themselves would exacerbate the differences already in existence, which we would wager were the effective cause of the failure to reach an accommodation. Those sections that fail to amalgamate from the outset must not be marginalised or labelled as 'scab'. Scabbing is inconceivable other than in organisations that blatantly betray the workers' cause during strikes, by means of denunciations or other serious actions that well merit the label [...]

We believe that this is a faithful reflection of the will of congress on this point, since, while we concede the relevance of the time factor in having these resolutions adopted in principle, we also mean to see them implemented, as briefly outlined above, within a reasonable time frame; which will rule out the endless negotiations that might outwardly be caused by a troublesome focus on personalities.

Let us allow time for the establishment of *sindicatos únicos*, but, once these are in place, let us also set a period of grace within which the unaffiliated can revise and amend their performance prior to their being excluded from the broad workers' movement.

Some congress accords

Motion 7: In battles between capital and labor, unions affiliated to the Confederation are obliged to give preference to direct-action methods, as long as there are no bona fide circumstances of genuine *force majeure* requiring recourse to different approaches.

Motions 19 and 22: Professional politicians can never represent workers' organisations and the latter must see to it that they are not based in any political premises.

Motion 21: The unions have an imperative duty to see to it by all permissible means that the women—partners, daughters, etc.,—living alongside them and working alongside them in some industry or trade, are organised into unions.

In mixed trade unions, the steering committees should be mixed also, so that women take an interest in their battles and personally commit to their economic emancipation.

Motion 26: As long as there is a company in any given locality paying its operatives the set rate and employing unionised workers, no trade union shall provide labor to any other employer not meeting the same conditions. Nevertheless, when the work that needs doing is such as to be of direct benefit to the organisation, labor costs may be reduced with the consent of the comrades who are to perform it and of the unions to which they belong.

Motions 40, 43, 44 and 50: a) There is a duty upon every union member to do whatever he may to thwart the exploitation of minors. b) Under no pretext and in no sector will overtime be worked as long as there are members of that trade without jobs, and if the union, to which the comrade who is obliged to work overtime belongs, reckons it is strong enough to do so, it shall not countenance overtime under any circumstances. c) Those trades that have successfully imposed a maximum working day of eight hours are to help the rest to secure the same victory and then, on the say-so of their Federations, can target the introduction of the standard rate of pay, circumstances permitting.

Motion 47: a) Bodies that do not constitute professional or trade combinations for the purpose of standing up to capital should have no direct input into matters affecting the unions: but congress looks sympathetically upon those that uphold a social ideal consonant with the interests of the proletariat working outside of the unions and on behalf of the emancipation of the producer class. b) Rationalist teachers, having rendered sterling service to the working class and being a necessary factor in the struggle for emancipation, may have a direct input into union business, as long as they are organised as a body.

Motion 48: No comrade who is not from a given trade or locality may be appointed to committees and federations within a locality. But when it comes to regional congresses or gatherings, a comrade from the locality wherein the delegating union is based or the one where the meeting is due to be held may be appointed as delegate [...]

Motion 37: This working party is minded that the most practical means of boosting the dignity and the morale and profiles of 'handicapped' comrades is for the Regional Committee to have an input into handicapped organisations, supporting these materially, taking a hand in centres of production (already or yet to be established) where handicapped persons engage in manual tasks, as well as having an ongoing, general input into artistic and musical associations.

It is our belief that by so doing and by drawing them into our bosom, this organisation will largely be able to avert begging and, on the other hand, will also avert their having to ply for trade on the streets. Provided that the local committees first draw these comrades into the broader workers' organisation, it wrests them away from those reactionary protective agencies currently manipulating them according to their whims.

As a result, this working party believes that it would be extremely useful to introduce collective workshops. Said workshops should operate under the administrative supervision of the workers' organisation.

With an eye to technical operation from the industrial point of view, those nominated for this task should themselves be handicapped persons versed in the various industries in which said workshops might be engaged.

Such problems as might arise in terms of proper development and expansion relate to the distribution and sale of manufactured goods, and in order to do away with this difficulty, the Municipality should, at the urging of the working class, be applied to for a number of fixed outlets in the busiest parts of the city, as long as those outlets are no blight upon the city's appearance or the free movement of citizens. As well, outlets should be located at the gates of the markets, in conditions akin to those outlined earlier in this resolution.

As a result, therefore, it is our view that in order to do away with street begging, such workshops and fixed outlets should be set up, where the public could go to purchase manufactured goods. As to the internal operation of such workshops, this should differ from what we might regard as collective workshop activity.

By which we mean that the essential point is to furnish the handicapped with raw materials and that the full product of the manufactured goods should be paid to the individual manufacturer, except for a small deduction to cover commission, lighting and workshop rental costs.[15]

The statements above offer an economic breakdown of demands designed to do away with exploitation in the future society and to repudiate politicians and Leninists. These were binding upon the CNT's trade unionism: an ability to open wage-earners' eyes to hard and fast goals, handled by dedicated, steadfast syndicalists capable of standing up to repression; an eye for the detailed, practical implementation of resolutions; a wide-ranging vision taking in women, children and the disabled. Linked to which, the anarcho-syndicalist leadership was fully alive to its revolutionary mission as well as to the dangers surrounding it, and equipped itself with sound tools.

The *sindicato único* gathered all the workers of the same firm or locality (if the locality was small enough) under one roof. There was a community of interests and solidarity between skilled workers, specialists and labourers whose differing degrees of skill and pay rates tended to divide and split asunder. Solidarity was not restricted to the mythic slogan "Workers of the world unite", as it was inside the UGT and European-style trade unionism (long forgotten these days in France, Germany, etc.), and workers stuck together regardless of work distinctions.

Brief review of the historical backdrop

Knowing how CNT personnel operated, one can better understand anarcho-syndicalism's élan in Spain's past.

---

15 *Memoria del Congreso de Sants en 1918. Nuestro parecer Sobre algunos de los acuerdos adoptados* [being the National Committee's commentary on the Sants regional congress in 1918], extracts taken from Manuel Lladonosa's *El congrès de Sants* (Barcelona 1974) pp. 171–174, 179–181 and 184–185. Many of these accords were then passed at the national plenum of the CNT's 1919 congress.

The ideas of the International reached Spain thanks to an Italian deputy dispatched there by Bakunin (on the basis that he enjoyed free rail travel), who conflated the all-embracing ideas of the International with those of Bakunin, who in turn was in favor of encouraging the spread of unionisation by the workers through the Alliance.[16] When Marxists took exception to this conflation, a split with the UGT (*Unión General de Trabajadores*/General Workers' Union) resulted. The UGT grew rapidly from a membership of 57,000 in 1905 to 148,000 in 1933.

Between 1900 and 1911, the history of the Spanish labour movement was punctuated by many events: The colonial war in Morocco triggered a mutiny by recruits in Barcelona in 1909, in the wake of which the anarchist educationist Francisco Ferrer was executed by firing squad. Anarcho-syndicalist groups, ever-present since the introduction of the socialist ideas of the International Working Men's Association in 1868, finally began to coordinate. Thanks to this, the CNT had a membership of 30,000 when it was launched in 1911.

One glaring mistake made by the CNT was that it turned a blind eye to colonial exploitation in the Spanish territory in Morocco, and failed to campaign for and alongside the victims of exploitation in the Maghreb. Ángel Pestaña was alone

---

[16] The Alliance (*Alianza*) was a body that coordinated hand-picked militants to accelerate and further the advances made by the workers, and kept these safe from politicians during the act of revolution, which it believed was well within the capability of the masses. Marx and Engels reckoned that, initially at any rate, the proletariat needed to be committed to the political struggle (for several years or even decades). They did not believe in the capacity of the working man. As formulated by Lenin, this meant that the Party's role was to introduce the elements of science and consciousness, or order and discipline. Bakunin was opposed to future leadership structures: "Were the International able to organise itself as a State, we, its heartfelt, impassioned supporters, should turn into its most rabid foes". See *Bakunin Crítica y Acción* (Libros de Anarres 2006). For this very reason, the Alliance was at no time a party in the Leninist sense.

in raising the issue at the 1931 congress, although he did not table a motion through his trade union.[17]

The upshot of the First World War was that Spanish industry serviced the belligerents, and that exploitation of wage-earners surged as a result. In August 1917, the CNT and UGT made contact with each other and decided to mount a revolutionary general strike together. It failed, thanks to the chicanery of the socialists, summarised thus in the Spanish Cortes by Indalecio Prieto: "Sure, we gave weapons to the People. But it is also true that we did not give them ammunition".[18] In order to foment and orchestrate future labor disputes, the CNT espoused the *sindicato único* format.

The efficacy of the new format was borne out in 1919. Catalonia's power company, La Canadiense, was brought to a standstill by a strike mounted in solidarity with eight bookkeeper employees (over their being taken on as permanent staff at a lower rate of pay).[19] That solidarity then spread to many power plants and textile plants. The government declared a state of emergency in Catalonia and conscripted the workers who nevertheless refused to return to work. Their demands were for a pay increase, an eight-hour working day and half pay for days

---

[17] Pestaña declared: "I move that the Confederation should seek for the protectorate zone in Africa the very same political and social conditions as other regions of Spain are to enjoy. That the Moors in the Spanish Protectorate be deemed citizens just as we are, and enjoy the same rights and the same duties and be shown the same respect as any of us. That all our social legislation be enforced there, that the view not be taken that within Spain there is one region whose inhabitants enjoy a lower status [...] the impact of this resolution might prove revolutionary in that it might trigger enduring malaise among the Moroccans who are under the rule of other countries". *Memoria del Congreso extraordinario celebrado en Madrid los días 11 al 16 de junio de 1931* (Barcelona 1932), pp. 85–86.

[18] José Peirats, *La CNT en la revolución española* (Toulouse 1953) Vol. I, p. 18.

[19] Albert Balcells, *El sindicalisme a Barcelona (1916–1923)* (Barcelona 1961), p. 69.

spent on strike. That strike began in January at La Canadiense and by the end of February it affected the whole of Catalonia. The strike dragged on into March, and between 24 March and 7 April there was a general strike in place. On 14 April, the employers' union caved in to all of the demands, including the release of 3,000 arrested workers. Some 100,000 workers had taken part in the strike in Catalonia.

That strike, entirely the handiwork of the CNT, is an example of that organisation's effectiveness; that year its membership numbered 755,000, which is to say, nearly 10 percent of the working population. In Catalonia alone, the CNT had 252,000 members by 1920, whereas the UGT had 211,000 in the whole of Spain.

In 1922, a CNT delegation was dispatched to the launch of the Third International in Moscow, and decided not to affiliate to the new International in light of the situation of anarchists and the Russian workers. Two Marxists in the delegation—Andrés Nin and Joaquín Maurín—then quit the CNT, and went on to launch the POUM.[20]

But more serious developments were afoot: the Catalan employers, out for revenge over the La Canadiense strike, armed men who gunned down trade union officers, including the man who had been the inspiration behind the strike tactics—Salvador Seguí. This was the era of *pistolerismo* (pitting the 'hired killers' against the syndicalists). In response,

---

20 The POUM (*Partido Obrero de Unificación Marxista*/Workers' Party of Marxist Unification) was an amalgamation of four Marxist groups active since 1930. One had been led by Andrés Nin, who, between 1921 and 1929, had been a supporter within the USSR of the dissident Bolsheviks and Trotsky—although he fell out with Trotsky in 1933 when Trotsky insisted on his entering the PSOE. The amalgamation was supposed to form a CP that would not be under Moscow's thumb. Amalgamation was achieved in 1935 after a year of fraught discussions with an eye to the 1936 elections. The USSR-backed CP regarded the POUM as a gang of Trotskyist and fascist traitors, and Trotsky regarded them as bourgeois revisionists.

the defense groups were formed. There was all-out struggle between 1919 and 1923.

These were the days of Mussolini and military dictatorships across Europe (Hungary, Bulgaria), and the Spanish employer class needed a strong government. General Primo de Rivera took power in 1923, and not one political group lifted a finger to oppose him. The CNT opted to disband and take its structures underground, though at a local level the unions carried on with their activities, sometimes under a different designation.

During the Primo de Rivera dictatorship, the PSOE and the UGT not only failed to oppose the regime, but actually collaborated with it. This explains why the Mussolinian model, followed in Spain, never ruled out the parliamentary road: another effort was to wipe out the CNT by means of state sponsorship of the UGT. Thus the UGT's general secretary, Largo Caballero, was seconded to the Ministry of Labor as councillor of State. But the dictatorship had no trade union policy; the workers were not taken in. Between 1920 and 1926 the UGT stagnated, with only a slight rise in its membership from 211,000 to 219,000.

Where the *cenetistas* (CNT personnel) stood was something of an unknown quantity as far as their adversaries were concerned. In fact, since 1927, the CNT had been flanked by an anarchist federation, the FAI (*Federación Anarquista Ibérica*/Iberian Anarchist Federation, the aspiration being to embrace Portugal as well, though this was never achieved, due to the Salazar dictatorship's repression), the aim of which was to further the spread of anarchist ideas inside the CNT and across the country.

The dictatorship failed to live up to the ambitions of the Spanish employers who did not take to Mussolini-style *dirigiste* economics; the left-wing political parties began to stir, and disputes took a more bitter turn. The 1930–1931 period was crucial, for the regime allowed a measure of trade union reorganisation, doubtless on account of possible tensions arising from the 1929 depression. By around 1930, the UGT membership stood at 277,000.

From the Interior minister, General Mola, and following overtures made by Pestaña, the CNT secured the right to organise. Mola went on to become the organiser of the 1936 coup d'état and, in particular, was behind the orders that left-wing leaders be executed en masse and out of hand, without trial.

This was the backdrop against which the April 1931 municipal elections were held, with a clear victory going to the republicans, whereupon a Republic was proclaimed on 14 April 1931. King Alfonso XIII was no more keen than the employers to be forced into a direct confrontation. He abdicated and left the country. Given that a left-leaning military coup had been put down harshly in December 1930, the right opted to let the left bring discredit upon itself and suffer the impact of the 1929 crash, which was already making itself felt in the land. When this failed to come about, those same forces resorted to violence in 1936.

Over and above any difficulties faced at the top of the trade unions (of which more anon) the workers unionised in their droves: the UGT grew to 1,200,000 members and the CNT to at least 800,000. With that sort of following, the CNT national committee's secretary was officially the Confederation's only full-time and paid officer (see the "sham pyramid" below for a more nuanced picture). In fact there were only about twenty comrades who received emoluments or wages for their work—a very small number compared with the UGT.

The CNT as a harmonious whole, and the sham pyramid

The leadership, CNT cadres and FAI cadres alike, was drawn from the ranks of the working class and moulded by anarcho-syndicalism, just as they had been from the very beginning under the First International in Spain. The 1870s had seen the emergence of Anselmo Lorenzo, Tomás González Morado (both type-setters) and the like. The creation of the CNT in 1911 brought to prominence men like Galo Díez, José Negre (railway worker) and Manuel Buenacasa (carpenter). 1916–1918 threw up militants such as Salvador Seguí (painter and decorator), Ángel Pestaña (watch-maker) and Juan Peiró (glass-blower). During the Primo de Rivera dictatorship, up popped a group that included Ricardo Sanz, Buenaventura Durruti (metalworker), Juan García Oliver, Francisco Ascaso (these last two waiters), Antonio Ortiz (carpenter), etc. Come the establishment of the Republic, in came the likes of Mariano R. Vázquez (construction worker), Cipriano Mera (bricklayer) and David Antona.... During the civil war along came José Peirats (bricklayer), the Sabaté brothers (Quico Sabaté was a plumber) and Raúl Carballeira, some of whom were to lose their lives in the struggle against Francoism between 1948 and 1960.

From 1870 to 1936 and beyond, there was an uninterrupted succession of tried and tested syndicalists, all of working-class extraction. Those seventy years of militancy and working class self-education in both city and country, from Andalusia to Asturias and Catalonia, constituted the strength of the CNT. This was a mighty strength not comparable with and utterly different from what Russia had to show.

In Russia during the nineteenth century, there had been only three flare-ups of agitation: initially, the so-called Decembrists (anti-tsarist agitators drawn from the ranks of the enlightened bourgeoisie), then the exiles drawn from that same class and converted to socialism—like Herzen and Bakunin—and finally the *narodniks* or Populists, the offspring of the bourgeoisie who turned to the people with social ideas that were very often entirely theoretical.

Practically speaking, workers only had the twenty-five years between 1880 and 1905 to generate their own cadres. The ensuing repression decimated the educated classes and left little scope for the emergence of a fresh crop of youngsters—up until 1917, at any rate. And of the revolutionary leaders, not one was of working class extraction; they were petit bourgeois intellectuals like Lenin or Trotsky or Bukharin, etc., and their chief concern was with devouring one another at the expense of the workers, just as Makhaiski had forecast that they would, back in 1905.[21]

Leaders drawn from the bourgeoisie never posed a problem for the CNT as it had very few of them: we call to mind the doctors Pedro Vallina and Isaac Puente.[22]

The second factor accounting for the CNT's strength was its organization, which was rooted in three things: direct action and the *sindicato único*, federalism and globalism.

Direct action, as defined and spelled out by the French anarcho-syndicalists at the beginning of the twentieth century, means rejecting State interference in negotiations with the bosses, and insistence upon all demands being met. In the face of it, the bosses are left with only two options: to give in, which meant success for the union and more members for it; or to stand firm, which usually triggered a flurry of strikes. Time and again the boss would hire scabs and strike-breakers who had to be persuaded to show solidarity. A violent response from the bosses, in the form of drafting in scab labour, often triggered violent pressures by a number of groups or individuals that would persuade the bosses to cave in to worker demands.

A typical example of this was the La Canadiense strike mentioned earlier. The very same tactics persisted between 1931 and 1936. When employees of the Telephone Company across Spain came out on strike, the peasants' union in Ronda decided to support them, and its militants severed

---

21 Makhaiski or Makhayev took the view that militants of bourgeois extraction were out to seize power for themselves, on the pretext of backing the workers. See Alexandre Skirda *Le Socialisme des intellectuels, Jan Waclav Makhaiski* (Paris 2001).

22 Not until the 1930s did Federica Montseny join the CNT, since she had previously espoused a critical line on anarcho-syndicalism.

many of the telegraph posts across the region. These were union members, most of them illiterate but with a clear and effective political outlook. Lots of folk, highly educated by the standards of formal bourgeois culture, lacked any such sense of the practical.

Federalism guaranteed great flexibility of action, which was crucial given the differences between the regions. Each *comarcal* (county) or local committee was free to embark on action without having to consult with central committees that might have been more or less *au fait* with the issues. There was a example of this in 1934: the CNT and UGT could not agree on a joint approach. In Asturias, though, the two UGT and CNT regional organisations entered into a pact of alliance (which just goes to show how influential anarcho-syndicalist tactics were within the UGT), but within the Asturian regional CNT, the CNT's local federation in La Felguera rejected the pact. This might, at first glance, seem like a contradiction and a weakness, but it reflected the local situation and actualities of the UGT and CNT. In Aragon between 1934 and 1936, cooperatives and farming ventures were boosted, which was unheard of in other regions.

The third especially distinguishing feature is what we might refer to as *globalism*.

The CNT never restricted itself to trade unionism and its halls were the venues for literacy classes or Ferrer Guàrdia-type schools for the young. Ever since Francisco Ferrer Guàrdia faced the firing squad in 1909, his schools had carried on with his work under the aegis of the CNT across Spain (except that now they were directed at workers' sons and daughters, whereas Ferrer had also targeted the offspring of the bourgeoisie).[23] Funding support came

---

23 Ferrer Guàrdia was a free-mason, and in that capacity, urged a de facto alliance between the atheistic, left-leaning bourgeoisie and the workers' movement, a nonsensical view in that it involved no real pursuit of social revolution nor attempt to end wage slavery. Free-masons were quite commonplace within the CNT. One

from some unions, and the teachers, as a rule, were militants who did their teaching at the end of their working day. The study of Esperanto was also very commonplace, as were studies in vegetarianism, naturopathic medicine, contraception, sex education (from 1910 on), women's emancipation and excursions. All of these activities were mirrored in reviews, as well as in the trade union press. Allow me to offer a small selection of the latter from 1932: *Solidaridad Obrera* (Barcelona, a daily newspaper), *Tierra y Libertad* (Barcelona, a weekly), *La Tierra* (Madrid, a like-minded weekly), *La Revista Blanca* (Barcelona, monthly), *Nosotros* (Valencia, monthly), *Redención* (Alcoy), *Acción* (Cadiz), as well as newer publications like *CNT* (Madrid, daily), *Orto* (Valencia), *Solidaridad Proletaria* (Seville), *La Voz del Campesino* (Jerez) and so on. Not to mention pamphlets published under the auspices of unions or individuals and like-minded series, such as the (monthly) *La Novela Ideal*.[24]

Such multifaceted activity was neither redundant nor overdoing it. There was a point-by-point challenge to Catholic culture: starting at birth when first names like Acracio, Floreal, Germinal, Helios, etc., or Luz, Libertaria, Alba, Acracia, etc. were given—rather than Jesús, Salvador, Ignacio or Iñaki (after Jesuit founder Ignatius of Loyola), or, to take some female examples, Covadonga (the first mock-historical victory over the Muslims, featuring Santiago Matamoros, butcher of the unbelievers), Amparo (the protection of the Virgin Mary), Soledad or Dolores (a reference to the suffering of the Virgin), not to mention the litany of locations where there had been

---

resolution moved at the 1926 Zaragoza congress—but not mentioned in the official summary published in exile in France—recommended that free-masons should not hold positions of responsibility, as borne out in the August 1983 written testimony of Manuel Fabra, a free-mason and CNT member, and of Ramón Álvarez, a CNT member hostile to free-masonry.

24 Renée Lamberet, *Mouvements ouvriers et Socialistes (chronologie et bibliographie): L'Espagne (1750–1936)* (Paris 1963).

apparitions of the Virgin, places popularising names such as Pilar, Begoña, Guadalupe, Montserrat, Nuria, etc. Later, after death, atheists or poor Christians were excluded from Catholic graveyards. Even the preferred literary authors such as Tolstoy, Zola, Multatuli and Panaït Istrati[25] were different from the writers favoured by most bourgeois.

Another target for criticism was marxism (of the Leninist variety), its theory and practice within the USSR, which were depicted as what they were: the new ideology of the exploiter classes, a cloak donned so that they might continue their rule over the workers. The lessons of Bakunin, Kropotkin, Reclus, Rocker and Nettlau were published in book and pamphlet format. And there were lots of books and pamphlets examining marxism from the theoretical viewpoint (Bakunin, Kropotkin, Cafiero and Rocker) as well as from the practical, including the writings of Russian anarchists (Yartchuk, Gorelik, Voline, Arshinov, Makhno) and those of a number of *cenetistas* who had been to Russia (people such as Pestaña, Pérez Combina, Martín Gudell and Horacio Prieto). Not to mention propaganda arriving from Latin America (Mexico, Argentina and Uruguay), relations with which were very close indeed.

However, the CNT fell well short of flawlessness: hence the notion of the sham pyramid.

In hierarchical systems, power and the ruling class sit at the top and the exploited majority make up the base. The whole set-up might be represented as a pyramid, a battery of orders emanating from the top down.

But what has this to do with the CNT, which, in theory, adopted a more horizontal arrangement?

Some things in history represent anomalies: the creation of the FAI, anticipating the provisions of the Arshinov Platform, i.e. control of the trade union by an outside, foreign body (See Appendix IV below), the flirtations with alliances in the 1920s and the damaging controversy between *faístas*

---

25 Multatuli, who was a Dutch writer, and Panaït Israti, who was Romanian, were well known to older CNT members.

and *treintistas*. A few remarks about the latter should help explain the two preceding ones.

Certain *cenetistas* had their suspicions as to unspoken horse-trading going on between a group accused of reformism (Peiró and Pestaña and the so-called *treintistas*) and the republicans. The FAI became the home of attacks on reformism. In actual fact, a third tendency emerged, a group made up of Durruti, Ascaso, García Oliver, etc., who craved social revolution and cashed in on the popularity of the FAI whilst setting up a group that was answerable to nobody.

In what way was this falling-out any different than the falling-out between Trotskyists and Stalinists at around the same time?

The pro-Stalin Leninists or the pro-Trotsky faction who were in the gulags with the Italian-Croatian former-Trotskyist Antón Ciliga, fell out over matters relating to tactics and moves designed to seize control of the levers of the organisation, manipulating meetings and congresses as if the rank and file workers—whom they all purported to represent and lead—were brainless and incapable of articulating their opinions.[26]

Inside the CNT, the opinions of all the membership were actually sounded.

The tactics of attempted revolution, heralded by numerous spontaneous ventures spearheaded by the rank and file (see Appendix II below) demonstrated that some of the membership was in step with the FAI, but that there were serious and highly damnable shortcomings when it came to laying the groundwork for attack.

In fact, the Spanish left could not bring itself to introduce the social and economic changes the country so sorely needed, even from the point of view of a forward-looking capitalism,

---

[26] This was a logical Leninist stance, comparable to that of bourgeois politicians when their proposals are rejected at the ballot box. But in the USSR, the workers were already in the know; hence the sensitivity of the observations in Antón Ciliga in his 1938 book *The Russian Enigma*.

if only for straightforward surgical reasons and out of the merest regard for the lives of the majority of the population. The workers, hungry for immediate, real and definitive socio-economic changes could not understand the snail's pace. The masses craved change and yearned for social revolution.

At the grassroots level in Asturias in 1934, a formal alliance had been brokered, as we have seen, between the UGT and the CNT. And out of a socialist-organised uprising there spontaneously emerged a workers' alliance, under the UHP. To all workers, the UHP became a synonym for immediate revolutionary social change.

All of this ensured that the insults and mutual abuse swapped between the *cenetista* bigwigs (well-ensconced leaders barely—or not at all—answerable to the rank and file) were outweighed by the mutual reconciliation that culminated at the Zaragoza congress of May 1936. But the gulf between the rank and file membership and the leadership was not tackled, no more than by rotation of offices, which was not so much part of CNT practice as a response to police action when the unions were forced to fill vacancies created by the arrest of comrades.

In reality, within the CNT there were two lines on revolution and libertarian communism (see Appendix V below): that of the bigwigs who sought a revolution from above on a date of their own choosing, and that of the grassroots members out for immediate direct action designed to trigger a thoroughgoing social change in the workplace, in the *barrio* or at village level.

From the stances adopted in 1936–1939 and in 1944–1948, we may infer that the bigwigs believed in the value of alliance with some of the bourgeoisie—and later, even with the monarchy—as a means of directing and bolstering the CNT. This was utter nonsense, as would have been obvious had they actually explored writings and experiences of Bakunin, Kropotkin and anarchists who had emigrated from the USSR. This was all the more nonsensical when they had themselves witnessed the treachery of German socialists and like-minded trade unionists, calculated to eradicate revolutionary workers (Spartakists and direct actionists), and were aware of US intervention in its Central American backyard.

The CNT bigwigs emblazoned a superficial anarcho-syndicalism and anarchism (see Appendices VI, IV and V), which explains how they could so glibly and lastingly enter the governments of Catalonia and Spain (respectively, September 1936–May 1937 and November 1936–May 1937, and again from April 1938 until March 1939).

It is telling that there has been no analysis of the CNT's collaboration in government between 1936 and 1939, not in exile (pending a congress within Spain) nor within the Peninsula (driven by the need to organise first and foremost and to head off controversy), for which reason the polemics endure, and theoretical confusion persists. This is why it is important to know the actual numbers of militants on the payroll of the Organisation. As Pestaña has it:

> The claim in public that we are against paid officials, and the private understanding that in the day to day running of the organisation we have them, strikes me as an act of hypocrisy out of place in our group where we are forever claiming full responsibility for our actions.
>
> Officially, we have no paid officials today, but the editors of *Solidaridad Obrera* are paid.[27] Off the record, under the table, so to speak, there are two paid and permanent posts on the National Committee; one or two—more often two than one—on the Regional Committee of Catalonia; two

---

27 Pestaña attended the 1931 congress as representative of the administration of *Solidaridad Obrera*, which consisted of its editorial board (three employees), its administrators (three employees), its printing staff (five??), its panel of contributors (three), foreign correspondents (three), making a total somewhere between twelve and seventeen. See *Memoria, Congreso extraordinario celebrado en Madrid del 11 al 16 de junio 1931* (a multi-copied text, no place, no date cited, published in France), 11th edition, p. 108.

paid posts within the Barcelona Local Federation; and a number of Barcelona unions, some of which also have two or three paid officials. But let us repeat that this is off the record and such payments are justified by invoking the tasks they perform.

Not that the Catalan organisation is alone in having paid officials: the practice applies to virtually every region of Spain.[28]

Having thirty-odd paid officials out of a membership of about 550,000 and a catchment area twice that size is a trifling matter in terms of material benefits, but it is huge in terms of influence and the exercise of power over the rest.

That situation was flying in the face of the 1919 congress, which had decided that only the general secretary would be paid (approximately the wage of a skilled worker). But the "non-remuneration policy operated a selection of leaders among the most dedicated, men who owned nothing and remained entrenched in their *refus de parvenir*".[29] With the upshot that most of the CNT officials carried out their trade union duties after the day's work was done and sometimes had to lay out money for the travel essential to keeping in touch.

Another weakness was the rejection, for fear of bureaucratisation, of the federations of industry for which some militants lobbied. According to the militants, these federations had to be organised along the lines of horizontal and vertical trusts (for, say, the metalworking, transport industries, etc., embracing all of the unions engaged in them), these being better suited to the concentration of capital whilst also offering a foretaste of the unions taking over the running of the economy themselves. Without a shadow of a doubt, they would have enabled a clearer appreciation of what needed

---

28 Ángel Pestaña in *Solidaridad Obrera*, No. 409, 24 April 1934, reprinted in *Ángel Pestaña, Trayectoria sindicalista* (with foreword by Antonio Elorza) (Madrid 1974), pp. 678–679.
29 Maura Romero, writing in *Government and Opposition*, 1970.

collectivising. And all the propaganda books and pamphlets peddling libertarian communism (above all those from Isaac Puente, inspired by Besnard) described a post-revolutionary regime, organised by and for the workers, without the transitional period called for by the Marxists, and with federations of industry and agriculture and inter-related regional bodies.

Another drawback was follower-ism and leader-ism, even in the absence of bureaucratisation. This was manifest in culture, in the expertise—be it economic, political or technical (e.g. in the manufacture of explosives)—that some militants had acquired, despite exhausting toil for poverty wages. Such militants possessed experience very often superior to the bourgeois professionals who operated in the same field (such as that displayed by Peiró when he unmasked police skullduggery during the years of *pistolerismo* in Barcelona), and so they wielded an intellectual sway over many union members.[30] In fact, this is commonplace in group sociology, as is evident in the case of José Díaz, who defected from the CNT to the Communist Party along with the membership of his trade union, the dockworkers of Seville; as well as Andrés Nin and his influence in Lérida; Stalin and the Georgians; Trotsky and the Russian Jews; and so on. Structures and a grounding in anarcho-syndicalism were therefore not enough to thwart this deviation, although

---

30 A shrewd French (though actually Russian-born) observer at the 1931 congress, Nicolas Lazarévitch, noted: "As to the National Committee, it was taken to task for having failed to intervene with due vigour and forcefulness in response to the repression in Seville. The speeches were very violent, and some very harsh views were expressed. In spite of this, all it took was for Peiró, the director of *Solidaridad Obrera*, to adopt a hang-dog look of an accused man standing before the court and acknowledge his mistakes for the heartstrings of delegates to be given a tug and for them ultimately to decide not to proceed with any changes to the organisation's leadership bodies". N. Lazarévitch, *À travers les révolutions espagnoles* (Paris 1972), p. 20 (first published in *La Révolution prolétarienne*, No. 121, November 1931).

they did minimise it: the stream of militants whom we have named proves that the mere existence of a leader was no impediment to the training of leadership material.

The breaking dawn and shortsightedness

The UHP articulated the deep-seated yearnings of the Spanish workers, as did all the attempted revolutions since January 1932. Above and beyond party political squabbles, currents and factions within each current, reality itself cried out for social change.

Contrary to the experience elsewhere in Europe, Spanish workers had known no profound changes in the feudal, Catholic, landed-property system because of the bourgeoisie's failure to force the pace. The absence of left- or right-wing politics and the tentative, timid and sluggish tactics of the republican governments from 1931 onwards merely fuelled their impatience. The Second Republic of 1931 proclaimed itself to be "a democratic republic of workers of all sorts, organised into a regimen of Freedom and Justice" (Article 1 of the constitution). It boasted, "The Spanish state has no official religion" (Article 3) and that "Spain abjures war as an instrument of national policy", in addition to a long litany of moderately interesting measures. This was empty rhetoric bereft of economic equality and with the admixture of brutal, even criminal repression by the forces of order. But the poor took for granted that the Republic was now a reality and that it was poised to work in their interests.

Against this backdrop of expectations and demands with regard to social change, the apparent defeats suffered by libertarian communism in 1932, in January and December 1933, and the UHP in Asturias in 1934 actually proved to be glimmers of hope, paving the way for further attempted revolutions.

In 1936, the left came together in order to win the elections. The CNT discreetly urged recourse to the ballot box and the figures clearly suggest it had an impact: in 1933 the left claimed 3,200,000 votes, 20 percent of the turn-out; in 1936 that figure rose to 4,800,000, or 35 percent—meaning an additional 1,600,000 votes. Of course, we also have to include in this figure a number of returned economic migrants—who had left as the result of the aftermath of the world depression in 1929—plus younger, newly qualifying voters and the franchise granted to women in 1931.

What might the CNT input have been? The figure of 1,000,000 votes, which was bandied about by the CNT itself, strikes me as acceptable.

The left secured a slender 1.1 percent majority with a fifty-three-seat[31] margin over the right, thanks to the system of proportional representation in use. Actually, the right retained much of its enormous clout.

The most remarkable change was the strides made by the Communist Party during this period, with fourteen deputies returned as against just one in 1933. Just to review the results: the Party took 12,900 votes in Málaga in 1933; by 1936 this had risen to 52,750. The 3,000 Communist Party voters in Cádiz in 1933 soared to 97,000. Oviedo's 16,830 swelled to 170,500 and so on. There was a baffling paradox in that the membership of the Party, according to the Party's own sources, sat at between 17,000 and 30,000,[32] and nationally the Party had taken 1,800,000 votes. The only explanation is that it raked in CNT voters, and, in fact, thirteen of its fourteen deputies came from regions where anarchists were in the majority.

This political faux pas by the *cenetistas* (boosting their fiercest ideological foe) can be explained by their grudges against the UGT and the PSOE.

The Popular Front got a rapturous welcome, and pressure from the people secured the much-wanted release of political prisoners. As in 1931 there were no thoroughgoing

---

31 See Manuel Cruells *El 6 d'octubre a Catalunya* and Javier Tusell *Las elecciones del Frente Popular* (Madrid 1971).

32 *Historia del Partido Comunista de España* (Paris & Warsaw 1960), p. 111.

reforms announced. The police continued to open fire on workers. The government was incapable of taking effective action. Right-wing outrages proliferated, thanks to the handiwork of the Falange, a pro-Mussolini group led by José Antonio Primo de Rivera, the son of the man who had been dictator from 1923 to 1927. Tensions were running high on the left, as highlighted by the headlines in *Solidaridad Obrera* between 1 and 18 July 1936:

> Should the UGT fail to come up with a prompt response to the cordial appeal issuing from the Extra-ordinary Congress of the CNT, the responsibility for what may ensue will fall entirely upon the heads of the socialists.[33]

> The venture is a mighty one, especially with the trapeze-artists of the POUM on the scene. But enthusiasm on your part, plus pressure from the Confederation will steer you to victory.[34] (There is a cartoon by Gallo showing hands bound with manacles bearing the initials UGT.)[35]

> (Another Gallo cartoon shows a woman gagged—the revolutionary press—and a man carrying a hammer and sickle urging her to be quiet: behind him looms a monster marked with a swastika.)[36]

> Enough! Only lunatics and agents provocateurs can imagine a connection between fascism and anarchism [...] Let the gentlemen from the Popular Front watch their step![37]

---

33 9 July 1936, front page headline.
34 12 July 1936, apropos of a strike in Sardañola at the Uralita (cement) plant.
35 14 July 1936, p. 1.
36 15 July 1936, p. 1.
37 16 July 1936, p. 1.

Lack of vision in fraught times and the counter-revolutionary behaviour of Spanish marxism opened the gates to fascism.[38]

And another Gallo cartoon, at the foot of a photograph from the CNT construction strike in Madrid, a fiefdom of the UGT: two pistols marked UGT and CNT are trained on each other with the caption: "No!"[39]

The army's attempted coup d'état was the logical consequence of the republican government's passivity. Yet the CNT had, months earlier, anticipated the course that events were going to take:

[...] Right-wing elements are ready to trigger an army revolt [...] Morocco seems to be the main concentration and epicenter of the plot [...] If the plotters light the fire, opposition must be taken to its ultimate consequences, and the liberal bourgeoisie and its Marxist allies must not be allowed to stem the flood of events, in the event that fascist rebellion is nipped in the bud [...] Fascism versus social revolution [...] Keep a watchful eye out, comrades![40]

---

38 17 July 1936, p. 1.
39 17 July 1936.
40 Statement from the CNT National Committee, 14 February 1936, as reprinted in Peirats, op. cit. Vol. 1. According to the review *Noir & Rouge* No. 41, p. 16, the statement was drafted by the CNT's then national secretary, Horacio M. Prieto. It is interesting to compare this outlook with that of Pestaña, by then leader of the Syndicalist Party: "Q. *Is the rightist menace—of a coup d'état—one to be reckoned with, for instance?* A. No! They have missed the boat. As far as the Right is concerned, the period of instability—which was very worrying at times—is over. A purge of the army and machinery of state will strip them of any chance of acting. Their current modus operandi—assassinations and terrorist attacks—is proof of their weakness". [Interview of 18 May 1936, published in *La Révolution prolétarienne*, 10 June 1936, p. 224]. There is anecdotal evidence in José Robuster's testimony, as it appears in Víctor

18 July 1936 marshalled all the usual enemies against a common foe (with the bourgeoisie and authoritarian left—with the odd exception—lining up against the libertarians).

Alba's *Colectivizadores,* to bear out just how shortsighted Pestaña was with regard to what happened in Barcelona on 18 July 1936.

Chapter Two
Catalonia as a Model: Self-Management Emerges in Barcelona; The First Contradictions

Catalonia was where anarcho-syndicalism organised best at grassroots levels, although there was a separation with the upper echelons of the CNT—a phenomenon that set the pattern for other regions.

The army was defeated mostly by the CNT-FAI and Civil Guard and Assault Guards, as well as by a number of Catalanist and POUM militants. Catalonia's Generalitat government, headed by Companys, had shown itself incapable of fight, even though it had been behind an outbreak of insurrection back in October 1934. "The proletariat armed itself; we did not have enough arms to issue to the proletariat".[1]

The Catalan CNT's regional committee found itself with almost complete mastery of the situation by 20 July 1936. A regional plenum of local and comarcal committees was hurriedly convened for that afternoon! In the wake of the attempted revolutions in 1932, January and December 1933 and in Asturias in 1934, and the publicity given to libertarian communism and the resolution passed on the subject by the Zaragoza Congress a month and a half previously, the policy to be followed was obvious, but the decision making conformed to Horacio M. Prieto's understanding of libertarian communism [see Appendix V].

---

1   Statement made by Companys to *News Chronicle*, carried in translation in *Fragua Social* (hereinafter F.S.), 23 August 1937, p. 7.

Marianet (aka Mariano Vázquez, secretary of the regional committee of Catalonia) later wrote: "[The CNT-FAI] did not let itself be over-awed by the climate, nor was it intoxicated by the swift, emphatic, resounding victory it had achieved. And amid this utter mastery of the situation, the membership looked at the wider picture and exclaimed: The towns in fascist hands must be liberated! Libertarian communism is non-existent. We must first thrash the enemy wherever he may be".[2]

At a gathering of some 2,000 militants on 21 or 22 July 1936, after Vázquez and García Oliver had announced that libertarian communism was being set aside, José Peirats made a highly critical riposte, which was cut short by Juanel who gave him a tongue-lashing.[3] Faced with such closed minds, Peirats walked out, as did the comrades from Hospitalet de Llobregat, except for Xena. Federica Montseny threatened to have them 'seen to'.[4]

Although the leadership sang the praises of alliance with the republican bourgeoisie and put their anarchist aspirations on hold, the rank and file, espousing Horacio M. Prieto's rationale and following the Isaac Puente line, was not interested in such considerations. Which explains the emergence of self-management in spite of everything, and despite all the leaders.

The 21 July 1936 edition of *Solidaridad Obrera*, on its front page, carried the following statement from the regional committee:

---

2 Mariano R. Vázquez, secretary of the Catalonian Regional Committee at the time, was co-opted on to the CNT National Committee as general secretary in late August 1936. See *De Julio a julio*, pp. 207, 208.

3 As reported to the author by a number of comrades in Bordeaux in 1974.

4 Ibidem. Montseny, who would later champion a firebrand anarchism while in exile, stated: "We were in the government but the streets were slipping from our grasp". This comment was published in Daniel Guérin's *No Gods, No Masters*.

In these grave times, it behooves each and every one of us to abide by the general watchwords emanating from this committee. We have a common foe [*illegible*] in fascism. We are taking it on. Our struggle is with it, and it is it that we must crush. Nothing more, nothing less. At the same time, cognizant of our responsibilities, we have determined that all essential supply services should remain in operation, as should communications, lest the people run short of basic foodstuffs, and lest priceless liaison be interrupted.

—Regional Committee, Barcelona, 20 July 1936

Note: This very morning we broadcast instructions over the radio for the bakers, milkmen, market employees, etc., to return to work so that vital necessities should not run short [...]

This statement, then, asserted that they had reverted to an almost normal economy, something that sat uneasily alongside the repeated exhortations to libertarian communism associated with previous essays on revolution.

Two different watchwords very soon surfaced: *Back to work*[5] and *Against looting*.[6]

At the same time, two campaigns were launched: 1) *Alliances* entered into with other sectors against the military,

---

5 See *Boletín de Información CNT-FAI* (hereinafter *B.I.*) 24 July 1936, *Solidaridad Obrera* (hereinafter *S.O.*) 25 July 1936, p. 4 and 26 July 1936 (See Peirats, op. cit., Vol. I, p. 169), 28 July 1936, p. 4. and 31 July 1936, p. 8.

6 Radio broadcast on 25 July 1936 (See Peirats, op. cit., Vol. I, p. 169: "Commandeered vehicles must be handed back", *S.O.*, 26 July 1936, p. 3. "Comrades of ours tried for holding up 'La Escocesa' have handed in the proceeds of seizures made from churches and the cathedral in Vich to the Generalidad government", *B.I.*, 28 July 1936: "Any individual of whom it can be shown that he has carried out trespasses against the people's rights will be shot by us", *B.I.*, 29 July 1936 and *S.O.* of 30 July 1936 (Peirats, op. cit., Vol. I).

despite the notable earlier resentments that still simmered;[7] and 2) *Protection for foreign-owned assets*, given the danger of intervention if this was not done.[8]

Meanwhile, with the military barely routed in Barcelona, the CNT-FAI decided to raise militias for the liberation of Zaragoza. Since the unions had taken over the lynchpins of the economy—metalworking, transport, energy services, communications, trade and provisions—from 24 July on it proved possible to outfit some 2,500 men and women.

Metalworking: On page two of its 22 July 1936 edition, *Solidaridad Obrera* announced that the CNT metalworking union was inviting "iron boilermakers and welders" to adapt production centres for "the armor-plating of trucks and other necessary tasks".

On 12 August, a journalist writing in the *Boletín de Información CNT-FAI* wrote: "In metalworking firms, as a result of the events in July, two new forms of administration have surfaced. One, involving worker management without restrictions of any sort, by means of take-over. The other represents a greatly attenuated bourgeois mode of administration through monitoring activity carried out by workers' factory committees".

By way of an example of straightforward take-over, let us look at the Torrens Company, which employed 500 workers

---

7   "The newspapers *La Humanitat, La Publicitat, El Diluvio* and virtually the entirety of today's press [...] are trying to downplay the contribution of the National Confederation of Labour and of the FAI to the fight", *S.O.*, 23 July 1936, p. 2. "Petty-mindedness on the part of those who see eye to eye when it comes to fighting fascism may have damaging consequences", in *S.O.*, 16 August 1936.

8   "Foreign warships off Barcelona", in *B.I.*, 26 July 1936 (Cf. Peirats, op. cit., Vol. I, pp. 179, 180). "The British consul looks to the regional committee and is given a list of all the British companies in Barcelona and has asked the secretary to do something [...] to ensure that said companies are not taken over or commandeered. The secretary thanked the envoy, for it is the wish of the regional committee that all foreign firms should be respected", in *B.I.*, 27 July 1936, p. 1.

and which armor-plated six trucks during the fortnight after 20 July 1936. And if we are looking for examples of worker monitoring, it affected several factories, inclining us to the view that this was the most widespread arrangement.

Barret S.A., with a workforce of 2,000, was not taken over because: "The Belgian consulate brought it to our attention that 80 percent of its capital came from the country it represents".[9] The inference is that it was not turned over to armor plating. At the Girona Company—with its 1,500 workforce—4 armored trucks were produced between late July and 6 August; at the Vulcano Company, with its 520 workers and joint CNT-UGT committee, trucks were being armor-plated and it was "working around the clock".

It should be said that, for blatantly ingratiating purposes, the Generalitat had passed laws decreeing the forty-hour working week and a 15 percent wage increase.[10] The CNT spoke out against the cut in work hours in a time of war, and against wage increases at a time of economic straits.

As might have been expected, torn between the two schools of thought, quite a few workers and collectives took the course of least resistance, boosted by the all too reasonable impression that the war would be over in weeks, since two days had been enough to see off the right-wing coup across one half the country.

So, in the factories listed above, the Generalitat's measures were, as a rule, implemented.

At the Vulcano plant, as well as at Maquinaria Terrestre y Marítima, the UGT also sat on the committee. The CNT made the running, but the UGT lent a hand after a while.[11]

---

9   *B.I.*, 13 August 1936, p. 2.

10 24 July 1936, *Butlletí Oficial de la Generalitat de Catalunya*, 26 July 1936. Reprinted in *Revista del Banco Comercial de Barcelona*, 25 July 1936, *Butlletí Oficial*, 26 July 1936, ibid.

11 *Colectivizaciones. La obra constructive de la revolución Española* (Barcelona 1937, republished by the CNT de Espana en el exilio, 1973) pp. 51, 65.

Transportation: Catalonia had three railway companies: the Madrid-Zaragoza-Alicante (MZA) line, the Northern line and Catalan Railways.

The MZA line: In 1936 the company was operating at a loss, primarily due to the high salaries paid to directors. The line was taken over by the UGT and CNT. When Spain was divided by the war, there was a 70 percent decline in traffic. The same source mentions a levelling-out of wages and reduction in fares.[12]

Catalan Railways: Operated at a profit, and high salaries were paid to the managers.

Northern Rail: An under-manager earned a minimum of 41,000 pesetas a year, and a porter 5.5 pesetas a day (about 1,650 per annum). According to a number of sources, an industrial worker was earning 10 to 12 pesetas a day (3,000 to 3,200 per annum).

Given this situation, it made sense to amalgamate all three lines, especially in wartime. This was achieved within a few days; the timetables were overhauled, rolling stock centralised and wages amended according to the principle of fairness, etc.

The article, "The future structures of the railways",[13] refers to electrification of Spanish railways, something that became a reality many decades later.

Transportation services in Barcelona presented a similar picture: they were centralized,[14] wages were standardised,[15]

---

12 *S.O.*, 11 August 1936, p. 8.
13 *S.O.*, 28 August 1936, p. 11.
14 The deed taking over the trams was dated 24 July 1936, and the one amalgamating the companies dated 30 July 1936. Documented cited by Walter Tauber, *Un cas d'autogestion: les tramways*, 1975.
15 Gaston Leval, *Né Franco né Stalin. Le collettività anarchiche spagnole nella lotta contro Franco e la reazione staliniana* (Milan 1952), p. 111 et seq.; *S.O.* 31 July 1936, p. 4: for the buses, see *S.O.*, 1 August 1936, p. 3, and 4 August 1936, p. 5: for the metro, *S.O.*, 6 August 1936, p. 2, and *B.I.*, 4 September 1936, p. 7.

hours were cut so as to provide work for the unemployed,[16] pensions were paid to retired employees,[17] a range of initiatives overhauled and reconciled time-tables, shift arrangements, spare parts, and a number of other practices that had been in place for years. And the workers made all of these improvements within days because they knew their trade, and could identify what problems needed resolution.

Energy sources: Initially, gasoline was distributed free of charge, and it was only after mid-August that it was priced, and rationing introduced.[18] It seems extravagant that unification of the railways should have been pursued while gasoline was free. One plausible explanation is that this might have been the result of different capabilities among trade unionists.

The water, gas and electricity companies were taken over by their trade unions towards the end of July.[19]

Communications: The Telefónica, a subsidiary of the US Bell company, was controlled by the CNT-UGT, which was to become a political issue in May 1937.

Commerce: Large stores, like El Siglo and El Águila, were impounded.[20] Barbershops and hairdressers were collectivised in mid-August.[21]

Provisions: The Damm brewery with its 610 employees, overhauled its payroll by cutting high wages and doling out a 70-pesetas pension instead of the previous 35-pesetas one.[22]

---

16 S.O., 22 July 1936, p. 2.
17 S.O., 15 October 1936, p. 11 and *Colectivizaciones*, op. cit., pp. 58–62.
18 B.I., 12 August 1936, p. 1: S.O., 13 August 1936, p. 7.
19 *Butlletí Oficial de la Generalitat de Catalunya*, 13 August 1936, p. 6; and Leval, op. cit., p. 127. Also Peirats, Vol. 1, p. 169.
20 S.O., 21 August 1936, p. 4 and S.O., 1 September 1936, p. 4, 5.
21 S.O., 23 November 1938, p. 2.
22 F.S., 21 March 1937, p 7; S.O., 19 January 1937, p. 2; *Nouvelle*

A workers' committee proceeded to re-open a pasta factory, which had closed down after it had gone bust.[23]

The nerve centre of Barcelona's food supply, as well as its greatest achievement, was the Borne market in the city centre.

Public Entertainment: Almost right after the failure of the attempted coup, there was a gathering together of musicians, actors, stage hands, etc., who decided to join the CNT. They launched an Entertainments Union and solved the problems of unemployment (500—of 1,500—musicians were unemployed), favouritism and wages. The Argentinean anarchist writer Rodolfo González Pacheco staged a number of plays, and numerous documentary films on the war and self-management were shot.[24]

After this short flurry of activity, there was a tremendous slowing down due to the contrary activity of the CNT-FAI leadership and the failure to take over the banks. The question of whether or not self-management was a spontaneous phenomenon has been left open. Chronology offers us one way to determine the answer since, if self-management began at around the same time in many firms, we may infer that the order came from above and the application was at the grassroots level; whereas, if things were less coordinated, the inference is that in each factory or workshop there was debate, delay and hesitancy until a final decision was reached.

This chronology falls into two distinct phases. The first, a period when there was no lawful authority, lasting until 8 August 1936, which saw the Generalitat government taking control of firms, and thus underpinning the activities of the

---

Espagne Antifasciste, 18 August 1938, p. 7; and *B.I.* (French language edition), 27 February 1937.

23 *S.O.*, 21 October 1936.

24 *Tierra y Libertad*, March 1937, reprinted in *Tierra y Libertad* (Mexico) July 1970.

rank and file committees.

Company Take-overs:

19 July Trams, Furnishings[25]

20 July Torras Company, Girona Company, Ribera Metals & Silver, Hispano-Suiza, Maquinaria Terreste y Maritima, Vulcano Company,[26] Northern Rail, the El Siglo store

21 July MZA

22 July Metro

23 July Public Entertainments

24 July Catalan Railways[27]

25 July The Transatlántica Company,[28] Water Services[29]

27 July Xalmet Company[30]

28–31 July Light & Power,[31] Sanitation[32]

---

25 S.O., 19 August 1939, p. 12 mentions the 19th of August, and *Colectivizaciones* mentions the 24th, but since such transport was essential, the 19th looks like an acceptable date. As for furnishings, see A. Lapeyre, *Le problème espagnol* (1946) pp. 22–24.
26 S.O., 22 July 1936, p. 2 (as for the Vulcano Company, B.I., 12 August 1936, mentions the 22nd).
27 *Colectivizaciones*.
28 S.O., 15 October 1936, p. 11 (S.O., 18 August 1936); *Colectivizaciones* says 27th.
29 Peirats, Vol. 1, p. 169.
30 Located at No 6, Calle Pedro IV, Barcelona (See Salamanca Archives, *A.S.*)
31 Peirats, Vol. 1, p. 361.
32 Leval, op. cit., p. 122.

1 August García García Industrial Foundries[33]

2 August Pompeia Bookstore[34]

3 August Gabernet Advertising[35]

5 August Spanish General Bookstore Co.[36] Escampa-Unión Publishers[37]

7 August Publicitas,[38] Field Steel Erectors[39]

This makes a total of twenty-six firms: nine involved in metalworking, six in transport and eleven in the service sector, covering a wide range of activities and spread over a lengthy period of time. At the García García Company, the owner offered his firm to the workforce.

As for the second, later period, one might have expected that there would have been a surge in take-overs. Instead, the take-overs continued but usually at a slower rate.

Metalworking and Automobile industry:[40] Between 11 August and 31 August, eleven firms were taken over through the imposition of an audit committee: six by the CNT and one by the UGT, plus three joint CNT-UGT take-overs and one of indeterminate complexion. In September, there were twenty-three cases of take-over: eight by the CNT, eight joint CNT-UGT operations, and seven of indeterminate complexion. Among this total of thirty-four cases, we find fourteen

---

33 Located at No 9, Puig Xiriguer, Barcelona, *A.S.*
34 Located at No 5 Conde Casanas, and No. 4 Rambla Flores, *A.S.*
35 Located at No 62, Calle Pelayo, *A.S.*
36 *A.S.*
37 *A.S.*
38 *A.S.*
39 *A.S.*
40 *A.S.* for everything hereafter.

CNT committees, one UGT committee, eleven CNT-UGT committees and eight of indeterminate persuasion. In nine instances, the cited motive was the absence of the employer (six CNT committees and three UGT committees). In eight instances, the employer voluntarily 'gifted' his firm to his workforce (two CNT committees and six committees of no particular political persuasion).

In several instances, firms shared the same street but did not follow the same pattern. Thus there were Nos. 6, 172 and 295 in the Calle Pedro IV; there was a CNT take-over on 27 July; on 1 September there was a joint CNT-UGT take-over; and on 15 September there was a take-over of indeterminate hue. Something of the sort happened with Nos. 419, 533, 574 and 674 in the Calle de Corts. On 28 August we find a CNT take-over, a UGT take-over in late August, a CNT-UGT take-over on 10 September and another joint take-over on 28 September.

The Clothing Industry: Undated records, fifteen take overs; we have three of CNT provenance, eleven on behalf of the CNT-UGT and one on behalf of the CNT-UGT plus another organisation. In August there were eleven cases, starting on 12 August: five from the CNT, three from the CNT-UGT, one from the CNT plus another body and two of undetermined provenance. In September there were nineteen instances: two emanating from the CNT, and seventeen from the CNT-UGT. Thus, out of forty-five take-overs, there were thirty-one joint CNT-UGT committees and ten CNT committees.

In three instances the employers gifted their firms or entered into a partnership. As with the other industries, we find different arrangements on the same street: on the Ronda de San Pedro there were five CNT-UGT cases in August—on 20 September and on 8 and 13 October. On the Calle Trafalgar, Nos. 6, 15, 36 and 80 were involved: there was one CNT committee, three CNT-UGT committees involved in take-overs on 31 August and 7, 9 and 14 September.

Printing Trades and Paper-mills: In August, starting on the 13th, there were twenty-nine instances: twenty-one CNT, seven CNT-UGT and one CNT-UGT-POUM. In September, there were thirty-nine take-overs, most of them during the first fortnight, and thirty-two were UGT and seven CNT-UGT. So, out of sixty-eight instances, the UGT was in the ascendancy on fifty-three committees, as against fourteen CNT-UGT committees and one for the CNT and POUM.

The UGT's ascendancy had no impact on the features set out earlier. As far as the employers went, there was one who was made 'technical director'. There were also variations between firms in single locations. On the Ronda Universidad, there were two cases of take-over on 21 August, one on 26 August, one on 1 September—all four emanating from the UGT—and, on 22 September a joint CNT-UGT take-over.

Whilst there was a glaring absence of directives, the reference to employers 'voluntarily gifting' their firms remains suspect. Fear and opportunism must have played a large part. However, special mention must be made of the stance adopted by the *Federació de patrons perruquers i barbers de Barcelona i Pobles limítrofes* (Barcelona and Outskirts Wig-makers' and Barber Employers' Federation), which made contact with the CNT's barbershop employees' union on 9 August to discuss collectivization. On 11 August there was an extra-ordinary meeting of that employers' Federation:

> Following a short debate and clarification of a number of related points, a vote was taken and the contents of said document were unanimously and unreservedly endorsed by acclamation on every count. At the same time it was resolved that once collectivisation came into force the aforesaid employers' associations would automatically be disbanded, their members becoming, *ipso facto*, members of the Barcelona and Outskirts Barbers' Sindicato Único, enjoying all of the rights and obligation pertaining thereto.

On 14 September, collectivisation of that industry was formally enacted into law, with the employers' assets and those of their Accident Fund transferring to the collective.

From the preceding list of events, we may deduce that, alongside the UGT,[41] the CNT seized the nerve centers of the Barcelona economy, as borne out by the decisions taken by the Regional Committee. So what was the political impact?

Let us take a look at statements emanating from the UGT, the CNT[42] and from the Generalitat. Companys was asked by the *News Chronicle*:

> Just supposing that the Catalan people were to champion anarcho-syndicalism. Would the Government of Catalonia go along with that?
>
> That is not how I see things. The democratic bourgeoisie, free of any interest in finance capitalism, has no right to override the will of the people. Should that happen, the bourgeoisie would be obliged to go along with it.[43]

As for the CNT, on Sunday 9 August 1936, there was a huge anarchist rally held in Barcelona, involving Vázquez, Montseny and García Oliver, at which the official line of the anarchist 'notables' was made public.

> Given the abandonment of many of the industries vital for the economic reconstruction of the revolution we are compelled to go further than we had intended.

---

41 The UGT was a partner, but usually a sleeping partner. See *Colectivizaciones*, p. 52. In the suburbs, in Tarrasa, a wave of collectivisations began on 11 August and ended on 5 October 1936, as can be deduced from Ragón, *Tres anys difícils de guerra civil* (Terrassa 1972).

42 *Pleno Nacional del Transporte (UGT)* (Valencia) and Abad de Santillán, *Por qué...* (op. cit.), pp. 68, 69.

43 *F.S.*, 23 August 1936, p. 7.

Let us take on the responsibility, discarded without any thought of extracting the least advantage from it.[44]

To put this another way: Gentlemen of the bourgeoisie, if there is libertarian communism, it is the doing of the rank and file, but we, the leadership of the CNT, are doing our damnedest to apply the brakes to it.

On the international scene, we face the threat of foreign intervention [...] Let us offer them no excuse, however [...] When the consuls came calling upon us, we swiftly marked out foreign-owned firms so as to preclude anyone's tampering with them. And when such has been the desire, we have even posted our own sentries to ensure respect for such foreign interests.[45]

In other words, we are the multinationals' trustworthy brakes and firewall against the working class.

I call upon the entire proletariat to remain at its post in production and to shirk no sacrifice. We have to bear it especially in mind that our brethren on the front place no limits upon their sacrifices.[46]

This is not the time to go around calling for the forty-hour week or 15 percent pay rises.[47]

---

[44] Actually, in this quotation, Federica Montseny is telling the politicians that the CNT agreed, much against its will, to take over the reins of the economy and was doing so without any self-serving interests. See Montseny in *S.O.*, 11 August 1936, pp. 4–5.

[45] Vázquez, ibid.

[46] García Oliver, ibid.

[47] Vázquez, ibid: Franz Borkenau, a shrewd observer of events, argues in *The Spanish Cockpit* (London 1937), p. 92, that he could not find this statement in *Solidaridad Obrera*. He was mistaken.

That is, discipline and obedience, enforced by a faker who, in the same breath, can speak of the militias on the front-line and of the capitalists they faced. Small wonder that Peiró, the erstwhile *treintista*, was to opine:

> It is right and proper to take the measure of comrade García Oliver's integrity in facing up to present and future reality. We may be sure that lots of those who heard that comrade's address at Sunday's rally will not forgive him for his honesty in stating that at the present time—and in the near future, we might add—there can be no thought of the thirty-six-hour week, nor of the forty-hour week.[48]

So, as may be deduced from the quoted declarations of the leadership of the CNT (leadership in every sense of the word), there was absolutely no intention of confirming and conserving the workers' capture of the means of production. The issue was: how would the membership and the workers respond? The very emergence, persistence and spread of (horizontal, anarcho-syndicalist-style) self-management goes some of the way towards providing an answer.

---

48 *Perill en la reraguarda*, p. 22.

Chapter 3
A Brief Survey of Self-Management in Other Regions of Spain

Forcible or voluntary self-management?

Coercion is the logic deployed by the thug in order to carry on exploiting the vast majority of the population, just as the Spanish Republic retained the monarchy's Civil Guard corps, sustaining it and bolstering it in its defence of the landlords and capitalists with a newly created Assault Guard. In the USSR, in order to sustain the new mode of exploitation, the new ruling class agreed to steps designed to preserve its power on the pretext that it was paving the way for the arrival of the 'new man' and the egalitarian society yet to come (Lenin's and Trotsky's Red Army, the establishment by Lenin of the Cheka in December 1917, along with the concentration camps that Stalin merely improved upon, for example).

Some historians well disposed towards capitalism or Leninism have accused CNT personnel of having imposed libertarian communism violently and at gunpoint, by conducting themselves like thugs and killers—that is, by adopting the conventional modus operandi of those very same historians' capitalism and Leninism. This is the traditional ploy of the polemicist, knowingly or unwittingly rubbing other people's noses in his own shortcomings.

Since truth is revolutionary, we need to look into the situation in Aragon in 1936—that being the only region where there could have been CNT bullying in the imposition of libertarian communism as the Confederation's militia columns arrived on the scene.

As we have seen before, there are two main criteria by which we can gauge the authentic wishes of the collectivists: a shaky, zigzagging chronology (the very antithesis of an order sent out by some central committee as in the case of the Stalinist collectivisations in the Soviet Union) and the prior foothold enjoyed by the CNT unions.

In an earlier study, in 1975–1977, I chronicled twenty farming collectives established between July and September 1936, as cited in the press and in CNT publications. Re-examining things now, the following data come to light.

Huesca Province, Aragon: nine collectives, six of them represented at the CNT congress held in Zaragoza in May 1936. Three more were founded between 31 July and 5 August, one with a CNT militia present; four were created between 13 and 28 August, one in the presence of a militia column and another where there had been a previous experiment in libertarian communism in 1933; and a further two dating from 18 September—with a militia column present—and 16 October. From which we may infer that the presence of CNT columns was not a factor in the quick emergence of collectives, nor was there any sort of directive at work here.

Teruel Province, Aragon: seven collectives, three represented at the Zaragoza congress. Another four were created between late July and 5 August, two with columns present, as in the case of Calanda[1] where there was an attempt at libertarian communism in 1933; one established on 9 August with a column present and where there had been an earlier attempt at libertarian communism; two in October, one with a column present and where there had been a previous attempt at libertarian communism in 1933. We may also take

---

1 Calanda was the hometown of Luis Buñuel and family. Even though the CNT member and surrealist artist Ramón Acín financed Buñuel's first movie, *Las Hurdes*, with his lottery winnings, Buñuel was not particularly fond of the CNT.

A Brief Survey of Self-Management in Other Regions of Spain

it for granted that the presence of the columns was of no particular advantage since these were in three villages where their presence was not necessary, given that the CNT had had a decided foothold there back in 1933.

Zaragoza Province, Aragon: four collectives, which had had no representation at the CNT congress in Zaragoza in May 1936, plus four early ventures, all of which were in the presence of the Durruti Column. The latter's eminent powers of persuasion must be self-evident.

What form did pressures on the inhabitants take? How were relations with the CNT?

Let us begin with Zaragoza province.

A militia column arrived in Lécera on 6 August in search of provisions, only to find that this was precluded by the way the village was organised. Item One on Durruti's proclamation referred to the need to gather in the harvest. In Bujaraloz, another proclamation of Durruti's on 11 August 1936 announced, "from the issuance of this notice the big landowners' private ownership of the land is hereby abolished" and, as for the militias, "the citizens of Bujaraloz [all 3,000 of them] are to afford them enthusiastic and unconditional support in material as well as moral terms".[2] The tone is very positive: the enthusiasm is spontaneous and natural, not like support commanded by the clique in place. In Gelsa, with its 2,500 residents, the peasants suggested that the wheat be harvested without delay, and "in order for the village to answer this call en masse, a proclamation was posted stressing that anyone failing to hand over all manner of foodstuffs and clothing items but hoarding these with an eye to profiteering, or against the eventuality of shortages, will be chastened by the ultimate punishment".[3]

In wartime, measures of that sort from an invading army are commonplace. But I am taken aback to find that the CNT's policy was not tempered, as the Makhnovists before

---

2   *S.O.*, 14 August 1936, p. 8.
3   *S.O.*, 16 August 1936, p. 12.

them had suggested, by a prior denunciation of potential abuses and indeed by affording the populace the right to kill any assailants purporting to be militians.[4]

As for the other provinces, we have this account from an observer (a critical Marxist) in Fraga:

> From [some peasants] I learned details of what had happened. The executions were not the handiwork of those villagers themselves but of the Durruti Column. They rounded up all who were suspected of engaging in reactionary activities and these were taken away in lorries and shot [...] What became of the possessions of those executed? The homes, of course, had been commandeered by the committee and stores of foodstuffs used to feed the militia [...] It was obvious that in this village the agrarian revolution had not arrived as the result of impassioned struggle by the peasants but rather as an almost automatic by-product of the executions.[5] These were just another incident in the civil war.[6]

---

[4] Leaflet and part of Item 2, Alexandrovsk, 7 October 1919: "Without meddling in the civic life of the population, the Insurgent Army will take some crucial steps against the wealthy bourgeois class as well as against Denikinists and their followers. Such steps are to be carried out in an organised way. Persons turning up in order to commandeer and arrest in the name of the Makhnovists, bearing no mandate or signature from the unit commander and the commander of the army inspection agency, should be immediately placed under arrest and dispatched to the unit staff or inspection agency. The same policy should be applied to looters and assailants who may even be executed on the spot". In Alexandre Skirda, *Nestor Makhno, le cosaque libertaire 1888–1934: la guerre civile en Ukraine 1917–1921*, Paris (4th edition, 2005), pp. 455–456.

[5] Gabriel Jackson, *La República española y la guerra civil*, p. 248, n. 18. "In separate conversations I had with two monarchist landowners, one of them a university lecturer and the other a lawyer, I heard a vigorous defence of Durruti's active opposition to the murders". [See Appendix XIV.]

[6] Franz Borkenau, *The Spanish Cockpit* (1937) (Spanish translation,

A Brief Survey of Self-Management in Other Regions of Spain

As well, the issue of suspicious persons in the republican camp became more acute when word broke of the fascist massacres carried out in Badajoz and Seville, with 'reds' being slaughtered according to the instructions previously issued. "It is to be borne in mind that action must be violent in the extreme so as to break the enemy as quickly as possible, he being strong and well organised. Naturally, all of the leaderships of political parties, societies and trade unions unsympathetic to the *Movimiento* are to be jailed, with exemplary punishments inflicted upon said persons in order to snuff out rebellion and strikes".[7] The toleration shown towards counter-revolutionary families in many collectives deserves much credit (see the example of Utrillas below).

Not every village had a CNT militia: on the Aragon front there were also columns belonging to the POUM (anti-USSR leninists) and PSUC (Catalan communist party). We have an example of an anarchist collective faced with each of these.

In Sariñena (population 3,600) the same witness[8] reported that the church had been torched, that executions had been carried out and notarial deeds burned, but that the anarchists had not commandeered all holdings, having confined themselves to expropriating four extensive ones. The peasants were using commandeered farm machinery that had been placed at everyone's disposal: "It was clear that the seized machinery should be for collective use".

Paris, p. 197) 12 August 1936, pp. 97–98.

7 General Mola, 25 May 1936 (the coup had initially been scheduled for June 1936), cited in Julián Casanova *Anarquismo y revolución en la Sociedad rural aragonesa 1936–1938* (Madrid, Siglo XXI, 1985, p. 103). The same historian supervised *Morir, matar, Sobrevivir. La violencia en la dictadura de Franco* (Barcelona 2002) wherein he states that some 50,000 reds were executed, and 10,000 children handed over to rightwing families (p. 27). Historian Francisco Espinosa claims that the repression in this zone was part of a plan of extermination and terror, a carefully prepared genocide.

8 Ibid., 13 August 1936, p. 102 et seq.

Meanwhile "Relations between the anarchist village and the POUM militia were far from good. But even so, and with many fewer deaths, the anarchist nucleus had secured considerable improvements for the peasants and was also astute enough not to try to force collectivisation on the more recalcitrant part of the village, instead waiting for the example set by the rest to have an impact".[9]

It is worth noting that, whilst Fraga was unrepresented at the Zaragoza congress, Sariñena were represented by forty-five members.[10] The *Pravda* correspondent cited the formation of an anarchist collective in Tardienta,[11] the PSUC column's base. Tardienta had 135 CNT members out of 1,900 residents in May 1936, at the time of the Zaragoza congress.[12]

In Utrillas (population 2,500) there was no militia presence but a public gathering made the decision to launch a collective. It is important to note the difference of attitude towards opponents here; some were shot as a result of a decision made at the gathering, whereas others were left unmolested. Some fled to the fascist lines, as a result of which 150 suspects were rounded up. Many were released after a vote, but thirty-two were remanded into custody. According to the pamphlet from which we have borrowed this likely-sounding report:

> Some militians on the front got wind of their still being detained and tried to influence the village, in that they reckoned that, being enemies, these should be shot, but since the village decided against this, they respected that decision.[13]

---

9 Ibid., p. 103.
10 *S.O.,* 6 May 1936, p. 3.
11 Mikhail Koltsov, *Diario de la Guerra de España* [1937] (Paris 1963), 12 August 1936, p. 25 et seq.
12 *S.O.,* 6 May 1936, p. 3.
13 Op. cit., p. 47. The Utrillas collective is mentioned in *Cultura y Acción,* 24 October 1936, p. 4.

A Brief Survey of Self-Management in Other Regions of Spain

As we can see, a core of anarcho-syndicalists, no matter how small, was able, without assistance from outsiders and with the acquiescence of the population, to establish a collective. But this was feasible only in smaller locations, because in Barbastro with its 10,000 residents and 444 CNT personnel,[14] work proceeded at a much slower pace.

> The bigger the population, the less collectivised it is. The smaller the village, the deeper runs the spirit of communism.[15]

So there was no over-arching plan, but there was in every village—with or without a militia presence—improvisation. In Alcolea (population 2,350), the collective was launched in September; in Mas de las Matas (population 2,300), they waited for the backing of the law in October, whilst in Binéfar (population 5,000) and Lagunarrota (population 600) they were set up in August 1936. By contrast, Graus had to wait until October, as did Barbastro, and in that city it spread from a farm collective in October, to bakeries, shoemaking and printing in November and to medicine, pharmacy, carpentry and so on by December.[16]

> One interesting and useful fact is that in Aragon monuments given over to religious worship were pressed into economic service. In erstwhile monasteries there were now stables, a reading room (Alcañiz) and schoolrooms (Alcorisa and Calanda). In former churches, food warehouses were set up (Alcañiz, Oliete, Calanda and Mosqueruela), sometimes with shops (butcher shops in Calanda, imported goods and hardware in

---

14 *S.O.*, 6 May 1936, p. 3.

15 Agustín Souchy, *Entre los campesinos de Aragon. El comunismo libertario en las comarcas liberadas* (Barcelona 1937) and *Fragua Social*, 18 July 1937, p. 4.

16 Leval, op. cit., p. 247.

Mosqueruela, a restaurant in Bujaraloz) or cinemas (Alcorisa, Peñalba, Alcampel).[17]

Two speeches lifted from the published minutes of the 20 September 1936 regional plenum of the Aragonese FAI membership, held in Alcañiz, show the understanding and critical vision at the time:

> [The delegate from] Fraga states that the social revolution must not be confounded with partisan revolution [...] We have no desire to impose a dictatorship, but rather wish to resist one being foisted upon us [...]
> [Puebla de Hijar] declares that some villages are in disagreement with the way they are being mismanaged, and that some of the comrades holding positions on committees ought to disassociate themselves from the situation created and should not be so authoritarian, since, by being so, they are not anarchists.[18]

From which I deduce that the representative from Fraga (a renowned rationalist teacher, Alberola) was arguing that libertarian communism was for all and that no obstacles should be placed in its way. And the Puebla de Hijar delegate was highlighting the abuses committed by CNT personnel, as flagged up in the villages. Thus there was open criticism coming from without and from within the CNT.

On the basis of that evidence, my conclusion is that collectivisation was imposed by force in only a few instances and imposed by outsider CNT personnel, and that the collectives

---

17 Bernard Catllar, *Problèmes de la construction et du logement dans la Révolution espagnole, 1936–1939: Barcelone, Aragon (Documents recueillis et traduits par l'auteur)* (Toulouse, June 1976, multi-copied text). See the quotation from Anselmo Lorenzo in Appendix V below.

18 *Memoria* (Barcelona 1936), pp. 11–12.

where there was a presence of non-CNT columns from outside were seriously constrained.

By contrast, the Aragonese CNT personnel, conversant with the situation, seized their chance with but few abuses (See Appendix XII) and managed to implement their ideas with the endorsement of the majority of the peasants. In the cities and business sectors, collectivisation was a slower process. Whenever the UGT was around it too started to put its ideas into practice, and there were some joint CNT-UGT collectives.

The trend among the bigwigs drew one of the earliest protests against deviation:

> [Having pointed out that on 9 August a comarcal plenum of the Valderrobres unions had been convened.] We sent word out everywhere. We also announced it at the regional plenum of unions in Caspe; bear in mind and let us not forget what happened in Russia to our anarchist comrades.... Whether or not Aragon is in a position to introduce libertarian communism I cannot say. I do know that the time has come to do away with every vestige of the obsolete *ancien régime*. I do know that throughout Upper and Lower Aragon, off their own bat and as of one mind, community life is being organised with the greatest possible freedom. And this without a word said about libertarian communism.
>
> We would never have imagined that the anarchist newspaper *Tierra y Libertad* would be the one to try to pour cold water on Aragon, as comrade Marianet [Mariano R. Vázquez, secretary of the CNT national committee] did at the plenum in Caspe. It is easy [to say] that we, the CNT membership from Aragon, Rioja and Navarra, have forgotten confederal tactics; what we have not forgotten nor do we forget is that we are experiencing something that nobody can deny. *After all that time spent preaching that in Spain a regimen of Freedom and Justice could be introduced, we stand firm in our belief that the time has come to prove it. Which is*

more or less what we are doing. The movement has to point the way by getting on with it.[19]

Of course, the emphasis has been added by me, and the Aragonese comrades were so right that they brought about a change of mind. Among the line-up of the Alcorisa collective, up until it was ended by the Francoist push in March 1939, was a lawyer and a veterinary surgeon, one of whom had a bad leg as a result of a bullet wound inflicted by the village's CNT personnel during the attempted revolution in 1933. Though they may have had deep-seated grounds for hostility to the new dispensation, these people of intellectual and bourgeois extraction threw themselves whole-heartedly into the collective by helping to re-float it after Líster had swept through. One of them explained self-management to the 'individualist' circles, eager to divide up the collective's lands, in these terms: "Once upon a time, I had more lands. Now when I climb to the top of the hill, I own them all because the whole lot are collectivised". Unfortunately, they could not follow his meaning.[20]

In Aragon, self-management was economically and socially different from what it was elsewhere in Spain. Life there was poor, and agriculture was not as complicated as it was in Levante (with international exports, and a wide variety of produce). The self-management proposed by the CNT was flanked by medical services and upgraded educational provision, two services that had been very precarious in the villages prior to July 1936. In the overall picture of self-management,

---

19 Julián Floristán (Valderrobres, Teruel), 6 September 1936, *S.O.*, 9 September 1936, p. 3. The closing remarks hark back to Isaac Puente's pamphlet *El comunismo libertario*, pp. 52–53.
20 According to the collectivist Vicente in *Autogestion*, 1972, No 18, p. 155 and reprinted, unaccredited, in Ratgeb, *De la grève sauvage a l'autogestion* (Paris 1974), pp. 96–97. "Not to mention that unwarranted anti-communism, omissions and misrepresentation are distinguishing features of verticalism".

there was common cause between the 300,000 collectivists and some 150,000 inhabitants who were not collectivists, and this with a battlefront very near and a strategic requirement to see to the upkeep of militias.

General Líster's dialectics

Municipal elections were held in Aragon in January 1937, the outcome being as follows: the CNT took 51.5 percent of the council seats against the UGT's 27.1 percent, and the rest went to the political parties. Of these, Izquierda Republicana took 9 percent, the 'Popular Front' (without further definition) 6.5 percent, the PSOE 2.4 percent, Unión Republicana 2 percent and the Communist Party 0.75 percent. The PCE's share of the seats was distributed as follows: in Huesca 0.8 percent, in Teruel 2 percent, in Zaragoza—to be precise, in Caspe alone—it took 5.5 percent.[21]

These are interesting figures because, in August 1937, in a wonderful exercise in dialectical materialism, the communist General Líster's division stepped in to disband the Council of Aragon and demolish the collectives, acting on oral instructions from the socialist Indalecio Prieto. In an act of supposed 'liberation',[22] Líster reintroduced agricultural smallholders (or *kulaks*, to borrow the PCE jargon) who, at around the same time, were being annihilated in the USSR through the almost complete extermination of that category of farmer. Quite a few collectives were reconstituted once Líster had moved on, but the bubble of enthusiasm had burst.

Líster's interference was an issue, even for the communists themselves, as is apparent in this testimony from the

---

21 Graham Kelsey *Sindicalismo y Estado en Aragón 1930–1939? Orden público o paz pública?* (Madrid: Gobierno de Aragon. Institución Fernando el Católico Exma, Diputación de Zaragoza/Fundación Salvador Seguí, 1994).

22 Enrique Líster, *Memorias de un luchador I. Los primeros combates* (Madrid 1977), p. 263.

Institute of Agrarian Reform (even with all of the tact one might expect of an official document):

> When the Republic's government disbanded the Council of Aragon, the governor general sought to banish the deep-seated unease in the heart of the peasant masses by breaking up the collectives. Such a move represented a very serious mistake, and led to tremendous disorganisation in the countryside. Those unhappy with the collectives, and who had good grounds for being so if the methods employed in establishing them are taken into consideration, exploited the governor's ordinance in order to attack them, seizing and dividing up all the fruits and assets they possessed and ignoring those that, like the collective in Candasnos, had been set up without violence or coercion and that had a life of their own and were exemplars of organisation. True, the governor was out to make good the injustices that had been done and to plant in the minds of rural workers the belief that they had the protection of the Republic. But the upshot was completely the opposite. The measure simply added further to the confusion, and the violence swung the other way. As a result, all farm work ground almost to a complete standstill and, when planting time came around, one-fourth of the land was not ready for seeding.[23]

This statement can be supported by three things: The PCE's lead-up propaganda claimed that the Aragonese were being oppressed by self-management. Shortly after Líster swept through, the PCE gathered some witness statements,[24] but these were so few in number that they were not published. Thus the communist rapporteur from Castejón de Monegros claimed, "The CNT chair, Mariano Olona, is a highly dangerous individual. He is currently in this area, and

---

23 *La revolución popular en el campo*, cited by Bolloten, op. cit., pp. 202–203.
24 Salamanca Archives, 397B.

his home is a haven for security personnel bent on introducing communism" (further evidence that the PCE was accepting right-wingers into its ranks).

Officially, the Aragonese Communist Party had to backtrack: "We communists cannot deny our revolutionary credentials and so, today, we should pay the utmost heed to the collective organisation of labor as a first step towards the creation of a free and strong Spain".[25]

The type-written minutes of a "meeting of social delegates from Aragon", held in Caspe on 7 February 1937, reads: "[Delegate from Huesca speaking:] 35,000 of the 60,000 pesetas owed by a collective in Sena village have been recovered. As for the collectives that may be disbanded on account of their damnable methods, the period leading up to their break-up should be put to good use in collecting from them or making them cough up the debts they owe to the Institute, since, if this opportunity is allowed to slip, there will be no way of ensuring payment".

"[Delegate from Mora de Rubielos speaking:] In Monteagudo del Castillo, the Smallholders' Council is returning livestock and land to the rebels, and collecting 6,000 pesetas from the collectivists who had handed them back 'on the grounds of a fear that the others are on their way'. He asks that the press offer guidelines as to how the Examination Councils should be organised in such a way that their existence is known in the villages, since many villages are unaware of them".

"[Delegate from Zaragoza speaking:] Collectives have been reorganised in Bujaraloz, in Candasnos, in Peñalba, La Almalda, Castejón de Monegros, Lécera, Azuara, Pina, Sástago and elsewhere".[26]

We have three fundamental points to make: the campaign against collectivisation was still ongoing in February

---

25 *Boletín Interior*, Provincial CP Committee, printed, August 1937.
26 Salamanca Archives, 373B.

1938, it triggered a political deviation and self-management survived in spite of all the obstacles.

It is important that we underline the views of those witnesses (see Appendices VI and XI) who claim that the resuscitated collectives were the better for it and people doubly determined and, wherever excesses had taken place, it proved all but impossible to refloat them. With regard to this last point, we might list the collectives that were refloated—according to CNT sources: Alcolea, Alcorisa, Calanda, Gelsa, Más de las Matas, Peñalba, Pina and the Barbastro comarcal federation with its thirty-odd collectives.[27]

The resuscitation was all the more impressive when one considers that the CNT adopted a laissez-faire line, as no less a figure than Joaquìn Ascaso declared: "Despite the defeatist views of the CNT, we would have taken up arms to defend our Council, because we saw it as the revolution, and today we remain the very same anarchists and revolutionaries that we were before".[28]

Adopting a reductionist approach and discounting all factors specific to Aragon, we can embrace the critique of the French anarchist André Prudhommeaux: "Wherever the redistribution was so straightforward as to take on the appearance of barter, where the population amounted to only a few families, a village and its fields, capitalism was expropriated entirely. In doing so, the peasants were not furnishing proof of their ideological superiority, but they faced such general conditions that collective organisation of production was only feasible if distribution was effected in accordance with communist principles. It was the distribution of farm produce that pushed the peasants to take production under trade union control. They could not have acted in any other way".[29]

---

27 Peirats in *Espoir*, 31 August 1969; *CNT* (Toulouse) 16 November 1952; A.S. with regard to Gelsa, Mas de las Matas and Pina.

28 *L'Espagne Nouvelle*, 29 October 1937.

29 *L'Espagne Nouvelle*, 24 December 1937 [unsigned].

Strictly speaking, the changes feasible in certain circumstances are easy, the object being to shift from the poverty imposed by capitalism to the satisfaction of a range of pressing and fundamental day-to-day needs. Not that Isaac Puente's *Comunismo Libertario* had ever said anything different. Collectivisation in Aragon was based on national agricultural output—of wheat, sugar beet—and a population that had no 'modern' needs (refined consumer goods, entertainment, rest, etc.). Barter and wartime economics could be implemented fairly easily (although it will not do to over-state this). Levante and Catalonia, by contrast, were regions where there was less stark contrast between the classes, with national and international export and import trades in agricultural and industrial produce, and, there, collectivisation proved more problematic, and therefore raised more interesting issues.

Valencia according to the Catalan CNT template

19 July 1936 in Valencia followed a very specific course. The military was besieged inside the barracks by the popular forces, neither venturing outside nor surrendering; and the popular forces were in no position to attack, having no weapons. A general strike had been declared and a committee, made up of the Popular Front and the CNT, formed. The government was insistent that the local garrison was loyal and it sent in a Junta and lobbied for the strike to end.

Meanwhile, the CNT national committee in Madrid was demanding arms from the government. When the government refused, the CNT of the Center region and of Catalonia shipped supplies down to Valencia, where the Junta and Committee alike refused to arm the people. Plus "the CNT and the UGT had ordered a return to work", from which only transport workers were exempt. But the workers refused to comply with these instructions. The CNT's decision to storm the barracks brought some clarity to the situation once and for all.

Our deduction from these telling events is that the government did all in its power to thwart and control all authority beyond its own. As in Catalonia, the CNT was more concerned about alliances than about social gains, deciding upon a return to work that it then had to postpone in light of the workers' insistence upon attacking. An unsettling paradox for a proletarian organisation.

Bearing in mind that the working party reporting on the rural question in Catalonia largely took on board the wishes of the peasants of Levante, that working party, in putting its signature to the report, agrees to those items it regards favourably and offers these for the approval or consideration of the Congress.

1. The Regional Peasants' Federation declares the Institute of Agrarian Reform to have no remit in relation to seizures, and states that such seizures and the awarding of loans and wages falls within the remit and under the control of the CNT and UGT, whose agencies are to thrash out an agreement on overall control of the agricultural industry [...]

6. Should there be any possibility of introducing socialisation within a village without running the risk of aggravating the problems we have mentioned, this should proceed across the board and immediately, and should the majority of peasants in a village dissent or if there is anyone in disagreement with this, the unions are to respect cultivation by smallholders along said lines* and shall proceed to impound the remaining land under union supervision

(*)In principle they are to be allowed to till the soil, as long as this does not hamper or create difficulties for the proper growth of the socialised sector [...]

8. To conclude this motion and in faithful reflection of the widespread federalism that the CNT has always championed, this working party sees merit in demanding

the widest possible freedom for each peasant locality in choosing the manner and timing of the implementation of the accords above.[30]

The November 1936 plenum in Valencia was certainly the most interesting of all those reported in the libertarian press during the civil war, since *Fragua Social* carried the full minutes of the proceedings—even the most tiresome items (something for which it was later taken to task).[31]

In Levante, the CNT had 300,000 members at that point, whereas in May 1936 it only had 50,000 and, going back to the aftermath of the [treintista] split, just 20,000. As it happened, in the voting, the motions on the abolition of wage slavery (Item Seven) and the militias (Item Two) were of a markedly non- or anti-CNT bent:

> Woodworkers, Alcoy: says that the majority of the delegations voting for Item Seven did so because they were only recently set up and are not conversant with the Confederation's norms. And it is the villages that are familiar with them that must stand up and challenge it.[32]

> [Segorbe, speaking on Item Two:] Let me say that this entire plenum, regrettably badly advised by the Regional Committee, is proceeding along plainly reformist lines.[33]

Vilanesa: Trial Run for May 1937

One leading and repeated criticism levelled at the November plenum was: "The workers have taken over the industries and

---

30 *CNT-AIT Congreso regional de campesinos de Levante* (Valencia) 18/20 September 1936.
31 *F.S.*, 8 December 1936, p. 9, Column A.
32 Ibidem, 13 November 1936, p. 6.
33 Ibidem, 14 November 1936, p. 7.

have not improved the economic circumstances of the villages one bit". As well as, "Yesterday's bourgeois has turned into today's *forty* bourgeois".[34]

The latter criticism should be understood as meaning that, say, in a firm with a staff of forty, self-management, in the absence of solidarity and commitment, could have spawned forty selfish interests. The hyperbole was meant to point to the greater sacrifices made by rural CNT personnel. In a national context, it was also discernible that deviations deserving criticism could loom in the countryside.

And at a peasant plenum, in December 1936, it was stated: "The differences between the peasantry and city workers must not continue".[35]

Within months, the verbal criticism gave way to armed violence. Curiously, the pretext was afforded by the Ministry of Trade, then headed by Juan López from the CNT of Levante. A decree issued by him assumed control of all foreign exports. The collectivists rejected this, and the government sent in the security forces.

The strained relations and mutual distrust that existed between the police and the collectivists, between the collectivists and the CNT, are plain from this description of the clash.[36]

On 8 March 1937, in Vilanesa [Valencia] shots were exchanged between police and CNT personnel over the ownership of some premises. After some hours, things settled down and police withdrew from the village. Meanwhile, other CNT personnel from the comarca had arrived and attacked the Guardias on sight. Valencia

---

34 F.S., delegate from Albalate dels Sorells, 20 November 1936, p. 6.
35 F.S., delegate from Puero de Sagunto, 6 November 1936, p. 10.
36 Report from the CNT National Committee, signed by Vázquez, Valencia, 22 March 1937, reprinted by the Catalan regional of the CNT in the note convening a regional conference, signed by Valerio Mas, Barcelona, 27 March 1937.

A Brief Survey of Self-Management in Other Regions of Spain

dispatched reinforcements and more CNT personnel arrived. The CNT national committee, which was in session, as was the Valencia government, dispatched a delegation to secure a cease-fire, and entered into talks with the Interior Minister, Ángel Galarza, no friend of the CNT. Even though all of this was happening within a fifteen kilometre radius and the means of transport and communications were still in operation ["it is a ten minute car ride from Valencia to the scene"], hours later, matters were still as they stood at the outset, in terms of gunfire and truces. In Valencia, Alfara, Moncada and Gandía, there were gun-battles, and in Utiel a strike was called. The Iron Column was threatening to go back into the rearguard.[37]

In the end, with the death toll at four CNT personnel and eleven police, an agreement was hammered out, however reluctantly:

> We had previously issued specific instructions to the Region, calling for an end to the comrades' hostile stance. But nowhere were these believed or heeded. The Gandía comarcal replied by telephone, defying us and uttering a number of epithets insulting to the National and Regional committees.

Within days a plenum had been called to look into the situation. It opened on 16 March with representation for 46,000 out of a total of 120,000 members.[38] After some "fraught moments", an agreement was arrived at whereby a call was issued

---

[37] Peirats, op. cit., Vol. II, p. 78. In October that column had left the front in order to attack the bourgeoisie's foundations (records and Civil Guards) in the rearguard. See Peirats, Vol. I, p. 242, and Bolloten, *La revolución Española (sus orígenes, la izquierda y la lucha por el poder durante la guerra civil)* (Barcelona 1980).

[38] Report cited in note 36 above.

for prisoners to be freed, the Assault Guard was mobilised for front-line service and arms returned. Before then, the national committee had justified its own stance and called for discipline ("instructions... not believed nor heeded"). So the internal operation of the CNT was becoming more authoritarian.

Alongside these developments, the Communist Party had embarked upon a campaign of anti-anarchist agitation,[39] with

---

39 The line that "As far as Catalonia is concerned, the mopping up of Trotskyist and anarcho-syndicalist elements is under way and will be prosecuted with the same vigor as in the USSR" is commonly attributed to *Pravda*. The quote actually comes from Camillo Berneri's "Open Letter to comrade Federica Montseny" and was taken up by anarchist propaganda such as Garcia Pradas's *Rusia y España*, p. 71. Even historians have endorsed the quotation's 'truth' by reprinting it, e.g. Hugh Thomas *The Spanish Civil War* (London 1977), p. 302; Gerald Brenan, *El laberinto Español* (Paris 1962), p. 245; James Joll *Los anarquistas*, p. 245. Now that quotation is false, since the Russian text by Koltsov in *Pravda* (17 December 1936, No. 346, p. 5) reads: "In the recent happenings in Catalonia and beyond, we acknowledge the provocations by the Trotskyists followed by the very same comrades who, with the aid of the Hitlerite police, murdered comrade Kirov inside the Soviet Union. Fortunately, though, we will thwart the schemes of the Trotskyists in our own country. Our people long since woke up to their enemies in the front lines as well as in the rearguard". The POUM paper, *La Batalla*, carried on its front page, on 5 January 1937, a report from the Mexican Febus news agency, datelined Moscow, to the effect that "the entire Soviet press cherishes the hope that the purge undertaken in Catalonia against the Spanish Trotskyists and anarcho-syndicalists will be carried out with the same vigor as in the Soviet Union". So the misrepresentation originated with an anti-USSR Leninist source. The version carried by *La Batalla* was rebutted on 8 January 1937 in a note issued by the Soviet consulate and signed by A. Korobizin: "In the Soviet press there is not, nor can there be, any attack mounted on the fraternal movement of the workers of Spain banded together into the CNT"(!!!). For all that, the adulteration of this text, presaging the May Events of 1937, precisely mirrored the mentality of the Spanish communists, in that several PSUC militants declared to Ilya Ehrenburg—an intellectual and Stalin's envoy in Spain—in 1936: "Better the fascists than the anarchists". See the extract from his memoirs in *Odyssey*

A Brief Survey of Self-Management in Other Regions of Spain

the backing of the republican bourgeoisie. From verbal and written polemics to the spilling of blood was but a step. This became apparent in May 1937 in Barcelona with the murders of Camillo Berneri and his bodyguard Francesco Barbieri.[40] Berneri had been the spokesman for anarchists opposed to the dereliction and compromises of the CNT-FAI leadership.

Just as May 1937 in Barcelona showed the CNT national committee's laissez-faire attitude, so in Aragon the Aragonese CNT membership failed to resort to arms in their own defense (see Appendix XI).

Review (New York) December 1962, p. 50, and translated in *Novy Mir* (Moscow) 1962.

40 Berneri was an anarchist, a one-time philosophy teacher from Italy, a political refugee in France and subsequently a volunteer in Spain. As editor of the newspaper *Guerra di Classe* published in Barcelona, he made his name for his analyses of Soviet imperialism and criticisms of leading CNT personnel. See Carlos M. Rama *Camillo Berneri. Guerra de clases en España, 1936–1937* (Barcelona 1977). Barbieri was involved alongside Severino Di Giovanni in the fight against fascism in Argentina before fleeing to Europe and making his way to Spain to assist the revolution.

Chapter Four:
Organising Self-Management across the Nation

The economic context

The CNT-FAI had been anticipating prompt implementation of its socio-economic program. The adjective 'totalitarian' was bandied about, but its meaning in those days was very different from the one it has today; it was a synonym for all-embracing, all-encompassing. Despite the change of outlook in the higher echelons, the rank and file still kept faith with the anarchist approach:

> We believe that a scheme for collectivisation should be informed by a totalitarian outlook in terms of its program. But when it comes to its implementation, this should be a phased process to be carried out over consecutive phases as an ongoing project.[1]

Unfortunately, local efforts only managed to provide exemplars from January 1937 onwards, long after the CNT-FAI leaders had presented the membership with the *fait accompli* of collaboration in government—that is, long after the economy had deferred to the republican bourgeoisie.

Agencies covering agriculture at the national level were formed belatedly, in June 1937, and it was not until January 1938 that an extended economic plenum was held, at which

---

[1] *Federación de la industria textil catalana, material de estudio*, early 1937 (private archives).

the problems of the new economy were broached: "This year and a half delay had deadly consequences for one of the most beautiful experiments in revolutionary history".[2]

What was the economic state of self-management? All in all, dire, given that the country was already grappling with very significant unemployment. It does not appear that Madrid or Barcelona had paid any great attention to this. The call was to resolve the war problem, even as it led to another problem in the shape of manpower shortages in some industries—chiefly the war-related ones. Indeed, the division of Spain into two zones wrought havoc with traditional economic industries. Come the air raids, electricity supply was restricted to the war industries. The following quotations echo some of the pressing issues:

> Three-fifths of the domestic consumer markets are in rebel hands [...] Nearly two-thirds of our workers [in Catalonia] are living, pretty much, on hand-outs.[3]

> [In Catalonia] there is an extraordinary number of collective and private firms whose workers spend most of their days doing nothing.[4]

From a Spanish textile and allied trades industry plenum: "[Catalan delegate speaking] Collapse is unavoidable, due to a lack of electricity, dyes and wool supplies". But, getting to the core of the issue, he stated that the truth "is quite simply that we need to turn to the government. We have no work. The government has no hard currency and, if it does, it is for battle equipment. This is the unvarying fact of the matter".[5]

---

2 *Examen crítico-constructivo del movimiento libertario Español*, p. 90 and *Le Combat syndicaliste*, 15 October 1964.

3 Fábregas, *Vuitanta dies al gobern de la Generalitat*, p. 85.

4 *Butlletí Interior de la UGT*, 15 January 1937.

5 *Memoria* (Salamanca Archives), November 1938, pp. 20, 21.

In addition to the war effort, there were the political frictions, and then self-management ran into certain abuses that were promptly exacerbated and sustained by the PCE. A range of CNT newspaper headlines help us to follow this process:

> Be it due to food scarcity, or driven by the selfishness of traders, the cost of consumer goods has soared very considerably since the fight against fascism started.[6]

> The scandalous price of basic goods.[7]

This is all condensed in Agustín Souchy's article "Economic problems of the Revolution", which stated essentially:[8]

> There are some things that remind us of capitalist mismanagement and these are as follows [...]
>
> 1. The peasants and agrarian collectives are getting no more for their produce than they did prior to 19 July 1936 [...] The prices of industrial products are rising at a dizzying rate.
>
> 2. The inexcusable differences in workers' incomes. Collectivised firms pay a weekly wage of 120 or—at best—140 pesetas, and the rural collectives an average of 70 pesetas. Workers in the war industries earn 200 pesetas a week or more. So it would scarcely be surprising if the collectives' attractiveness to workers were to be on the wane.
>
> 3. Lots of goods are unobtainable on the open market [...] Also, our economy is not as uniform and complete as the Russian economy,[9] because our collectives,

---

6 S.O., 27 September 1936.

7 F.S., 10 December 1936, p. 1.

8 S.O., 2 February 1938, p. 3.

9 As an economic model, the USSR being characterised by reformism and by politicisation at the workers' expense.

our cooperatives, etc., in city and country, make up barely one-half of the country's economy. A sizable part is still in the hands of the petite bourgeoisie. Plainly, the latter's position is today, in many instances, no better than that of the workers; but its business machinery is outside of the control of the proletarian organisations. The label "under UGT-CNT control" is, in most instances, more fiction than fact.

In spite of that somewhat over-stated conclusion, Souchy's assessment is a fair one, and the economic contradictions he was flagging were the logical outcome of the continual back-tracking.

The question of wages

Back in the days of the First International, collectivists and communists had been at loggerheads. The communists argued that the only way of exorcising the economic inequality that would simply be reborn via the collectivist precept of "from each according to his ability", was to embrace the principle "from each in accordance with his potential". In *The Conquest of Bread*, Kropotkin offered a crystal clear explanation of Bakunin's critical stance on Marx's *The Critique of the Gotha Programme*[10] as supporting wage differentials. And the marxism v. anarchism debate erupted again over wages in Spain's self-managed collectives.

In one way, CNT personnel championed Kropotkin's line by doing away with money in many Aragonese villages. But actually they retained the wage system whilst divesting it of its

---

10 Kropotkin and Makhaiski alike referred to "That labour power which therefore, over the same interval of time, materialises as relatively higher values. Such higher value, as compared to the norm, logically translates as superior work". See *El Capital* Vol. 1, p. 158 (Havana 1965). ["The Production of 'absolute' surplus value", being the section dealing with labour and its valorization.]

character as a lure and a differential between workers. The quotations that follow highlight the pragmatism of the collectivists:

> Is it your intention to institute this mode of consumption [the abolition of money] permanently?
>
> There is no way of knowing yet. Naturally, the safest thing would be for change to be made on the basis of improving upon the system. Everything done thus far has been done on a short-term and trial basis. In the early days, vouchers were issued so that necessities could be accessed. Later, we came up with this paper money [which is shown to us] and now we have switched to the producer's booklet. It is the best arrangement we have tried out, so far.[11]
>
> We should not be looking to some arrangement whereby there are pay scales dependent on the class of work needing done as a way of stimulating workers' productivity. There are other means of getting the producer to achieve normal productivity depending on his brawn and abilities, means that have absolutely nothing to do with such attention to chance attributes being mirrored in such a way by a hierarchy of sliding pay scales. And we do mean chance, in that, in the event of increasingly widespread specialisation, virtually every worker would be in a position to demand similar rewards.[12]

The Kropotkinian approach was reflected in the standard wage arrangements trialled in a number of Barcelona firms and that were not entirely convincing, as may be deduced from the minutes of the Catalan regional congress held in February–March 1938: "There are some who are unable to shake off such prejudices and find it unthinkable that an architect or a

---

11 Bujalance, Córdoba province, 25 September 1936, *S.O.*, 2 October 1936.
12 *Memoria del pleno national de Agua, Gas, septiembre de 1937*, p. 39.

bricklayer should earn more than a peasant. Until such time as we rid ourselves of such selfish thinking we will, ultimately, have accomplished nothing in practical terms".[13]

Faced with extreme instances of anti-bureaucratic prejudices ("Members of the administrative council earn 22 pesetas per fortnight less than the rest of the members of the collective")[14] and resistance to hierarchy ("Badalona calls for the abolition of the category of labourer. —Overruled")[15] the family wage was introduced across the board:

> The fair wage is the family wage because it provides an avenue to justice. The family wage will always be a boon to all those genuinely in need.[16]

> Long awaited and yearned for by all, the family wage was a miracle worker.[17]

> Wage differentials between men and women were retained. Some of the women pressed for equal pay, but this proved unattainable, even though there was a majority in favor at the meeting. The matter fell within the remit of the Council of Economy and of the trade union organisation, so it had to be a decision made across the board rather than applicable to a single firm.[18]

In the Barcelona Entertainments sector "there was also wage parity between men and women".[19] One former CNT

---

13 *Memoria...*, Op. cit., p. 58.
14 Tomelloso (Ciudad Real) in *Campo Libre*, 11 September 1937, p. 5.
15 *Pleno de Luz y Fuerza*, January 1937, p. 53.
16 Op. cit., p. 51.
17 *Pleno de locales y comarcales campesinas del Centro, 25 de octubre 1937*, p. 45.
18 Víctor Alba, *Los colectivizadores* (Barcelona 2001), La España Industrial, textile plant.
19 Op. cit., p. 218.

member explained "we used to pay the women ten *centimos* and the men fifteen. The women were paid less because, as a rule, in those days women were regarded as lesser than men and earned less than men. It was unfair for a woman to be paid less because she has the same needs as a man. But the CNT took this on board too".[20]

Gaston Leval sums up the attitude of the day:

> One gain of enormous importance was a woman's right to a livelihood, no matter what her role in society. In half of the farming collectives, the wage paid to her was lower than a man's wage, whereas in the other half it was identical. The difference can be accounted for if we bear it in mind that an unmarried woman rarely lives alone.[21]

The chief criticism here is that women were never looked upon as the equals of men, despite a number of reproaches emanating from *Mujeres Libres*.[22] Communists and socialists also voiced objections, but to no avail. In any event, equal pay for men and women needs to be accompanied by men's shouldering of some of the housework and the education of the children, if such equality is to be real.

There was opposition from a number of CNT members, either on the basis of ideological disagreements or because of the cost of living. Thus in Paret del Vallé, two CNT farm-workers resigned from the CNT and from the collective in order to join the UGT "because they refused to work for six pesetas a day".[23] In Carabaña (Madrid), the collective boosted wages to 15 pesetas, whereas elsewhere they stood at 6 or 8 pesetas. Later,

---

[20] Mercedes Vilanova, *Las maoyorias invisibles (explotacion fabril, revolucion y represion)*, Barcelona 1996, p. 336.

[21] Gaston Leval, *Ne Franco ne...*, op. cit., p. 315. Item 4 of "Principles and Lessons of the Spanish Revolution", but omitted from the French and Spanish editions by the author.

[22] Mary Nash, *Mujeres Libres*, Barcelona 1976, p. 153.

[23] 9 November 1936. See Salamanca Archives (A.S.) 2052.

following intervention by the regional federation, the wages in Carabaña were cut to 10 pesetas to restore some balance.

But the most serious problem was the issue of technicians: here there was a dual process. On the one hand, there was a degree of resentment by the manual workers, made manifest in the form of technicians being taken to task for the high wages they earned prior to 19 July 1936 and a consequent refusal to countenance further increases for technicians: "Another delegate from Catalonia complained that yet again, in yet another instance among many, it is going to be the technicians that suffer more than anyone else, given that, since 19 July 1936, they are the only ones to have had their pay cut".[24]

Besides, the UGT policy of raising already high wages was viewed as a 'ploy' designed "to encourage many to walk out and leave the manual workers to their own devices".[25]

A compromise solution was adopted in Catalonia's railways whereby a) there was a standard rate of pay of 5,000 pesetas a year, and b) in order to keep the technical personnel interested, there was a 2,000 pesetas annual pay bonus.[26]

The CNT followed suit and justified this approach at the expanded economic plenum held in Valencia in January 1938:

> Acknowledging the complementary requirements existing between the several categories of workers, we also call for the circumstantial[27] recognition of same, albeit that in the future the trend should be towards eradicating wage differentials between workers.
>
> Consequently, with regard to these basic considerations, we put it to the plenum [...]

---

24 *Pleno nacional de Agua, Gas, septiembre de 1937*, p. 43.

25 *Pleno de Luz y Fuerza, enero de 1937*, p. 73.

26 *Guerra di Classe*, 17 October 1936, p. 3.

27 As a rule, the use of this adjective was an attempt to explain away backsliding. See Salvador Seguí in 1919, in Peirats, *Los anarquistas en la crisis política*, p. 24 and *Manifiesto del Partido Sindicalista*, 1934, p. 7.

Basic Category, Labourer X.
Higher Category, Official: 20 percent bonus
2nd Higher Category, Specialist Official: 40 percent bonus
3rd Higher Category, Technical assistant: 70 percent bonus
4th Higher Category, Technical director: 100 percent bonus[28]

Now the reality far outstripped the resolution above. In the Barcelona construction industry, the wages scale as of May 1938 went: laborer, 150 pesetas a week; skilled worker, 180 pesetas (12 percent bonus); draughtsman, 675 pesetas (450 percent bonus); and architects and engineers, 1,500 pesetas (1000 percent bonus).[29]

The same trend can be found in self-managed agriculture.

Whilst wages on farms in Levante varied between 1.50 and 4 pesetas a day in April 1937 (with a top monthly wage of 39 or 104 pesetas, respectively), members of the FAI's regional committee were earning 400 (which is to say 1025 percent or 384 percent of the day laborers' minimum and maximum earnings).[30]

By comparison, in one FNTT-UGT (*Federación Nacional de los Trabajadores de la Tierra*-UGT) venture in Alicante, the secretaries were earning 750 pesetas in February 1938.[31] Given that the daily rate at the time must have been somewhere between 6 and 8 pesetas, that would give a monthly wage of between 156 and 208 pesetas, meaning a 480 percent to 384 percent increase, respectively.

To be fair, in the Centre region, the peasant federation did not attain anything like these percentages, but the general

---

28 *Acuerdos del pleno economico ampliado. El 1er congreso national de character constructive celebrad en la Espana antifascista desde el 19 de Julio, cuyas sesiones han tenido lugar desde el 15 al 23 de enero de 1938*, Barcelona 1938, pp. 10, 11; also in Peirats, Vol. III.

29 *Boletin del Sindicato Unico del Ramo de la Construccion*, 15 March 1938.

30 *Memoria del pleno de la FAI de Levante*, April 1937, pp. 95–96.

31 Op. cit., p. 73.

secretary still earned 560 pesetas compared to the 933 paid to an agronomist in February 1939.[32]

The UGT was spared the travails of the CNT, since marxism has no difficulty with wage scaling. Thus, in Catalonia, at the third UGT congress it was placed on record: "Congress must come out categorically against the standard wage and against the so-called family wage, these being regarded as anti-economic and utterly at odds with the requirements of the workers' day to day lives".[33]

The backwardness of this approach, of which there was no sign in 1936, is self-evident. What follows is a more clear-sighted critique:

> The standard wage robs the working man of any incentive to train since it brings him no reward. In Lérida we have the example of Construction. When collectivisation was introduced, equal wages were introduced for all workers, but with the passage of time, the skilled workers refused the responsibility for their specific work [...] Not only does the family wage amount to a rejection of reward and recompense for the skilled worker and his opportunity to train, but those bereft of an average education would make it their business to have enough offspring to increase their earnings, heedless of the consequences that this might have, not only upon the family per se, but also upon the economy in general.[34]

While the criticism relating to the absence of incentive can stand up, the attitude to workers "of average education" who would set about having children as a means of getting more money is an odd one. It presupposes a primitive mentality divorced from the political consciousness that enabled

---

32 A.S., 170M, February.
33 *Butlleti Interior de la UGT*, 15 September 1937.
34 UGT Lérida, translated from the Catalan, 24 August 1927, report, p. 29.

the workers—including and primarily those with "average education"—to take over the means of production in July 1936.

UGT members were doubtless rather underwhelmed by this propaganda, given that a pamphlet on the *Primer congreso de la federació siderometalúrgica de Catalunya* (First Congress of the Steel and Metalworking Federation of Catalonia) in 1938 was stressing the same point again. There were explanations about how to improve productivity, first of all through raw materials and then through "other incentives" such as "championships, competition prizes, shock battalions, promotions, elevation to positions of greater responsibility, better salaries, citations in the press, leave arrangements, travel prizes, etc".[35]

Here we have the banal description drawn from the Marxist-Leninist arsenal (so very similar to the capitalist one) perfected by Stalinism:

> It is intolerable that a rolling-mill operative should be paid the same as a blacksmith. It is intolerable for a train driver to be paid the same as a copy-typist. Marx and Lenin state that the difference between skilled labor and unskilled labor will endure even under a socialist system and indeed that this distinction should only be eradicated following the abolition of class distinctions. So, even under socialism, 'wages' ought to be paid in accordance with work performed and not on the basis of needs.[36]

The very existence of Spanish self-management, that is, of maturity in workers, demonstrates that there was no need for supervision and strict incentives, especially when we note that in virtually every economic and political decision made, the leadership—anarchist and Marxist alike—made gross and unfathomable blunders.

---

35 *Memoria*, p. 74, translated from the Catalan.
36 *Cuestiones del Leninismo*, Moscow, 1931, pp. 420–421.

The real issue is not the worker's incentive but his power. If the rank and file is in control, then self-sacrifice is possible. Unless it takes power, the rank and file will not countenance sacrifices, which is why it spearheads uprisings when it has had enough—as was the case in Berlin in 1953, Poland in 1956, Hungary the same year, and so on. Marxist-Leninist propaganda emanating from the Eastern bloc, Cuba and Asia (not forgetting Titoist Yugoslavia) can be countered with this testimony from the Cuban exile Nelson P. Valdés:

> Low productivity, absenteeism from work and so-called indiscipline are not the outcomes of a lack of consciousness in men and women who toil on a daily basis, but the direct consequences of a revolutionary government that has shared out social benefits but not distributed power. Since the workers do not make the decisions, they feel no responsibility. Just as before, they receive their orders from on high and sell their labor to those who control the means of production.[37]

The organising of self-management

The CNT very soon tried to define its stance as it applied to the overall private and self-managed economy. "Workers' organisations, chief among them the CNT, as well as the anarchist movement, should make ready to carry out a wholesale effort at economic reconstruction that must range from collectivisation through to socialisation of the land, mines and industry".[38]

Peiró came up with a better definition of the idea:

> If socialisation is carried out by the State, then it is nothing more than nationalisation; if it is the unions that bring

---

37 "*Burocracia y socialismo en Cuba*" in *Aportes* (Paris), January 1972, p. 51.
38 S.O., 5 August 1936 "*Cual ha de ser la actitud de la FAI en el momento presente*".

about the nationalisation of wealth, that is, of its creative sources, then, without a doubt, this is tantamount to socialisation. The difference, in any case, consists in whether it is actually the handiwork of the State or the outcome of the trade unions, and on this score the only problem is with the unions' equipping themselves with the capability [...] Are the unions equal to this mighty socialist role? [...] I say, emphatically not. And they are not because the industrial economy, closely bound up with the agricultural economy, is one and the same across the length and breadth of Spain. We have sound evidence of this in the economic phenomena being generated by the war, for it is the dis-organisation of the nation's economy [...] rather than the war per se, that is the reason why, economically, half of Spain is cut off from the other half [...] The National Federations of Industry, devised and so often promoted in CNT circles, have been espoused by the UGT, meaning that, assuming that that trade union grouping manages to shrug off the Spanish Workers' Socialist Party (PSOE), the UGT trade unions, should they decide to go for socialisation outside of the State, would be well placed to carry out this work of transformation [...] When we speak of socialising, only a few localised industries can escape the necessity of its being achieved nationwide, and in that case, our first thought should be for the appropriate agents of socialisation: the National Federations of Industry, to look no further than that segment of the economy.[39]

Up to that point the CNT had been organised into single sectoral unions that did not embrace all economic pursuits: "The Transport sector, for instance, was more of a partnership between the several industries it served, and survived as an autonomous trade union entity".[40]

---

39 *S.O.*, 17 January 1937, "*Necesitamos saber lo que hacemos*".
40 Peirats, op. cit, Vol. II.

With the move towards Federations of Industry, there were problems with the fairly deep-running rivalries between different trades unions: "I mentioned before that in fleshing out the *sindicatos únicos*, we run up against the same things. Everybody fighting his own little corner, so to speak. And now, when we try to flesh out the industrial unions, the same difficulties are cropping up".[41]

But the most deep-seated and worrisome problem was the shift in the direction of 'economics at firm level only'. "There are lots of collective ventures whose essential preoccupation has been with boosting wages and indeed cutting working hours and claiming wages for days not worked. Behaving as if the struggle was still against the bourgeois firm".[42]

The response came from the same source:

> The (Barcelona) Woodworkers' Union, fully cognizant of its responsibility and taking due heed of the times, wishes not merely to press ahead with the revolution but also to channel it by taking cognizance of our economy, the people's economy. To this end we gathered together all the small proprietors, the insolvent employers without the wherewithal to survive and took charge of all the microscopic workshops employing an insignificant number of workers, without asking them to which trade union Central they belonged, seeing them simply as workers who were idle, to the detriment of the economy [...] We set up confederal workshops with two hundred or more staff, such as had never before been seen in Barcelona and very few in the rest of Spain [...] We agree with collectivisation of all industries, but there should be one single fund, shared fairly. What we cannot countenance is that there should be poor collectives and wealthy ones.[43]

---

41 *Memoria del congreso de sindicatos de Cataluna*, March 1937.
42 *Butlleti Interior de la UGT*, November 1937, No. 21–22.
43 Peirats, op. cit., Vol I.

We come across the same vigor (in spades) in the concentration of workshops and worksites (from Barcelona's railways to its barbers) in the cities and, in the countryside, the concentration of machinery, the introduction or extension of irrigation works, consolidated exports of produce) against a backdrop of solidarity and mutual aid within one Federation and between the Federations (chiefly the Council of Aragon's) with coordination designed to resolve frictions and marshal effort.

Broadly speaking, come the revolution, solidarity outweighed selfishness. But sometimes CNT personnel could be very dour, and we offer the following as testimony rather than as hard fact:

> In Barcelona and nearly every town in Catalonia, each plant works and markets its products on its own account; each going after clients and competing with rival plants. This has spawned a working class neo-capitalism. The factory that discovered plentiful raw materials in the warehouses of the capitalist, or the employer expropriated or retained by the management committee as a consultant, is producing flat out. Others, less fortunate, are cutting back on production and on the living standards of their workers; still others must shut up shop, and the Catalan government pays their workforce for doing nothing.
>
> In business we find the same neo-capitalism, albeit on a lesser scale. Committees are being spawned in every business and in every company—the ex-owner even serves on them. The staff and owners come to some accommodation on how to exploit the customer.
>
> And so up pops the committee with all its shortcomings, of which we need not make a secret. Yet, in this initial stage, it is the sole manifestation that life goes on, since the bosses on the one hand and the unions on the other show no initiative. And life cannot grind to a halt. [...]

> We know of cases in Barcelona where the union representatives tried to get in touch with loss-making factory committees, which had no need to be such, only to be greeted at gunpoint. In other cases, where take-over was justified by excess profits that might have been used to help firms that were involuntarily operating at a loss, the same thing happened [...]
>
> The great lesson to be learned from such experience, which covers a three year period, is that, all in all (granted, of course, that there may have been a few exceptions unbeknownst to us) the committees spawned by the revolution [...] produced absolutely negative outcomes that brought the economy to ruination and engendered fresh forms of selfishness and exploitation. As for the trade unions, whenever they dared to go for socialisation, be it in Madrid or Levante or Catalonia, they met with gratifying success in terms of economics, freedom and justice.[44]

Clearly, this view is awash with a *dirigiste* brand of anarcho-syndicalism in contrast to committees 'plain and simple', and it carries within it the germ of the Marxist or authoritarian deviation, the belief that the masses are always wrong unless directed by the leadership committee of some group or other. Which is what happened to the CNT vis à vis the collectives—which, as we shall see, fought back—and vis à vis its own militants.

The logical outcome of crediting the rank and file with some inherent perversion (as Catholic leaders, capitalists and virtually all Marxists, Leninists or otherwise, believe, especially where peasants are concerned) was the introduction of the worker's record book or professional record book. A method for monitoring somebody's capabilities, morals and the place where he has worked. The idea appears to have originated with the French Second Empire

---

[44] G. Leval, *L'attivita sindacale nelle transformazuione sociale* (Milan 1948), pp. 36–40.

and it served an essentially policing purpose up until it was done away with in 1890. Now, from the 1930s on, the Italian and German fascists reintroduced the system. Horacio Prieto pushed it as a solution under the new revolutionary dispensation (see Appendix V below). Only days before the revolution M.R. Vázquez had this to say of it: "The professional record book facilitates State monitoring of all workers and furnishes it with a superb record for use when the time is right, when it can revoke the social status of those who are irksome to it".[45]

Not long after, by the beginning of 1937, the two trade union groupings, the UGT and the CNT, were beginning to favor the professional record book. First there was the confederal I.D. Card, which was to record "the industry in which engaged, the place of birth, the date he began working in the aforesaid industry".[46] Later, Madrid and Barcelona imposed the work certificate on all citizens.[47] And within the CNT, by the end of 1937, propaganda in favor of a confederal work certificate was underway, the slogan being: "It is no bother to any true worker to be asked for all the information required to authenticate his support for the people's cause".[48]

Lenin had written virtually the same himself: "Each worker has a work card. This document in no way degrades him, although today, it is, without question, a document authenticating capitalist wage slavery".[49] This fit with his theory of the one big union, membership of which was obligatory, and it accounts for the introduction of the professional record book in every one of the self-styled 'Marxist' countries.

---

45 S.O., 11 July 1936, "*Intervencionismo estatal equivale al fascismo*" (State intervention is tantamount to fascism).
46 *Memoria del congreso de sindicatos de Cataluna*, 2 March 1937, p. 395.
47 S.O., 23 February 1937, p. 6 and *Butlleti Interior UGT*, No 11–14, pp. 20–21.
48 *B.I.*, 8 October 1937; and *Nosotros*, 14 October 1937.
49 "Will the Bolsheviks survive in power? September 1917" in Adler, *Consejos obreros y revolucion* (Mexico, Grijalbo 1972), p. 127.

The final step was taken at the expanded economic congress held in Valencia in 1938. In the event of being dismissed several times over—from CNT factories!—the worker "is to have his curriculum registered in the work and trade union record books, any suspensions from work to be imposed are left to the discretion of the pertinent trade union, a course of action recommended as a last resort".[50]

The launch of so many Federations of Industry and the introduction of such controls on militants were carried through without any checks on the leadership. The UGT was less affected by the disagreements that had beset the CNT and FAI, than it was by a split (the PSOE had already had its own split between Caballero and Prieto) into a *caballerista*, pro-collective wing and a communist wing that favoured private industry.

Nevertheless, the UGT Executive Commission ordered "the taking of vigorous action against those unions failing to implement the government's dispositions".[51] For his part, M.R. Vázquez—a critic-turned-fan of the work record book—announced to the regional committees that "the electricity industry is to be militarised, and foreign capitalised companies handed back".[52]

Proof that the grassroots had no say appears in this statement by Vázquez: "There were two economic powers in Spain: one, the Jews, and the other, the Jesuits. That of the Jews was virtually entirely based on foreign capital. That of the Jesuits appeared, for the most part, to be domestic capital".[53]

Any militant would have said that such broad-brush ethnic slurs were nonsensical, since Kropotkin's wife was Jewish, as was Nettlau—the anarchist historian and specialist on Spain—and many Jews made up anarchist groups

---

50 *A.S.*, 1864M, October 1938.
51 *A.S.*, 1863M, October 1938.
52 *A.S.*, 593M, May 1938.
53 Ibid.

in the United States, as well as in Makhno's guerrilla formations. Individual error turns into collective blame when M.R. Vázquez, on behalf of the CNT, precluded any chance of recruiting left-wing Jews with this unashamedly racist affirmation: "It needs to be stipulated that we cannot unfurl a flag or strive for repeal of the old edict decreeing the expulsion of Jews from Spain and throw open her doors to all who would come and settle here. And this because that would unquestionably be one of the most anti-revolutionary decisions we could make. We are perfectly well aware that a capitalism of enormous significance will promptly gain a foothold here thereby reviving, as a result, the old systems of exploitation [...] Quite apart from this question of principle, all the recruitment, propaganda and information effort one might like can be carried out in the Sephardic world and circles, although we must agree that no Jew is a fascist".[54]

It was crazy for a CNT leader to be endorsing a decree issued by the *Reyes Católicos* 1492 and followed up by a second decree imposing the Inquisition throughout the entire kingdom. A number of Sephardic Jews had returned to Spain with the advent of the Second Republic and some—like the Turk, J. M. Estrugo[55]—fought on the republican side.

Grassroots versus Upper Echelons

Self-management organised from the ground up, spontaneously generated or, rather, looked to anarcho-syndicalist propaganda that adopted three approaches: *statistics* (as a means of monitoring the economy), *new technology* (in order to revamp the economy) and *education* (peddling a whole new outlook on the world).

---

54 20 May 1938; *A.S.*, 811B.
55 See *Los sefardíes* (Havana 1958), p. 33.

> Cullera states that a statistical commission should be set up, broken down into teams, and these teams together should form the local commission, and coordinate through comarcal, provincial and regional commissions.[56]

New technologies were introduced, which meant, first, the conversion of a consumer-goods industry into a war industry, which happened not just in Catalonia but also in Madrid (the Communist Party newspaper *Ferrobellum* describes this), Levante and Andalusia.[57]

At the same time there was a concentration of the transport sector, and exports of farm produce were brought under a single umbrella. Other industries followed the same trend.

A number of technologies previously unheard of in Spain were brought into play: technologies such as "portable bottles of pressurised gas" for vehicles,[58] fruit driers in Levante, poultry and rabbit breeding units in many villages, not to mention forestation management and irrigation works, which were similarly boosted.

Cultural endeavour could not be dissevered from the war effort, to the extent that it was the opportunity for self-management and the battle against capitalism that made it feasible. Thus, in the collectivist mind, self-management of the village, enlistment in the militias, the establishment of Ferrer Guàrdia-style schooling and birth control education were all different facets of the same thing.

> The view in Castelserás is that one of the very first considerations taken into account in this village was the running of schools, as today's children, who are to be the men of the future, have to have proper guidance and education.[59]

---

56 *Congreso regional campesino CNT de Levante, septiembre de 1936*, p. 8.
57 *Informe CNT-AIT*, November 1938, A.S., 568B.
58 *Memoria del pleno national de Agua, septiembre de 1937*, p. 45.
59 *Pleno regional FAI*, Alcañiz, 20 September 1936, p. 18.

Tailoring the school to the child and not the other way round, as has been the practice [...] Our school has no need to proselytise on behalf of a particular teaching or creed; it is enough that it should produce people with the aforementioned qualities and a lively sense of freedom, because we are sure that, if this is how they are, they will perforce be on our side and swell our ranks.[60]

The work of the CENU (*Consejo de la Escuela Nueva Unificada*/New Standard School Council) had yet to be undertaken, as were the anti-prostitution drives and campaigns of the Mujeres Libres. But there was a striking refusal to impose the same mental blinkers that the capitalist and Marxist authoritarians were accused of enforcing. Occasionally, there was a lapse into puritanism (see Appendix XI), as Ehrenburg and Kaminski[61] were quick to lampoon, but it was overlooked that "the most salient point about the anarchist movement was the tremendous dignity that it afforded man. Anarchism came to believe in such a man implicitly. It did not seek to help but to *do*. For example, there were ladies who assisted the poor drunkard; but the anarchists launched into a drive against alcohol abuse. Tackling the blight at its very root".[62]

Hence the further vandalism and attacks of the Communist Party on the rationalist schools as happened in the case of the 82nd Mountain Brigade, which banned the 115-child school of the collective in Ademuz.

---

60 *Ponencia de la regional de Asturias*, May 1937, A.S.
61 "They have done away with the old café; the puritanical collectivists saw it as a frivolous institution", A. Souchy, op. cit., p. 73; Ehrenburg, *Estampas de España*, on the eradication of prostitution, p. 18–19; and Kaminski, *Ceux de Barcelone* (Paris 1937). See also S.O., 25 October 1936; *Cultura y Acción*, 18 February 1937, p. 4; *Agitación*, 19 February 1937, p. 3; and *Tierra y Libertad*, 3 April 1937, p. 3.
62 F. Candel *Ser obrero no es ninguno ganga* (Barcelona 1968), pp. 72, 73.

***

The organisation and guidance provided by the trade-union bodies inevitably clashed with the collectivists' outlook. Also, the war was a great excuse for demands to be made and silence to be imposed: "And let no one think right now about pay rises or cuts in working hours. All workers, especially CNT workers, have a duty of self-sacrifice and to do whatever work needs doing".[63]

The first big criticism came from the peasantry:

> Industrial workers have been favoured financially even though some of them do not do a hand's turn; by contrast, peasants have not received the slightest help, although we are the ones that have actually put in all the hours of work possible [...] Neither the regional committee nor anybody else has spelled out what is meant by municipalisation; and since nobody has spelled it out, the peasants have no idea what to make of it [...] The same thing happened earlier when there was talk of establishing municipalities, for we were not told what their 'function' would be and it was the same story with the establishment of farming unions.[64]

The neo-capitalism detected at factories was also found in the farm collectives—to insiders as well as to the committees:

> [The Villena collective FAI group] We note that the individual trader has vanished and that we have opened the door to the collective trader. We now find one village pulling the wool over the eyes of another village as regards its produce, and this is deplorable.[65]

---

[63] *Memoria del congreso. de sindicatos de Cataluña, febrero–marzo 1937*, pp. 23, 24.

[64] Op. cit., pp. 23, 24, 58.

[65] *Memoria del pleno regional FAI de Levante, abril de 1937*, p. 93.

Esteban, from the Levante regional committee, endorses the views expressed by Gadea and states that a most deplorable selfishness has been implanted at village level. Villages bring their produce to the Federation when they cannot market them to the bourgeoisie or to the State. Some four million [pesetas] are owed to the Federation, and unless this is sorted out, disaster and disorganisation are on the cards.[66]

However this is one deviation that cannot be explained away in terms of the economic authoritarianism that arrived on the scene with the establishment of the National Peasant Federation: "Its accords are binding upon all its members and affiliates" (Article 14). [The peasant collectives and agencies] are to be subject to the national accords of the National Peasant Federation and its General Secretariat insofar as these apply to securing better harvests, the curtailment or eradication of rural blight and the conversion or replacement of crops that are uneconomic". (Article 26a)[67]

From late 1937 onwards, a campaign of opposition to the collectives was under way, a campaign to the effect that:

> The collective must not and cannot be anything other than the economic agency of the revolution and the new society created by it, the agent of which owes its birth to the trade union. The trade union as the founder of the collective has a duty to oversee it, to ensure that the revolutionary principles that led to its creation and launch are not misconstrued.[68]

Violently or otherwise, the collectives should be held answerable to the union and cling to an authentic

---

66 *Pleno de comarcales y sindicatos campesinos de Levante, 5 septiembre 1937*, p. 12.
67 *S.O.*, 25 June 1927.
68 *Federación regional de campesinos de Andalucía*, op. cit., 20 October 1937, p. 27.

understanding of the system of ownership which is to prevail.[69]

Naturally, there were instances in which the strike—the natural weapon of the exploited—was the solution:

> The carpenters have gone on strike due to their disagreement with the running of the collective, and the CNT-UGT Woodworkers' Sector states that, in light of the repulsiveness of all of the workers in that sector downing tools, without just cause or prior consultation, it not only condemns this move outright but is of the view that this is a move that could only be made by moles [*emboscados*], fascists and those devoid of consciousness.[70]

> After some days, Comorera issued the take-over [of public entertainments] order and our response was a general strike across the industry [...] The vast majority of the comrades repudiated the take-over [...] and suggested consulting the Executive Committee set up by the Organisation in Catalonia. This body, chaired by García Oliver, replied that, due to circumstances, we should defer to the take-over.[71]

As regards to the UGT, several workers in the railroad works in Gerona threatened to strike over the withholding of bonuses—though never actually struck—and as a result were sentenced to between six and eight years in prison for defeatism.[72]

All this bullying was in stark contrast to the passive acceptance of the sabotaging and undermining of the

---

69 Juan López, *El sindicato y la colectividad*, 1938, p. 12.
70 Translated from the Catalan in Ragón, op. cit, 1 November 1937, p. 248: Tarrasa.
71 *Enseñanzas de la revolución Española*, p. 164 e seq. (Madrid 1977).
72 Godicheau, *La guerre d'Espagne. République et révolution en Catalogne (1936–1939)* (Paris 2004), p. 286.

CLUEA[73] (see Appendix XII) and the forcible dismantling of the Council of Aragon, which is of course why no sanctions were ever imposed. One year on, the argument was still raging about what steps should be taken vis-à-vis those unions and collectives failing to implement national accords.[74]

Whilst the committees blundered or were slow to act (the Council of Aragon, according to its own bulletin, was still fussing over statistics in June 1937), vital measures were agreed, such as standardisation of accountancy practices in Levante. But other than in a few exceptional instances, it seems that the collectives were wrapped up in their work and failed to respond to official circulars: "The revolution will succeed through statistics".[75] "The peasants need to understand how important statistics are, for the making of purchases, sales and exchanges cannot proceed unmonitored".[76] "The importance of statistics in farming",[77] "Statistical Section: Circular (collectives are not responding appropriately)".[78]

The UGT seems to have been plagued with as many problems as the CNT, as is emphasised in a circular (no doubt dating from February–March 1938) from the Bajo Llobregat region: "Respected comrades: The plenum of the comarca's trade unions went ahead as scheduled. Said plenum had to be postponed to the 26th last month due to the failure of most of the unions belonging to this comarcal federation to attend, and it had to be rescheduled for the 2nd of this month, when a goodly number of unions were similarly absent [...] It was embarrassing to note that, after that interval, some 80 percent of the comarca's unions were still failing to comply with a requirement vital to the proper functioning of this committee".

---

73 Comité Levantino Unificado de Exportación de Agríos/Unified Farm Produce Export Committee of Levante
74 *F.S.*, 2 October 1938, p. 2; and *Vida*, 15 October 1938, p. 2.
75 *F.S.*, 1 November 1936, p. 1.
76 *S.O.*, 29 April 1937, p. 9.
77 *Vida*, 22 October 1938, p. 4.
78 *Campo Libre*, 14 January 1939, p. 7.

In any event, the problems with gathering statistics fail to account for the inability of each union, and of the republican government itself, to provide overall figures for the numbers of collectivists in the various sectors of the economy and information regarding the collectivists and their families. Though surveys were carried out,[79] it looks as if no one made the findings public. Needless to say, the figures bandied around in exile are far-fetched.[80]

The collectives' problems: smallholders, frictions, abuses

Let start off with a minor issue: the issue of travel, of people leaving the confines of the collectives, since this matter has been misrepresented by a Belgian Catholic reporter heavily under the influence of the propaganda of the PCE (as those of limited intellect customarily are). Émile Hambresin writes— in a left-leaning Catholic review—about a sick woman who had been refused permission to leave the Membrilla collective to go to Ciudad Real:

> This example affords some insight into the unbearable dictatorship exercised by the committees. The most trivial aspect of life was subject to their oversight. Many peasants were of the opinion that the new anarchist dictatorship was as unbearable as the old feudal dictatorship.[81]

Let me make a few points here: Hambresin lifted this example from anarchist sources (but fails to credit them) and gets the wrong collective. Actually, Souchy recounts that in the Albalate de Cinca collective, there was a woman who wanted to go to Lérida to consult a specialist and the committee insisted that she produce a certificate from the collective's

---

79 CNT in *F.S.*, 29 May 1937, p. 16, repeated in *S.O.*, 9 December 1937, p. 7; Agrarian Reform Institute, see *F.S.*, 15 June 1937, p. 4.
80 *Espoir*, July 1975.
81 *Esprit*, February 1938, p. 687.

doctor, on the grounds that people were habitually abusing exit permits. Souchy's conclusion was that the doctor's opinion would have resolved the issue.[82]

Now, in Membrilla the very opposite occurred; the narrator writes that a woman applied for leave to consult a specialist in the city and "without any red tape, was promptly handed the cash for her trip".[83] Besides, Kaminski[84] mentions, in relation to Alcora, that travel was not a problem. In April 1937, a circular was issued by the Aragonese regional federation asking each collectivist transferring between one collective and another to do so with authority so as to avert frictions.[85] Describing the Villas Viejas collective,[86] *Campo Libre* stipulated that journeys that were deemed useful were reimbursed whereas the costs of any others had to be defrayed by the collectivist himself.

This minor misrepresentation is yet another proof of premeditated hostility to self-management.

The underlying issue—the cornerstone of all the incidents—was the issue of smallholders. Plainly, the Communist Party stirred up frictions, but self-management was put forward as an economic model and set itself the task of doing away with smallholdings. So it is important that we steer clear of generalisations that complicate or simplify an issue that has already been sufficiently misrepresented by Leninism with its theory that peasants, first and foremost, seek personal ownership of the land and only then will agree to cooperation.

For one thing, in quite a number of instances the collectivists were smallholders who then pooled their holdings. Initially, it is true that they were a minority who were later

---

82 Op. cit., p. 92.
83 *Colectivizaciones*, p. 214.
84 H.E. Kaminski, op. cit. (Paris 1937).
85 *Nuevo Aragón*, 22 April 1937, p. 6.
86 25 December 1937, p. 4.

followed by the other peasants, either out of enthusiasm, under duress or out of opportunism. We are speaking here of a first phase that lasted roughly until 1937.

From 1937 on, thanks to the stance adopted by the republicans and the PCE and thanks also to the law, there was no compulsion or opportunism involved in falling into line with the collectivist minority. And we find clashes breaking out (Vilanesa, La Fatarella and Cullera) although the collectives not only survived but proliferated in Castile, Santander and Levante.

So self-management was a phenomenon embraced and adapted to each situation. The very fact that the Madrid government and the PCE drafted in an army general to smash collectivisation in Aragon is indicative of just how deep-rooted collectivisation was. There is further evidence in the form of the minute books of collectives: in three of these consulted at the Salamanca Archives we find new members joining, belatedly and in an ongoing process, which shows that peasants were coming around to the idea on reflection and through experience. The La Torre (Valencia) collective was launched on 17 September 1937 and it registered fresh members on 14 October 1937, 2 December 1937, 22 December 1937 and 20 January 1938. Villacañas (Toledo), a CNT-UGT collective, registered new recruits on 25 April 1937 and 26 December 1938. Campo Leal (Ciudad Real) did likewise on 26 January 1939.

The collectives have been accused of not surrendering land to ex-collective members reverting to individual farming. From the documentation consulted, it looks as if actually there was broad and complete freedom there.[87] However, at the Alicante UGT congress in February 1938 the decision was made not to surrender "any collectivised land to malcontents wishing to break away from it for reasons not justifiable in the estimation of said collective".[88]

---

[87] Alcorisa, 1 December 1936; Cuevas de Cañart, 24 September 1937 and *A.S.*, 373B.

[88] *Memoria*, op. cit., p. 66.

In fact, it emerges from the Communist Party of Aragon's own documentation that it was those who were quitting the collectives that were guilty of abuses by taking more out than they had pitched in.

Another serious problem was frictions between collectives, especially indirect frictions. One instance of direct friction was between Albalate del Luchador (formerly Albalate del Arzobispo) and Alcorisa (two collectives in Teruel province) over the costs of power supplied by a power station under CNT and UGT control. Another grievance was hypothesised in exile, according to J. Llop: "Had Balsareny and Ascó carried through their hydro-electric schemes [...] we might have faced a major clash in terms of bickering over water".[89] Indirect frictions were—as we see it—clashes between regions (unrelated to self-management) such as Aragon and Catalonia over, say, power supplies[90] and, finally, the way several collectives traded with the State rather than trading through trade union commercial channels".[91]

Economic *abuses* between collectivists and abuses of power within a collective[92] also played their parts. It should be borne in mind that earlier, as in Liria, not every collective was perfection: in Teresa de Cofrentes[93] there was 'confusion', in Corral de Almaguer (Toledo)[94] "a caricature of a collective", but, all in all, the criticisms were few.

The problem of power abuses by the collective's committee would have emerged over time and was hinted at in the statues:

---

89 R. Porté, *CNT*, 10 September 1950; in the view of J. Llop, Leval's claim, op. cit., p. 130, that there was a dam under construction in Flix, is mistaken.

90 *Pleno de Luz y Fuerza*, January 1937, p 75 et seq.

91 The same view was articulated at a November 1938 national plenum of the textile industry, p. 23.

92 For Ascó and Trivisa see *Le Monde libertaire*, July 1936; and for Alcorisa and Fraga, see Leval, op. cit.

93 García García, op. cit., p. 19.

94 A.S., 910M.

Accords passed by the steering council shall be binding upon members of the cooperative.

The council shall be elected for a four-year term of office and will face re-election (half in December 1939 and half in December 1944).[95]

It seems that this was the model followed in Castellón. In Castile, Andalusia and Aragon, committees enjoyed no such rights to dictate.

The sanctions recorded in the minute-books are understandable (alcohol abuse, "inadvisable conduct with a female comrade") or, frankly, worrying: "Any collectivist absenting himself from the assembly—held weekly—may be liable to a 1 peseta fine [the wage stood at 5 or 6]" or "for his conduct towards the council at this meeting" or "expelled as an undesirable". But a broader sample would be needed.

Temporary shortcomings due to wartime conditions? Inevitable committee-ocracy? Impossible to say. Such problems did exist and were combated within an economic context that was indisputably fairer and more varied that the pre-self-management one.

---

95 A.S., printed matter in 1561M and two pamphlets dealing with Castellón and Segorbe.

Chapter Five:
Self-Management under Attack

On many occasions the war was invoked as an argument for some alleged unity against fascism, with weapons being retained in the rearguard for an attack upon enemies in the days to come.

Here are two examples, the first in September 1936 in Aragon, which applies to both the rearguard and the front lines:

> I don't want to be taking any more phone calls at one or two o'clock in the morning saying that such and such a village has risen up or that some other village has done likewise. I reckon the time has come for this war to be taken seriously. Just as it is being taken seriously in the forward positions, so it should also be taken seriously in the rearguard and when I say 'rearguard' I mean from the very first village behind our forward positions stretching right back to the Plaza de Cataluña in Barcelona [...] I am surprised that on the few occasions I have left the front lines I left them for Lérida only to be told: Durruti, things can't go on this way. We are ready to go in with guns blazing. What is that all about? [...] Only last night we were looking at ways and means of helping the comrades, just as we had agreed to pull back from Monte Aragón to lend a hand to the comrades from the parts between here and Perdiguera and Peciña. I had a phone call at one o'clock in the morning. Durruti? Barbastro town here. *What's going on?* Nothing. Two

hundred *aguiluchos* [*faistas*] have shown up and everybody here is ready to kick up a rumpus. What's happening? Well, the Civil Guard and Carabineros have pulled out of Barbastro and all hell is about to break loose. I told them: You nitwits! Here we are planning to dispatch three hundred men into the sierra to risk their lives and you are bothering me with problems in the rearguard? I called them names, and they needed me, on the phone, to sort matters out [...]

Rovira [POUM]: What I say is that if I get wind of you mistreating one of my people, I'll muster a *centuria* and hunt you down.

Durruti: If we mistreat him...

García Oliver: Now, let's not mexicanise the struggle.[1]

The second example dates from around February 1937 and the republican government, according to Largo Caballero—prime minister from September 1936 to May 1937—when there were scarcely any differences of opinion between the factions:

The operation would open with an attack on Peñarroya, seizing the Córdoba-to-Extremadura rail line and, pushing further into that area, severing communications with Madrid province. Simultaneously there would be a thrust via Guadalupe designed to cut the roads near the capital. For this two-pronged operation we needed to muster forty thousand men. The Russians who visited me daily to talk about the war and brief me on the shipment of arms, were happy with the plan and gave me the names of brigade commanders, communists, to take command of the units due to be deployed. But the General Staff and I had already made the appointments to those commands. The requisite preparations were made: stores of equipment,

---

1 Verbatim report of meeting of political and military leaders in Aragon (Hoover Institution, USA), pp. 9–10.

quartermaster arrangements, medical arrangements, etc. I instructed them to ask the actual air force chief [the aircraft, pilots and commanders being Russian] for a written memo of the number of planes that might be deployed and the response was that we could count on ten planes. Ten planes for an army offensive putting forty thousand men into the field: I interpreted this as pay-back for having failed to appoint communists to positions of command.[2]

Pressure from the USSR undid the social tactics of the Communist Party of Spain, which had played its part in the uprising in Asturias and had, back then, taken an insurrectionist line:

Our task is to win over the bulk of the proletariat and prepare it to take power [...] Which means that we must focus our efforts on organising workers' and peasants' committees and setting up soviets.[3]

In July 1936, for the sake of international and national considerations and because of Russian interests that had absolutely nothing to do with the Spanish situation, the very same spokesperson—Dolores Ibarruri—this time announced:

What is being carried through in this country is the bourgeois democratic revolution mounted over a century ago in other countries such as France [...] We communists champion a system of freedom and democracy. Alongside the republicans, socialists and anarchists, we shall, no matter what the price, prevent Spain's sliding backwards

---

2 Largo Caballero *Correspondencia secreta* (Madrid 1961 [written in 1946]), p. 275.
3 Dolores Ibarruri, late 1933 in Moscow, as cited in Bolloten, op. cit., p. 89.

and turning her back on progress.[4]

In actuality, the communists did all in their power to oppose take-over measures:

> In the initial moments of confusion, at the time of the rebel uprising, no organisation other than the Communist Party dared to call for respect for the small property-owner.[5]

The short and most certainly incomplete chronology that follows plots the rise of the CP and USSR to power through a proliferation and escalation of clashes. Note, too, how the CNT's participation in the Catalan and republican governments provided no ease.

30 October 1936: Communists open fire on members of the (self-management-championing) Iron Column attending a funeral (upwards of a hundred were hit).[6]

13 November 1936: Gun-battle in Fortuna (Murcia) between CNT and communist personnel.[7]

1 January 1937: The CNT- and UGT-organised workers' supplies committees in Barcelona are disbanded.[8]

Late-January 1937: Clashes between collectivists in La Fatarella (Tarragona).[9]

---

[4] Ibidem, p. 87; and *Mundo Obrero*, 30 July 1936.
[5] Julio Mateu, *Por que se constituye la Federación Provincial Campesina* (1937).
[6] *Línea de Fuego*, No. 37.
[7] A.S., 1061B, letter from the CNT National Committee to Federica Montseny.
[8] *L'Espagne Nouvelle*, 17 September 1937, p. 1.
[9] A.S., 1340B, *L'Espagne Nouvelle* 17 September 1937, p. 1.

3 February 1937: The Generalitat outlaws collectivisation of the dairy industry.[10]

3 February 1937: Clashes between CNT and UGT personnel in the Cullera collective (Valencia).[11]

8 March 1937: Clashes (see above) in Vilanesa.

17 April 1937: Anti-CNT shoot-out in Puigcerdá (an important CNT collective).

May 1937: Armed police raid intended to clear out the Barcelona telephone exchange, which was in the hands of UGT and CNT personnel. The CNT remains passive: ministers Montseny and García Oliver step in to douse the flames, bringing severe pressure to bear to ensure that armed CNT personnel do not arrive from Aragon to help their comrades in Catalonia.[12]

June 1937: Attacks on the collectives in Mora, Mascarate, Perales de Río (Toledo) mounted by Líster's brigade.[13]

July 1937: Incidents in Ascó (Tarragona) in the wake of the Líster Brigade (See Appendix VII).

August 1937: Collectives destroyed in Aragon by the Líster Brigade and the Council of Aragon (disbanded) abolished.

---

10 García García, op. cit.
11 *Umanità Nova* (Rome), 20 December 1964, p. 2; testimony of Umberto Marzocchi.
12 *Confederación*, 11 June 1937, p. 4.
13 José María Marcet Coll, *Mi ciudad y yo* (Barcelona 1963), p. 37: "Its installation, of unmistakable military significance, fell intact into the hands of the Nationalists together with all its magnificent equipment, which included state-of-the-art gear". This should be seen in the context of the imminence of the compact soon to be signed between the USSR and Nazi Germany, which facilitated the release of Soviet prisoners held in Francoist prisons.

October–November 1938: Government take-over of the Catalan war industries.

January 1939: Líster forgets to destroy an aircraft factory.

These notes show the incompatibility of the collectivised and non-collectivised sectors, the impossibility of political alliances between the ideologies involved and, above all, the lifespan of this experiment in self-management, the existence of which was entirely due to rank-and-file enthusiasm. It was down to the workers, not any rabble-rousing sloganising by the committee-ocracy such as 'better to die on one's feet than live on one's knees'—watchwords that were never acted upon by those who mouthed them (not least Dolores Ibarruri who spent years licking Stalin's boots).

Chapter Six
Self-Management's Outcomes: Overall Conclusions and Estimates

Any complete estimate of the active population in republican Spain has to take account of the shifting front lines. Up until the loss of the North in March 1937, the population might be reckoned at six million and, after that, at five million. Following the loss of Aragon in March 1938, this fell to about 4,200,000. These rough estimates enable us to work out some sort of overall percentage figures.

It has to be stressed that virtually all of the data is from the CNT, although the UGT also had important (though none more important) collectives in many provinces. Consequently, my calculations tend toward the minimum and are provisional.

What is glaringly absent is the overall figure for industrial self-management, especially in the war industries. Also missing are studies cataloging the UGT's achievements.

That said, I can offer this statistical break-down on participation in self-management:

Andalusia: The minimum number of farming collectives is 120, and the maximum 300. Using an average—210 collectives, with 300 people each—gives a total of 63,000 people.

Aragon: The figure of 450 collectives involving 300,000 is an acceptable one. Plus the UGT had a certain presence, with 31 collectives in Huesca alone.[1]

---

1 *Colectivismo*, October 1938.

Cantabria: Though minimum estimates, the figures offered are 100 farming collectives and 13,000 people.

Catalonia: The minimum figure for farm collectives is 297, and the maximum 400. If we accept the figure of 350, with an average population of 200, that gives us some 70,000 people. As for industrial self-management, the law set out the overall numbers of workers, though unemployment was a big factor. On the basis of 80 percent of the 700,000 workers in the province, that gives us 560,000 people. Which, adding in their family members, gives us a minimum of 1,020,000 people.

The Centre region: 240 CNT farm collectives involving 23,000 families, giving us a minimum of 67,992 people or thereabouts, to which must be added the UGT collectives (the same figure again—at least), leaving us with some 176,000 in agriculture. There were lots of industrial collectives in the cities and towns. I think it reasonable to accept a minimum figure of 30,000 people involved.

Extremadura: We have a figure of 30 collectives with an average of 220 people each, which gives us a figure of roughly 6,000 for the CNT and UGT together.

Levante: Our estimate is at least 503 collectives involved in agriculture, with 130,000 people. In industry, the minimum reckoning is 30,000, which, as in the case of the Center region, strikes us as reasonable.

Total: 758,000 collectivists involved in agriculture and 1,080,000 in industry. Giving us a figure of 1,838,000, which is, as explained earlier, a *minimum* estimate.

This estimate amends the ones I published in 1970 (2,440,000 and 3,200,000 respectively) and fits the estimates offered by Vernon Richards (1,500,000) but are in stark contrast with Gaston Leval's estimate of thirteen million and then "six, seven, eight million".[2] As a sample, let me take three periods with their respective percentage figures whereby the total figure of wage-earners involved in self-managed firms as against the entire active population can be arrived at, and which also needs to be adapted to take due account of the evolving developments in self-management and in the war.

For the July 1936 to March 1937 period, we have to take the view that self-management really began to function in mid-October (discounting Castile, which got its act together from late 1937 onwards), giving us a figure of 1,632,000 collectivists as against 6 million people overall: or 27.2 percent.

From March 1937 to March 1938 (without Cantabria and the Centre region at that point) we find 1,725,000 out of 5,000,000, or a percentage figure of 34.5.

Finally, between March 1938 and January 1939 (when Catalonia fell to Franco, when Aragon dropped off the map, when Levante was thrown into disarray through breaches of the front lines, but with the Centre still operating flat out), we come up with 1,450,000 out of 4,200,000, or some 34.5 percent.

Self-management was the mainstay of the economy and emblematic of revolution, despite the ascendancy gained between the beginning and end of the war by the anti-self-management camp (ranging from out and out Francoists to a motley crew of saboteurs spearheaded by the Communist Party and the Soviets).

---

2 Vernon Richards, *Enseñanzas de la revolución española*, p. 88.

Chapter Seven
Conclusions about Self-Management in 1936–1939, and Broad Reflections

On 18 July 1936, the forces of the right triggered their coup. The date was well chosen, for the left—the workers, as well as the CNT, deep down—were split.

However, in many instances the politicised and conscious workers, most often CNT members, put up a ferocious fight and managed to thwart the would-be coup makers in Catalonia, Asturias, Castile and Levante. By 21 July, the map of Spain had been divided into two zones and to the misfortune of the CNT, Galicia and part of Aragon and Andalusia had fallen to the other side. Furthermore, the forces of the left felt compelled to keep quiet about their differences, the better to resist the enemy—or so the theory went. And thus was born a reluctant alliance of republicans, (initially loyal) Civil Guards, quite a number of army officers, socialists, communists and trade unionists from the UGT and CNT, all united, for the first and last time, behind the UHP logo.

In actual fact, some people obeyed the government and did their duty (like Aranguren, the general in charge of the Civil Guard in Barcelona, Miaja, and so on), while others followed their class instincts and threw in their lot with the Francoists (like many Civil Guards and like the intellectual Gregorio Marañón, who had been a CNT supporter in the summer of 1936). Left high and dry, republican-minded bourgeois refused to throw their weight behind the people's revolution and hoped to negotiate with the rebels as a way of preserving capitalist hierarchy. The socialists were divided against one another and with republicans in order to grab a share of power. In complete contradiction to what they had been saying only a few years earlier (see Appendix XV), the USSR's cat's-paw Communist Party argued that what was happening in Spain was a *bourgeois* revolution (a Spanish version of 1789) and that workers would have to wait to see what Spain's future held in store. Rank and file CNT members and quite a few UGT personnel and unaffiliated workers pushed for social revolution, while the CNT's own bigwigs allied themselves with the politicians, postponing social change until *after* military victory (as if the fighters and economy were likely to render victory possible in the absence of immediate social change).

This confusion fostered misunderstandings and led to armed clashes within the republican camp in the course of what some saw as a civil war and others as a revolution.

With the blessing of the Pope,[1] fascists and Francoists, the rebels had raised the standard of a war of religion, and launched into a massacre of thousands of leftists and workers, in an out-and-out class genocide. They were aided and abetted by Italian and German fascism and with the connivance of Great Britain and the USA. It was a replay of the policy of annihilation deployed against captured Paris Communards by Thiers and General Gallifet (when some 30,000 children, women and men were shot down, not to mention the oth-

---

[1] "On 16 April 1939, fifteen days after the war had ended, [Pius XII] broadcast a radio address to Spaniards [the very first radio address by Pius XII to the world following his appointment as Pontiff of the Catholic Church] in which, addressing himself to 'Catholic Spain', he said: 'It is with immeasurable joy, most beloved children of Catholic Spain, that we address you to express our fatherly congratulations for the gift of peace and victory which God has deigned to bestow upon the Christian heroism of your faith and charity as displayed in so very many selfless sentiments...'" See http://galeon.hispavista.com/razonesespanola/r116-cru-htm.

Conclusions about Self-Management in 1936–1939

ers arrested and deported to New Caledonia). This was social warfare designed to uphold a capitalism under threat of revolutionary change, which was being sabotaged from within, by the military hegemony of the Soviet Union, which in 1938 placed a freeze on aid in order to pursue the pact it signed with the Nazis in 1939.

At grassroots levels, among the UGT and CNT workers, such matters were less of a consideration. There was a belief that the war would be over within a matter of weeks. Durruti pushed this line, and people made their preparations with this in mind. They had to ensure that industry was kept up and running so that it could be converted for war purposes and they had to see to it that the cities were kept supplied. They pulled it off: neither bread nor milk ran short (as Kropotkin had insisted they must not in *The Conquest of Bread*).[2] In Barcelona the CNT and the FAI laid down a marker as early as 24 July 1936 when they raised a 3,000-strong column of volunteer militias for service in Aragon, complete with armoured trucks, kit, quarter-master and auxiliary services and so on.

Only one week earlier, workers had been leading humdrum lives, and for the vast majority of them, the previous Sunday had been just another Sunday in July.[3]

A month before, in France, amid all the euphoria surrounding the left's election victory, workers had taken over the factories, only to desert them, induced to do so by promises of a forty-hour work week and legislation about holiday pay.

One inside observer stressed:[4]

---

2 See the Introduction to this book.

3 For instance, the POUM leader Jordi Arquer (in an unpublished interview), and the Reus chapter of his party held a get-together for a *gargolada* (snail roast).

4 Simone Weil, a philosophy teacher who—in order to familiarise herself with the life of the working class—went off to work in several factories in Bourges (a very Catholic city associated with the arms industry) from 1932 until 1937 and later in Paris and northern France. Out of this experience came her book *La condition ouvrière,* from which this quotation is borrowed.

Although there is no agreed strategy, the leaderships are not joining forces and not seeking common ground in their demands. Indeed, one often comes across a startling ignorance of what is happening beyond the nation's borders. Up until now, worker internationalism has been more talked about than practised.[5]

Little by little, shop stewards are beginning to look to workers like agents of trade union authority. The workers were passively obedient for years, with little experience of trade union democracy, and are used to waiting for their orders.[6]

The French CGT of the day, shaped by the Communist Party and, previously, by reformist jingoists during the First World War, operated along top-down lines, of course. This accounts for the absence of direct action and horizontal initiatives, even when employer authority, to all intents and purposes, suddenly vanished in the summer of 1936. In Spain, by contrast, there is no denying that the CNT's structure and the rounded education it offered its militants accounts for the speed and maturity of the social organising that supplanted capitalist rule. Even though it looked—and still does—simplistic in the eyes of CNT bigwigs and capitalist economists,[7] the libertarian communist approach was enough (not that it claimed to be a panacea in any case) to open militants' eyes to their entrepreneurial and creative potential.

---

5 Written on 30 July 1937, and contradicted by the 30,000 French who volunteered to fight in Spain. Weil spent several weeks as a volunteer with a CNT column in Aragon and later in Barcelona, which, oddly enough, she omits here.

6 *La condition ouvrière* (Paris 1951), pp. 271–272, from June 1936.

7 One answer might be that, essentially, current capitalist economics relies on speculation, fictitious data (two sets of company books, national expenditure inflated so as to cover up the thievery at the top) and wars (future or past) and the rest is claptrap.

Conclusions about Self-Management in 1936–1939

In Barcelona, for instance, there were several transport companies (the main ones anyway) that amalgamated in the wake of the coup attempt. Several railway companies also amalgamated. In these, the workers resolved matters relating to time-tabling, accounts, the numbers and quality of spares to be manufactured—or for the manufacture of which provision would have to be made if they could not be got from foreign suppliers—as well as a range of newer issues (old age pensions, cultural activities, free schooling and military transport).

In Barcelona, healthy shops and work-spaces promoted by the CNT and, in some instances, by the UGT, were inaugurated as replacements (as Anselmo Lorenzo had anticipated happening, see Appendix V below) for the sort of lethal workshops still in operation all around the world to this day—those with the approval of neo-liberal capitalists or the acquiescence of Chinese Marxist-Leninists.

At the same time, wage-earners bettered their working conditions (collectivisation in agriculture and adaptations to work-rates in industry). Spontaneously, they acted in the cultural sphere (setting up schools and libraries), given that illiteracy levels were high.[8] Great strides were made in terms of healthcare, especially in the agricultural sector; in Aragon medical treatment was free of charge and the doctor lived in the collective. Elderly workers received pensions (a very far cry from the norm in Spain and France today).

An important point here was the absence of hatred: writings on the subject of libertarian communism, and Kropotkin himself, had stressed that collectivisation was for the good of everybody, including former foes (see Appendix V). In the villages operating under self-management, widows, Civil Guards' families and the families of rebels killed during the coup were respected and catered for; they were all equally entitled to the collective's stores.

---

8   This was reflected in Barcelona, July 1936, where the deeds setting up collectives were signed by a thumb-print 50–60 percent of the time.

Marxist-Leninists, with their obsessions about plots and sabotage by capitalist agents operated—and still do—along very different lines. They pigeon-hole and keep files on people, holding generations of ex-bourgeois at a distance (the way Catholics did for centuries with Jewish converts) and establishing social pariah categories (those of bourgeois or *kulak* extraction), who have to pay for their redemption with moral and physical prostitution to the Party fat cats. Common practice for any brutal medieval-style regime down through the ages.

On workers' emancipation, Spanish anarcho-syndicalists looked primarily to the First International, and believed it needed to be the workers' own doing. As a result, they strove to eradicate social inequalities by setting up a shared compensation fund that covered both poor and prosperous collectives, agricultural collectives and industrial ones, as well as collectives in the service sector. Thus, the Barcelona hairdressers' collective funded the purchase of an engine to pump water to the town of Ascó (Tarragona)—an engine that operated even after 1939.

No attempt was made to impose an arrangement whereby everybody was required to show the same commitment and levels of consciousness, but there were shortcomings:

First, in a number of collectives, agricultural and industrial alike, there was a sort of psychological self-absorption as collectives tended to share profits without a thought for the war situation or the opponents of self-management. This led to a sort of neo-capitalism in some collectives that might be described as a move away from one boss to many bosses—namely, all of those serving on the self-management team in some firms. The anarcho-syndicalist trade unions fought back by establishing liaison between collectives under threat of sanctions (such as cutting off of supplies). This was a genuine reality and was corrected.

Another flaw was the absence of comrades qualified to handle the book-keeping. Here, as in the compilation and passing on of the statistics vital for the establishment of horizontal and vertical coordination, shortcomings were due to the inadequate training available in the school system, the time squandered on countering anti-self-management propaganda, the unrelenting pressures of the war and the constant siphoning of personnel for front-line service.

Nevertheless, agricultural output was maintained (not being dependent, like industry was, on raw materials or spares from outside the country), thanks to the hard work of women, the elderly, and young people generally.

The reach of self-management depended on three factors: the CNT leadership, the law and the return of the bourgeoisie.

The CNT-FAI's abandonment of self-management was one of a host of concessions, the upshot of which might be summed up by this public admission in September 1936:

> Had we to talk about the cavalier approach to everything that could have been achieved and was not achieved over these two tragic months; if we had to speak of the squandering of the opportunity that existed to amass all of the offensive weaponry that was missing, even as the Bank of Spain up in Madrid held millions upon millions in gold in storage; had we to express our rage and our powerlessness [...] then there is a lot that I could say, but I prefer to say nothing.[9]

Second, the republican and Catalan legislation that discriminated against and pushed self-management into second place (cf. The October 1936 law on collectivisation in Catalonia, and the skullduggery of the communist minister of Agriculture), that failed to acknowledge the lawfulness of the revolutionary act of seizing land for collective use, hobbled chances of securing funding.

---

9   Federica Montseny speech from 20 September 1931, cited in *F.S.*, 22 September 1936. The gold in question vanished, USSR-bound, on 25 October 1936.

Finally, the May 1937 events in Barcelona meant a boosting to the petite bourgeoisie's grip on the economy, thanks to the communist and Catalanist parties and the assault on UGT and CNT trade unionists. This was underlined a short time later—that August—by the pressures of the division commanded by the communist Líster, which were designed to undermine and ruin the self-managed economy in Aragon, right when the wheat harvest was due.

***

Viewed alongside the international experience, the self-management witnessed during the Spanish revolution is a model that none can ignore. One Spanish former-communist-turned-socialist said:

> As the civil war and revolution of 1936–1939 recede further into the past, the most significant point about their political legacy, the one that retains the greatest relevance and theoretical interest in the current struggle for communism, is the self-managerial effort made by the Spanish proletariat at the urging and initiative, in most instances, of the anarcho-syndicalists.... Shortly before his death in Moscow [in February 1921], Kropotkin ventured to say that the Bolshevik experience was an object lesson in "how not to make the revolution". But how was it to be made in such a way that the steps taken to eliminate the old society not become obstacles to the creation of a communist society? This is the great issue of our day, and awareness of it is the precondition for the first step towards a resolution.[10]

The point is well made, but remains rather mealy-mouthed, compared to answers offered in early-twentieth century USSR:

---

10 Fernando Claudín, *Movimiento Libertario Español*, 1974.

Kronstadt: *Resolutions of the General Assembly of the Crews of the 1st and 2nd Flotillas of the Baltic Fleet, held on 1 March 1921.*

Having listened to reports from the delegates dispatched to Petrograd by the general crews' assembly to take the measure of the situation there, the Assembly has determined that there is a need:

1. For proceeding immediately to the re-election of soviets by means of secret ballot, given that the current soviets are not expressions of the will of the workers and peasants. The lead-up election campaign is to be conducted with complete freedom of speech and propaganda among the workers and peasants.

2. For freedom of the press and of speech for all workers and peasants, for the anarchists and for all the left socialist parties.

3. For freedom of reunion to be guaranteed for trade union and peasant organisations.[11]

Makhnovists are workers who raised the standard of revolt against Denikin and against any yoke, all violence and falsehood, no matter their source. Makhnovists are those workers whose toil enriches, fattens and underpins the reign of the bourgeoisie, in general and, right now, the Bolshevik bourgeoisie, in particular [...] Workers themselves must freely elect their soviets; soviets that carry out the wishes and decisions of those workers, which is to say, executive and not authoritarian soviets.[12]

This points to the consciousness and creativity of Russian workers, who operated through their free soviets and coordinated according to need and through horizontal decision-making

---

11 Alexandre Skirda, *Kronstadt 1921: prolétariat contre bolchévisme*, pp. 179–181.

12 Makhnovist flyer dated 27 April 1920. See Alexandre Skirda, *Nestor Makhno*, op. cit., pp. 459–460.

processes. And even earlier, these were largely the practices espoused by Mexican peasants between 1910 and 1917, in accordance with their native collectivist tradition and after the anarchist style of the Flores Magón brothers' Partido Liberal. In the Spain of July 1936 there was no doubt as to the approach to be adopted vis-à-vis the politicians. However, most of the CNT leadership, whether or not under the sway of the FAI, collaborated with people whose ineptitude in handling the wage earners had been demonstrated.

So why did they act in such defiance of their rank-and-file members? They were imbued with a top-down outlook and authoritarian mind-set, and failed to grasp the real meaning of a libertarian revolution. On very different grounds, one CNT member who resisted the compromises and betrayals from July 1936 onwards, came up with this considered opinion:

> Nobody wants to play down the issue that confronted anarchists on 20 July 1936 when they found themselves with a situation on their hands and had no idea what to do with it. Where they were found wanting is not in their repudiation of an anarchist dictatorship but in having plumped for counter-revolution instead. The dilemma articulated—dictatorship or collaboration with government—is a phony one. From the anarchist point of view, dictatorship and collaboration with government are one and the same thing. And the choice between two things that are the same is no dilemma at all. Dictatorship is counter-revolutionary and the State is counter-revolutionary. Now, if the government contains anarchists, on the one hand the government's counter-revolutionary power is boosted but, on the other, the revolutionary opposition is weakened. From which it follows that simply by the anarchists' not collaborating in government, the revolutionary opposition might have been bolstered and the State's counter-revolutionary power weakened at the same time.

Would the war have been lost that much sooner? Knowing that would require proof that the State lifted a finger to win it once it spotted its chance to do away with the revolution [...] So, instead of the question, 'What was feasible?' let us pose this one: 'What should *not* have been done?' and we will have solved half the problem.[13]

The clarity of that message aligns with Bakunin's declaration:

Before we can accept you, you must promise us that: 1) Starting right now, you will subordinate your personal interests and, indeed, family interests as well as your political and religious beliefs and displays to the supreme interest of our association: the struggle of labor against capital, of the workers against the bourgeoisie in the realm of the economy. 2) To never compromise with the bourgeois for self-serving reasons. 3) To never act in your own interest over the masses of the workers, which would instantly make you bourgeois, an enemy and an exploiter, since the entire difference between the bourgeois and the worker is that the former always looks to his own advantage outside of the collective good, and the latter neither seeks nor aims to succeed other than in the company of all who labor and are exploited by bourgeois capital. 4) That, at all times, you will be faithful to worker solidarity, since the slightest betrayal of it is deemed by the International as the greatest crime and greatest act of infamy that might be committed by a worker.[14]

Were the International able to form itself into a State, we, its sincere and zealous supporters, would promptly

---

[13] José Peirats, in the review published in exile in Paris, *Presencia* No. 5, September–October 1966.

[14] "The policy of the International", 1869, in *Bakunin. Crítica y acción*, op. cit.

become its bitterest foes [...] The International Association will only be able to turn into an instrument of emancipation for humanity after it has first emancipated itself. When no longer split into two groups — a majority of unseeing tools and a minority of learned mechanics — it has managed to inject the science, philosophy and politics of socialism into each and every one of its members.[15]

It is through the struggle against hierarchy and against the division of physical labourers and intellectual ones, and the insistence on rotation of offices and the revocability of officials, that the bureaucratisation that leads to dereliction and repression can be limited and eliminated.

What is happening today and what has the Spanish experience of self-management to offer us?

As opposed to the manipulative discourse about some ever-increasing democratisation of States and the need for capitalism to be co-managed — which the snake-oil salesmen of politics would have us believe amounts to 'self-management' (all wrapped up in some pink or green or Peronist packaging, and in face of the overlapping of economies, proliferating consumerism and the complexity of social life) — the hard facts and everyday reality suggest that the wretchedness and exploitation endured by 80–90 percent of the population of the planet sadly and relentlessly persist.

Only the grassroots approach in 1917–1921 Russia and in the Spain of 1936–1939 offer us a compass with which to escape the economic perversity thrust upon us.

And in the here and now there is a number of approaches open to us:

Refusal to play by the rules of consumerism and capitalism (working, resting and buying obsolete rubbish). Instead,

---

15 "The Organisation of the International", 1871, in *Bakunin. Crítica y acción*, op. cit.

standing by the exploited, as Bakunin recommended, means building ourselves a life with a sense of the social and the collective and being ready to engage with a struggle alongside others—prioritising activism and not wasting long hours on false liberations (excessive drinking, drug use, empty-headed books, obsession with animal rights, Esperanto, sexual communes and so on).

Self-management can make inroads into significant groups if pursued as a social and economic approach. This means the rejection of full time, permanent officials, and requiring that they spend half their day as wage-earners at their original calling, and that everybody takes his turn once every six to ten months (depending on how demanding the task may be), subject to recall by the rank and file in the event of differences of opinion that may frustrate progress.

Self-management also means reverting to something that socialists of the nineteenth century knew: that the employers follow up every rise in wages with increases to the prices of consumer goods. Thus any increase in wages has to be matched by a reduction in hours, productivity rates and years of pension contributions, as well as increases in retirement numbers and pensions.

Computer use facilitates the flow of information, and monitoring and usage by an indefinite number of groups and collectives.

Over and above opening minds to the fight against social and economic authoritarianism, self-management means refusing to countenance waste (medicines by the thousands when hundreds should suffice, over-consumption of meat and GM foods, items and machinery with built-in obsolescence, etc.), or unbalanced, unequal standards of living across the planet.

Trusting in the potential of wage-earners at grassroots level. The Spanish experience is a standing example in any fraught situation. In one of the last texts from *Solidarnosc* prior to the December 1981 military coup in Poland, one trade union leader wrote: "Doubts as to the ability of the working class and civil society to organise themselves disguise submission to bureaucratic authority. In 1936, after the masses of people crushed the Francoist rebellion, and following the flight of the bosses who were part and parcel of that rebellion, in Catalonia as well as in other regions of Spain the trade unions and workers' committees took over and brought the majority of industrial, business and transport ventures under social ownership".[16]

May 1968 in France, August 1968 in Czechoslovakia, December 1970–January 1971 in Poland. Countless instances of shops and supermarkets looted at the hands of the poor and marginalised in Third World nations and in the United States and Europe during the 1980s and 1990s. The intervention of the masses during periods of transition or a power vacuum in 1967–1969 in China, 1974 in Portugal, the late 1980s in Iran, 1981 in Poland right up until Argentina on 19 and 20 December 2001 came as blessed relief and liberation from the ennui and pressures of consumption, work, exploitation and conventional wisdom and was welcomed as endowing personal life with new meaning.

The liberation of all lives and society through self-management—so that we can have work that is purposeful and dignified—amounts to the creation of a new society, one that rejects absorption into capitalism, just as our Indian brothers have done ever since the Spanish invasion.

---

16 Zbigniew M. Kowalewski in *Samizdat 82* (Lausanne), p. 35.

Introduction to Appendices

The first three of the appendices that follow show that the traditional social and individual structures were being kicked over. Those are: religion ("Notes on the Spanish People's Superficial Catholicism"), fear of the forces of repression ("Revolutionary Uprisings in Spain, 1932–1934") and reorganising society in order to dismantle a regime of oppression ("One example of Monetary Reform and Scheme for Currency Circulation in a Social Economy").

The next two appendices ("The CNT and the FAI: Pressure Groups" and "The Two Libertarian Communisms") highlight the shortcomings of the confederal movement, which went on to infect and hinder the spread of self-management and swelled until it had a governo-centric outlook.

Appendix VI ("Notes on Governmental Collaborationism") presents an overview of the supposed 'necessity' for collaborationism, a necessity that quickly became a definitive feature of Spanish anarcho-syndicalism as articulated by all of its leading lights.

Appendix VII ("Making Sense of the Plenum of Confederal Militias and Columns") is an extraordinary documentary testimony to the lack of understanding between the National Committee and the most committed militants serving in a voluntary capacity on the front lines. It was a gathering first described by the upper echelons as an 'unlawful assembly'—and the very use of such terminology in the delicate circumstances of a revolution and war is itself nonsense—when it was an initiative emanating from the rank and file. Another extraordinary feature of it is the vibrancy of the proceedings and the fragility of the National Committee's politics of compromise.

The constructive revolutionary activity of the workers was displayed in concrete situations, ranging from basic units through to huge collectives, and included different phases in agriculture and industry, as can be seen from Appendices VIII to XIV.

In order to avoid repetition (in that the essential points have been incorporated into the text) I have dropped a couple of reflections from the 1999 French edition, which dealt with the questions of money and social welfare.

The last two Appendices ("Marx, Engels, the C.P., Councilism, Historians and Revolutionary Spain" and "Francoism, Transition to Democracy and Thoughts on Collective Management") grapple with some historical interpretations and with contemporary Spain.

Appendix I
Notes on the Spanish People's Superficial Catholicism

From the 15th century, Catholicism, as an exclusive religion, was imposed by force by the *Reyes Católicos* and the Inquisition. Before that there had been many long centuries of tolerance between Islam, Judaism and Christianity, usually coinciding with periods of economic and cultural boom. While the war against Napoleon relied heavily on the priests, by 1835 we find that, during popular uprisings against poverty, and during outbreaks of disease, the monastic buildings were looked upon as epicenters of exploitation and infection and were put to the torch. Hence the tide of arson attacks on religious buildings and the murders of priests, nuns, etc., in the republican zone between 1936 and 1939. In quite a few cases, CNT personnel opposed this, not least Durruti whose secretary was a priest rescued from the wrath of the people in one Aragonese village.[1]

---

1   See Monsignor Jesús Arnal, *Por qué fui secretario de Durruti* (Andorra 1972). The dedication to this book reads: "In memory of the man who was my friend and protector, Buenaventura Durruti Domingo, in token of my gratitude and affection". After stating that Durruti was neither a drinker nor a philanderer nor bloodthirsty, he sums up his personality thus: "He struck me rather as a good companion to all of those around him". He writes, "Thank you, Durruti! And may God, when he came to weigh up your failings, have taken into consideration the great delicacy with which you dealt with this priest. Many thanks!" For instance: "I was present at the questioning of rightwingers brought to the Column and the questioning never focused on their beliefs but rather on their deeds. Nor was the alleged offender the only person questioned: virtually all of the questioning was put to the village accusers who

Religion was always a easy career option: "From the mines of Alén we went to Castro Urdiales and my father took me from that place to Ponferrada at the age of ten [...] A practical man, he did not want his son to be a workhorse as he had been—those are his words—and he came up with the idea of having me study for the priesthood". This statement by Ángel Pestaña (*Lo que aprendí en la vida*) refers to 1896, and echoes a lot of testimony from Spain and France, and from literature, such as in Stendhal's *Le Rouge et le noir*.

The impact of the Great Depression and the emergence of the Republic had drastic implications for Spanish Catholicism.

> The undermining of family faith was reaching the alarming status of mass apostasy among the laboring classes [...] That year [sometime before 1930, we deduce], I was exploring the agrarian question in Spain and I spent months explaining Henry George's agrarian socialism to my students, who were in the final three years of Theology studies. When that was done, I assessed the outcome by telling them what a fright it was for me to discover

---

had shown up to hand them over. If the outcome proved in any instance to have been murder, then, without the shadow of a doubt, the village leaders deserve that much more blame, in that many committees conducted themselves that way [...] They were brought to Bujaraloz, into the presence of the *Jefe*, a few village residents accompanying the alleged offender. The first question put was this: —How has this man conducted himself in the village? —Very well! Was the unanimous response, without any hesitation. —And towards the workers in his charge? —Same response. The *Jefe*'s determination was swiftly made. —If he has behaved well towards the village and had behaved well towards the workers, what is there for us to do? Kill him just because he is rich? That is a nonsense. And turning to the alleged offender, he states: —I appreciate that you do not go out into the fields to toil like these people because you are not used to it, but there must be something that you can be doing in the village, such as, say, looking after the school. That way, you'll be kept busy. With which the case was closed".

that, unwittingly and unintentionally, I had made agrarian socialists of them! [...] I was eager to know why it had happened, and I could not come up with any other explanation than my pupils' social origins. Most of them were drawn from modest family backgrounds [...] So, scratch the surface of a seminarian's soul, just a little, and up pops a spokesman for the plebs, and he would look like a social revolutionary, were it not for the strong spiritual education received at the seminary.[2]

Leaving to one side the pertinence of the analysis of this Catholic theologian and sociologist for understanding the role of former priests drawn from the ranks of the populace in the French revolution and in nineteenth-century liberation movements in Latin America and, more recently, in Liberation Theology, what concerns us here is the abandonment of religion even by seminarians—those who are theoretically the future commanders of the faithful.

Here are some figures for the number of parishes without priests in each ecclesiastical province in 1934[3] (the italics show the areas that were republican after 18 July 1936):

Aragon: *Zaragoza* 206.

Andalusia: *Granada* 103; Seville 8.

Castile: Burgos 583; *Ciudad Real* 12; *Toledo* 323; Valladolid 221.

Galicia: Santiago 372.

Levante: Tarragona 156; Valencia 32.

Only Catalonia and Cantabria were fully 'staffed'.

---

2 Severino Aznar, *La revolución y las vocaciones eclesiásticas* (Madrid 1949), pp. 41, 24–25.
3 All data taken from Severino Aznar's study.

The numbers of seminarians who quit their studies in 1934:

Province	Number of seminarians	1930	1934	Percent of drop-outs
Aragon Zaragoza	1597	972	625	39.1
Andalusia Granada Seville	830 898	534 572	296 326	35.3 36.3
Castile Burgos Ciudad Real Toledo	116 1,295 401	60 760 689	56 535 712	33.3 48.2 41.3
Galicia Santiago	1,916	926	990	51.6
Levante Tarragona Valencia	1,720 1,052	993 557	727 495	42.2 47

As well, "The seminarians' desertion cannot be ascribed entirely to the effects of the revolution. Albeit more slowly, vocations were already being lost, and during the five-year period prior to the revolution these had shrunk by upwards of 20 percent".

The reasons for this, in Aznar's opinion, were 1. clerical poverty (sic!), 2. openings in business and 3. weakening faith.

In 1935, Cardinal Gomá declared, "We think we are living in the midst of a profoundly religious people preoccupied, so they say, with doing their duty by God and the Church, and yet there has been such a proliferation of cases of phobia towards godly things. There has been an undoing of the sense of religion in the country, which is powerless to react against the grossest acts of non-observance, so that our revised opinion is that, first, history and then convention had framed as a proper expression of the spiritual worth of our people".

During the civil war, Gomá himself drafted a *Collective Letter* to the Spanish clergy that was utterly supportive of Franco, and he exclaimed: "Why should we not believe that the God of our fore-fathers lives on, albeit hidden, in the depths of the people's souls?"[4]

Plainly, any faith, from apartheid in South Africa to Leninism, can be described as 'popular' as long as repression and re-education by means of schooling and policing actually work!

---

4   Op. cit., p. 61.

Appendix II
Revolutionary Uprisings in Spain, 1932–1934

We have already seen the expectations raised by the advent of the republic in Spain in April 1931. As well, we have seen the deep differences of opinion as to how this should be construed and how these differences split the leadership of the CNT into two camps. What we need now is some grasp of the social backdrop against which all of this was happening.

The figures are revealing: emerging from its underground existence, the CNT had a union membership of some 800,000 by 1931 (Pestaña's figures), the UGT had 277,011 in December 1930, increasing to 1,041,539 by June 1932. One factor to bear in mind is the founding, in April 1932, of the FNTT (*Federación Nacional de Trabajadores de la Tierra*/ National Land Workers' Federation) with 27,340 members, growing to 392,953 by June 1932—which is to say, accounting for almost 40 percent of the entire membership of the UGT.[1]

In order to tear down the centuries-old bulwark of hatred and poverty, the most class-conscious workers came up with the idea of organising with an eye to changing society in their favor. The British historian Paul Preston made this observation regarding Castile during the early years of the Republic, and I would apply it to the entire country: "There was little separating the anarchists and the FNTT's membership. In many villages, the local farm-workers' organisation would naively

---

1 *Memoria y orden del día del XVII congreso ordinario que se celebrara en Madrid los días 14 y siguientes de octubre de 1932* (Madrid 1932), p. 61. Also Edward Malefakis *Reforma Agraria y revolución campesina en la Espana del siglo XX* (Barcelona 1971), p. 338.

affiliate to the UGT, CNT and Communist Party alike.[2] On every side the fact that illiterate farm laborers joined the FNTT did not turn them overnight into degree-carrying Marxists and there was small difference between them and the members of the CNT in terms of political maturity or aspiration".[3]

Of course the "naivety" is inside Preston's head, and plainly these farm-workers were fed up with being exploited and craved a definitive change in society. So they joined the three organisations that, at that precise point, seemed to be standard-bearers of the revolution, thereby having some guarantee that at least one of them was about to embark on the struggle.

Preston himself shows how the workers' demands spurred on the UGT and PSOE, prompting Prime Minister Azaña to note angrily in his diary (late 1931): "If having three socialist ministers in the cabinet cannot stop a strike, what's the point?"[4]

There was a long rash of spontaneous social protests and trespasses against *latifundios* (landed estates) in the

---

[2] One temporary PCE slogan went: "Our watchword is 'all power to the workers, peasants, toilers'". And it also asserted: "That the masses are ready to fight and struggle with peerless heroism and immeasurable spirit of sacrifice, that much is plain and beyond question. What do we propose, what is our advice as revolutionaries to the struggling masses?" "Honest revolutionary anarchist personnel call upon the masses to implement 'the libertarian revolution' so as to achieve 'libertarian communism'. We should instruct the people in the real path to victory and what they ought to do". "Ours is a different watchword. The masses should seize political power. Our watchword is 'all power to the workers, peasants, toilers'. Unless power is taken there is no salvation from wretchedness, hunger and suffering, oppression and repression". (p. 31) in *Problema inspanskoy revoliutsiii* [Problems of the Spanish Revolution (paths of development and conditions for victory)], an anthology of collective texts compiled under the supervision of the central committee of the C.P. of Spain (Moscow, Partinnoye Izdaltelstvo, 1933, 259 pages).

[3] Paul Preston, *The Coming of the Spanish Civil War: Reform, Reaction and Revolution in the Second Republic* (London 1978), p. 61.

[4] Op. cit., p. 66.

countryside. The typical examples were Castilblanco (Badajoz) on 31 December 1931 (great New Year's gift) and Arnedo (La Rioja) on 5 January 1932—places where levels of social friction were low and where the UGT held demonstrations. In both cases the Civil Guard opened fire on demonstrators who posed no threat to them, and a single death provoked exaggerated retaliation resulting in the deaths of four Guards at the hands of peasants in Castilblanco, and eleven killed and thirty wounded in Arnedo. And over those few days there were gunshots traded and further deaths (eight) in Zalamea de la Serena, Épila (Zaragoza) and Safor (Valencia).[5] My own conclusion is that the banal demands of wage-earners for some change did not go down well with the rigid mentality of the bosses and their forces of repression.

Another point: twenty days after the shooting in Castilblanco, between 18 and 25 January 1932, there was an outbreak of very telling incidents in Figols (Barcelona).

The textile plants in the Llobregat district were on strike and in Figols the *Somatén* (the Catalan bosses' armed goons) threatened the peaceful strikers (including many women). A delegation from the textile union asked the (lignite) miners of the town to intervene, and the latter disarmed the *Somatén* goons, took over the town hall and launched a strike to press for improvements in the mines. The following day (19 January) the general strike spread, and libertarian communism was declared without any violence. Money was abolished, and barter on the basis of vouchers was introduced. At a general meeting in Figols at which "men, women and children over sixteen years of age" were able to vote, nine delegates were appointed to oversee the organisation of the commune. In stepped the army and, seeing that they were isolated, the rebels laid down their arms without a fight.[6]

---

5 All of these figures can be found in Julián Casanova, *De la calle al frente (el anarcosindicalismo en España)* (Barcelona 1977).

6 Eduardo de Guzmán (a CNT journalist in the 1930s), writing in the review *Tiempos de Historia* (Madrid) No. 14, 1976.

But the example they set spread to Berga, Sallent, Cardona, Balsareny, Navarcles and Suria. The army had restored order completely by 25 January. A few villages in Aragon (four) and Valencia (one) did mount a general strike.[7]

Casanova's treatment of the uprising in the Figols mining district in January 1932 is outstanding because, whilst the author is not concerned to highlight the fact, he captures all of the belief in revolution that was to come flooding back in 1936. "There were no preparations made [...] unsuspected strength [...] In Berga, Sallent, Cardona, Balsareny, Navarcles and Suria the mines ground to a halt and businesses shut down. In Manresa, picketing workers barred access to the factories and workshops [...] the revolutionary committee [...] spread the news throughout the area that 'libertarian communism is upon us'. And these were not inconsequential villages: Berga had a population of 7,000; Cardona of 6,000; Figols had 900 workers; Sallent a population of 4,653 and Suria 3,194 (according to the *Espasa Calpe* encyclopedia, 1920).

And during the poorly coordinated revolts promoted by the CNT in December 1933, Arnedo, which had previously suffered at the hands of the Civil Guard, experienced a peaceful attempt by some thirty men to institute libertarian communism. Symptomatic of the desires of the populace.

In Figols in 1932 and in Asturias in 1934, as well as in July–August 1936, we find a growing number of workers who (as in the days of the free soviets in Russia) did not wait for the leadership's okay—did not even consult them—and struck in order to make changes to their workaday lives, as if they were conversant with the statutes of the IWMA of 1864 and with the writings of Bakunin. How could that be?

Quite simply, it was because of the CNT's peddling to all the workers—through its activists and their example—the spirit of direct action, initiative and independence. And *faístas*, who pop up like 'the bad guys' in this movie, whether

---

7   Julián Casanova, op. cit., 1997.

in the eyes of José Peirats or those of the majority of 'level-headed' historians, reaped the harvest—a following among the class-conscious revolutionary youth. Who would not be sparing in their criticisms of the CNT's lack of groundwork, would make no bones about immediate revolutionary changes being the goal of the exploited classes of society, as witnessed in Asturias in 1934 and as gradually built up a head of steam in republican Spain from 1936 on?

In the wake of spontaneist peasant disturbances, efforts were made by certain organisations to work the fertile soil in order to trigger revolution.

Despite the CNT's de facto division (see the following appendices) and for all its internal organisational inconsistencies, the FAI egged the CNT into launching an armed uprising. The populace proved indifferent or rather "welcomed the revolt with enormous reservations".[8] *Treintistas* played no part in this revolt, nor in the one that followed, and then offered them no solidarity of any sort. However, in Levante—in Bétera, Bugarra, Pedralba, Ribarroja, villages with populations ranging from 1,500 (Bugarra) to 4,400 (Pedralba)—there were outbreaks of libertarian communism, which Peirats[9] has broken down into five points:

1. A bloodless insurrection and seizure of the town hall.

2. Siege was laid to the barracks of the Civil Guard who then surrendered or fled.

3. Libertarian communism was instituted: "the red-and-black flag was run up. Property deeds were burnt in the public square before crowds of onlookers. A proclamation or notice was posted announcing the abolition of money, private ownership and man's exploitation of his fellow man.

---

8   Peirats, *La CNT en...*Vol. I, pp. 64–65.
9   Ibid., p. 65.

4. Reinforcements of Guards and police were drafted in. The rebels more or less resisted them, depending on how long it took them to realise that the revolt had not spread throughout Spain and that they were out on a limb with their magnificent plans.

5. Captives were tortured by the forces of repression.

To which we might even add a sixth point: that nowhere was there violence carried out by the triumphant CNT personnel against property owners or the Guards and police. Tragically, the revolt was highlighted by the repression in Casas Viejas (a village in the province Cádiz, known these days as Benalup de Sidonia). There, the Civil Guard surrounded the home of CNT member Francisco Cruz Gutiérrez, nicknamed Seisdedos. All of the family was inside, and the Civil Guard eventually torched the house, killing eight people. Furthermore, the Guards made many arrests and responded to heckling by shooting twelve people dead. The right seized on the ensuing scandal, as did the CNT, to attack the Azaña government. The latter made excuses to the effect that if the Casas Viejas revolt had held out for one more day the entire province of Cadiz might have gone up in flames.[10] Word on the grapevine was that Azaña had ordered: "No wounded and no prisoners. Shoot them in the guts". It became a millstone around the necks of the republicans.

In the wake of the attempt at libertarian communism in January 1933, a man who was a *faista* at heart, if not actually a member of the FAI, wrote:

> We have to give priority to the countryside because the peasantry is ripe for revolution: all they need is some idea that will channel their desperation. And in libertarian communism they have found one. Ours will be a

---

10 See Jerome A. Mintz, *The Anarchists of Casas Viejas* (Chicago 1982).

profoundly humane, peasant revolution [...] In our action there is no hint of Blanquism or Trotskyism, merely a clear notion that the road ahead is a long one and that we must get a move on and move on briskly.[11]

The CNT mounted an intense abstentionist campaign in the run-up to the November 1933 elections: "Not the ballot box but social revolution". If the right were to carry the election, an uprising would be triggered. But few lessons had been learned from the events of January 1933.

When it came to deciding the date of the uprising, only some of the regional federations agreed to enter the fray, the rest still with lively memories of the repression in January 1933. Consequently, the uprising in December 1933 was confined to Aragon, La Rioja, Extremadura and Andalusia.

The January model was applied again to December 1933. In Aragon, in Valderrobres (Teruel), according to one who took part,[12] things went as follows: "Comrades carried out the task of burning property deeds, church records, municipal records etc. [...] There was a public proclamation to the effect that the use of money was henceforth cancelled [...] For five days we lived under libertarian communism, enjoying the acquiescence of the people and with the enemy at sixes and sevens or in a panic. A few people who were at odds with me even went along to the union and asked at the meeting if we might explain libertarian communism, and a number of them threw in their lot with it afterwards".

This account is borne out by the newspapers of the time, which referred to the burning of archives and the abolition of money.[13] In Logroño, lots of villages instituted libertarian

---

11 Durruti, in *La Voz Confederal*, quoted in Abel Paz, *Durruti*, p. 249.
12 "8 December 1933 and the Valderrobres comarcal" by Miguel Foz, in *Le Combat syndicaliste* (Paris) 28 January 1965.
13 See the bourgeois newspaper *El Sol*, 12 December 1933, p. 3; and 16 December 1933, p. 8

communism.[14] In Fuenmayor, a proclamation was issued covering Article Four of the model: "Libertarian communism has just been introduced throughout the length and breadth of the Iberian Peninsula", but also reflected memories of the repression in January: "And any who fail to abide by the new arrangement are to be shot".[15]

The unrest was quashed by the army.

At village level, the risings had been a success. In Teruel they involved villages with populations ranging in size from about 800 (Arenys de Lledó, Fornoles, Torre del Compte) to 3,000 (Beceite, Valderrobres). In Logroño they ranged from 2,000 (all but one of them) to 8,000 (Haro). In the cities—with the exceptions of Zaragoza and Granada—the uprising never amounted to anything more than a general strike. Based on the documentary evidence available to us we can state that nowhere did the forces of the left throw their weight behind the revolts. So much so, in fact, that the minister of the Interior was able to announce that the UGT had issued an order to work as normal during the CNT's sympathy strike.[16]

The balance sheet was negative. But following the defeat of the Left in the elections, by the beginning of 1934, the Socialist Party and the UGT, egged on by Largo Caballero, were espousing a 'revolutionary' stance, in the sense that they were talking about worker alliances and seizing power.

This trend found a welcome within the CNT, although most of the membership distrusted Largo Caballero (he was then president of the Socialist Party and general secretary of the UGT). Caballero had served as councilor of State under Primo de Rivera, and the UGT had embraced the Primo de

---

14 Ibid., 12 December 1933, pp 3 and 4 for Briones, Cenicero, Fuentemayor, Haro, La Bastida, San Asensio and San Vicente de la Sonsierra.

15 Ibid., p. 4.

16 Ibid., p. 10.

Rivera dictatorship. Flying in the face of other CNT federations, with the exception of its own La Felguera local federation (extraordinary evidence of CNT federalism at work), the regional CNT federation in Asturias decided to enter into an alliance agreement with the Asturian UGT in March 1934.

The Socialist Party and UGT were making preparations for an uprising. On 4 October 1934, Gil Robles and another two deputies from the CEDA (*Confederación Española de Derechas Autónomas*/Spanish Confederation of Non-aligned Rightists) joined the Lerroux government. The uprising began on 6 October 1934, with Catalonia and Asturias as the nerve centres.

In Catalonia, the Confederation was granted two days' prior notice of the impending revolt,[17] and once in power, the Catalanists moved to outlaw the CNT-FAI.[18] Within days, the central government had restored order.

In Asturias, the uprising was not only a success in the smaller towns, but the miners and workers captured Gijón and Oviedo (and its arms plant). Elsewhere in Spain, there were strikes but utter confusion prevailed. The socialist leadership appeared to wash its hands of what it had unleashed. Chastened by its experience in Catalonia and by the socialist stance, the CNT was not whole-hearted in its support for Asturias.[19] Dithering by the UGT and the PSOE seriously hurt the revolt, which was crushed by the *Tercio* (Spanish Foreign Legion) using Moroccan colonial troops.

It seems to me that what the socialists actually had in mind was to establish a disciplined military stronghold in Asturias as a lever to be used in political log-rolling. A shabby political gambit without a thought spared for the colossal

---

17 *El Congreso confederal de Zaragoza* (published in France 1955), p. 134.

18 Ibid., p. 135.

19 Ibid., p. 125. "In Granada [...] we did all in our power to back the rising"; "In Zaragoza, October was not supported because it showed no signs of being a revolutionary movement", p. 126.

defeat inflicted on the Socialist and communist parties in what by then had become Nazi Germany. And I see the following as evidence of this:

> On 5–6 October a tiny village was captured and a socialist councilor thanked us for our work, telling us that three days earlier, anticipating what would come, they had appointed a Revolutionary Committee [...] We were at odds with one another, and the socialists who fought disowned the councilor, and the Revolutionary Committee was appointed at that point. These are telling facts, indicative that once the revolution is under way the workers can be relied upon, even should they be socialists.[20]

Actually the revolt was all-embracing and became popular under the slogan of UHP (*Unión de Hermanos Proletarios*/ Union of Proletarian Brothers), which inspired such high hopes after and during the revolution.

Another feature of the Asturias revolt was that, for the first time, communists (from the PCE and what was soon to be the POUM) and socialists, in concert with the anarchists, put their revolutionary theories to the practical test in Spain, and those theories resembled the libertarian risings of 1932 and 1933.

> Money has been abolished, and a comprehensive 'war communism' prevails. The distribution of goods is directed and controlled by workers' committees that issue paper chits 'worth one kilo of bread', etc. Sale of alcoholic beverages has been banned.[21]

> Amid the clamor of the fighting, revolutionary committees even dealt with social works. Scarcely had control

---

20 Ibid., p. 151.
21 Edward Conze (a Trotskyist), *Spain Today. 1936, Revolution and Counter-Revolution* (London 1936), p. 100.

been seized in the villages than agencies were established to help tend to children and the elderly [...] Fighting and creation went hand in glove.[22]

The revolutionary order was manifest everywhere. Money was done away with. Each family will be entitled to a given amount of foodstuffs, depending on how many it comprises.[23]

The style of those three Marxist writers' assessments and their admiration for this new 'Paris Commune' is typical and moving. *Fighting and creation went hand in glove.* Within three years they were to be at dagger drawn with one another because the leaderships gave priority to their own interests over those of the workers.

It was no accident that Asturias threw up people's courts in communist areas, whereas in anarchist areas there was tolerance and good treatment.[24]

Taken together, January 1932, January 1933 and December 1933 highlighted the need for alliance to the anarchist movement. In 1936, Federica Montseny offered this summary of the 1934 uprising:

UHP. But we cannot walk away from criticism and analysis for the sake of some myth that may well turn out to be dangerous. The first suggestion at which that attempt

---

22 Jesús Hernández (communist), *Negro y Rojo. Los anarquistas en la revolución Española* (Madrid 1946), p. 127.

23 Joaquín Maurín, op. cit., p. 156,

24 Díaz Nosty, *La comuna asturiana, revolución de octubre de 1934* (Madrid 1974), p. 283 et seq., and Solano Palacio, *La revolución de octubre. Quince días de comunismo libertario en Asturias* (Barcelona 1936), pp. 140–195. "In Mieres, as it happened, manifestoes endorsed by the Revolutionary Committee were utterly defaced after they were posted. [...] José María Martínez, the soul of the revolutionary upheaval in Gijon, was mysteriously killed in the course of the fighting".

at a popular revolution hints is the action of the statist communists, cashing in on the fighting and the absence of libertarians, who were always in the front lines, to give their own preferred shape—a statist shape—to the new society that would have emerged from the revolution's success. In its failure, Asturias has its lessons to teach us too.[25]

Fine words, but all too poorly implemented within just months of their being penned.

---

[25] From Montseny's afterword to Solano Palacio's book, op. cit., pp. 195–196.

Appendix III
One Example of Monetary Reform and Scheme for Currency Circulation in a Social Economy[1]

Phase one of the current revolution will be an economic or monetary revolution, or it will be no revolution at all. Changes to the monetary system are even more important than getting the economy in order if what we are after is a biological and sustainable change to society.

The monetary system is an arrangement governing the measurement and comparative value of things, in the very same way as the metric system is an arrangement for measuring and comparing measurements.

Abolishing money in an organised society is an impossibility, since the need to compare and exchange things is an obvious human need, even for a man living alone. Like all systems for measuring and making comparisons, the monetary system is arbitrary. It is this arbitrary foundation to the monetary system that is susceptible to radical amendment or reform, just the same as the arbitrary basis of the metric system, in a number of countries, replaced the arbitrary basis underpinning the systems for measuring and comparing dimensions of objects pre-dating the French Revolution.

It needs to be understood that replacing the current monetary system by some voucher system does not amount to doing away with money: that is merely swapping that arbitrary basis for some other arbitrary basis for exchange. Can

---

1 This scheme was drawn up by CNT engineers and workers from the textile industry in Catalonia in late 1936.

anyone seriously believe that vouchers—necessarily different for each of the uses assigned to them—can successfully take the place of the present, well-nigh flawless monetary and financial arrangement regarded as the science of gauging the value of things, were it not for the continual intrusion of human emotion?

It needs to be understood that the present monetary and financial system must be reformed in such a way that all of its benefits—the outcome of the economic experience of many generations of human beings—survive, and that the shortcomings that mechanisation has frankly brought to light are banished as much as possible.

The current monetary arrangement offers no solution to the daily-increasing productivity of modern technology, in that it lacks gold reserves, and also, because of the distraint by individuals—over a long period of time, at that—no significant gold reserves and hard currency.

On the basis of the very same gold reserves currently in existence, we need to build a more flexible monetary system. The social and economic revolution thrust upon us by mechanisation is not going to be compatible with human potential until the day comes when it is understood that, for the first time in human history, productivity so exceeds the consumption permitted by our current finances that the attempt to cling to a monetary system whereby normal consumption of the accumulated wealth produced would require gold reserves or reserves of other precious metals on such a fantastic scale as to be unimaginable.

We need a monetary system whereby the quick exchange of monetary values and almost instantaneous automatic bank payments, provides the requisite minimum fiduciary guarantees with nothing more than the existing gold and precious metal reserves.

Radical monetary reform—which will make it possible to demolish the chief cause of capitalism and build up an economy with healthy, robust foundations—has to be based on a practical and actual separation of these two notions: consumer assets and production assets.

Demolition of the fetishistic power of money is not going to come about until the prevailing monetary system forces everybody to grasp this separation of ideas foisted upon us by man's basic instincts and the complexity of the modern economy. The property instinct in man is part and parcel of his nature; we need to work towards the satisfaction of that instinct in terms of the consumer assets man needs in order to fully achieve human freedom, and bolster his innate disposition to pool production assets, so as to generate a greater return.

On the basis of all of the existing gold and precious metal reserves that the contingencies of war and Revolution have left in the hands of the peoples of Iberia, we must create the following fiduciary arrangement. It is different in terms of how production assets and methodologies are handled and in terms of the purchase and usage of property and consumer assets, but only in terms of their relative exchange value.

1. Consumer currency: This will facilitate the unfettered handling, purchase, payment and usage of property and consumer resources and will serve as the instrument whereby a minimum of economic power is secured for each and every free individual, as they will be paid a family wage and whatever production bonuses may eventually be introduced in consumer currency.

Consumer currency will circulate openly as a standard currency in the form of paper currency with a value variable over time, the aim being to incentivise consumption and prevent hoarding, without utterly destroying personal or family savings. Paper consumer currency will be subject to discount by an annual or quarterly percentage yet to be determined, depending on whether the issue of bills occurs annually or at quarterly intervals.

Paper consumer currency will merely facilitate exchange of property and consumer goods and will absolutely not be applicable to the means and instruments of production.

The real value of paper consumer currency is to be set and promptly converted into production currency the moment it is returned to the production cycle: consumer industries, health and cultural agencies, personal savings funds, retail outlets, staff transport and the like. Once various bank payments have been settled in production currency, the currency will lose its entire value and be destroyed.

Annually, depending on the indexed collective wealth of the country and its potential productivity, the overall level and ceiling on personal and family consumption will be determined, and a list drawn up of consumer goods that will be normally and freely traded and accessed by means of paper consumer currency.

2. Production currency: This will represent the sum of trade in all industrial, commercial, financial and banking transactions in production assets, with absolutely no exception. There will be no visible and standardised trading in production currency-units, the value of which is to be constant and fixed and not subject to any sort of speculation.

The use of production currency will be mandatory in all dealings with production assets on the basis of written reckonings (cheques, letters, etc.), endorsed by seller and producer trade unions and overseen by their banking departments in accordance with the overall banking regulations.

All bank payments are to be carried out as normal by the speediest methods, in accordance with the New Social Economy's legislation governing banking accountancy.

Trade in production capital will be required, and will be vested entirely in the trade unions. Access, any more than the economic services of the political, social and judicial agencies strictly necessary to the new society, will be denied to any other natural or legal agent.

3. In the world market: Foreign Trade is to be based upon exchange, gold and other precious metals, which will in every instance be regarded as exchange assets until such time as an international currency is devised.

Appendix IV
The CNT and the FAI: Pressure Groups (1998 [revised 2005])

Since there is a lot of fuzziness surrounding this subject, both among professional historians (most of whom are in favor of a capitalist or Marxist hierarchy), as well as among a number of anarcho-syndicalist militants and certain Spanish CNT personnel (who sometimes also subscribe to the notion of hierarchy, being born politicians or having become obsessed with the notion that trade unionism is, ipso facto, reformist and having cried out for some imposed guardianship) we would need to lay down some sound guidelines.

The underlying rationale is a simple one: We have to show that, in terms of ideology, anarcho-syndicalism is just another movement like all the rest. Since the usual thinking is that the trade union ought to be an appendage of the political party, the FAI is the party and the CNT the transmission belt. The example normally invoked by all and sundry is Bakunin's Alliance within the IWMA.[1] Bakunin took the same view of the revolution and had misgivings about the centralising bent in Marx and Mazzini (who was an advocate of the nation state). In order to counter such deviations, teams of hand-picked militants had to keep a weather eye out, albeit operating as advisors and using persuasion rather than operating as some sort of a Cheka or adopting jesuitical means.

The line that depicts the CNT and FAI as mutually complementary is historically wrong, yet it is championed by lots

---

1   See Chapter One.

of Spanish CNT personnel who would like to offer us a triumphalist picture of their movement linking the two.

It would appear that the FAI was set up in March 1927 in Valencia in a period of dictatorship, with the ambition of including Portugal as well (hence the name Iberian Anarchist Federation). From the outset there was some ambiguity, the idea having been proposed by émigré anarcho-syndicalist groups in France and by an item on the agenda regarding the Arshinov Platform (whereby a minority would act as trade unionism's steadying hand).[2]

The groups represented in Valencia had no such outlook. They were unfamiliar with the Platform (and did not even get time to discuss that item on the agenda)[3] and confined themselves to coordinating the anarchist activities of the groups, without even bothering about the CNT. Actually, as a force inside the CNT the FAI only surfaced in 1929—that being its real birth date.

It's interesting to note how the Platform affected Horacio Prieto's conclusions in his 1932 pamphlet

---

2 Item 8 of the Arshinov Platform (the name by which the 1926 *(Draft) Organisational Platform of the General Union of Anarchists* is better known), concerning "Anarchism and Trade Unionism" proposed: "anarchists' task in the ranks of the revolutionary labor movement can only be performed if their efforts there are closely bound up with and compatible with the activity of anarchist organisation outside of the trade union. To put that another way, we have to enter the revolutionary trade union movement as an organized force, answerable before the anarchist umbrella organization for our work inside the trade unions and receiving guidance from that organisation. [...] Without burdening ourselves with the establishment of anarchist trade unions, we should seek to exercise our theoretical influence over revolutionary syndicalism as a whole and in all its forms (the IWW, the Russian trade unions, etc.). We can only accomplish this by setting to work as a rigorously organised anarchist collective and certainly not as little empirical groups bereft of organisational inter-connection or theoretical common ground".

3 Evidence of José Llop, interviewed by F. Mintz in *Movimiento Libertario Español*, Paris, 1974.

"*Anarco-Sindicalismo. Cómo afianzaremos la revolución*" ("Anarcho-Syndicalism: How We Shall Secure the Revolution") with its insistence on a disciplined revolutionary army, which would then "automatically disband itself", and with his opposition to anarcho-individualists and to "hermetic anarchism and anarcho-metaphysical orthodoxies".[4] Prieto's contention presupposed the leadership role of the platformist anarchist faction within the trade union being handed over to the CNT national committee, which would lead the workers in the direction dictated by the workers' interests.

It is my belief that this idea was the driver behind the performance of the two factions that surfaced within the Confederation and the manipulation designed to thwart the opposing faction without any explanation offered of the motives and guidelines at work.

When the political climate in Spain abruptly changed in 1929–1930, the FAI took on quite new dimensions. It was dominated by a school of thought that staked everything on an all-out-struggle approach, the idea being to winkle out of key posts within the CNT militants preoccupied merely with the pursuit of improvements.

The 1931 CNT congress allows us to gauge the repudiation of leftist politicians and the considerable inroads made by the FAI:

> [Arín, from the National Committee] We were invited, prior to the December [1930] revolt, to serve in the potential provisional government of the Second Republic [...] in some sort of fashion but along forcefully popular and direct action lines.
>
> [Peiró] I am intervening in this debate since I can hear voices being raised clamoring for little short of the heads of the National Committee. This is unfair. And cannot be asked for. I have asked for the opportunity

---

4   Op. cit., pp. 39 n.6, 37–38.

to speak, to state and affirm that not a single National Committee since 1923 and not one Regional Committee has failed to sustain contacts with political personnel, not with an eye to establishing the Republic but in order to put paid to a system of ignominy by which we were all swamped [...] Come the coup in January [1931] of which the Confederation had received no prior notice, we found ourselves in Barcelona with just eight hours' notification of the crisis. On the Sunday we were told: "The revolt kicks off tomorrow"; whereupon the National Committee summoned the comrades and made the requisite preparations. And since it had been agreed that the CNT would not make a move until it had seen the military on the streets and the artillery in position, once they came to us to tell us to take to the streets with our forces, we said no, since what we had insisted upon had not been complied with [...] The politicians didn't want to give any commitment to the CNT because they knew that the CNT required certain conditions to be met, one of these being, inevitably, the distribution of arms to the people.[5]

As stated by Arín, the National Committee of the time was obliged to make contact with political personnel, such contacts being handled by those individuals who purported to be representing the FAI.

[Arín in 1929–1930] Despite the resolution passed, the comrades from the Catalan regional, without prior consultation with the National Committee and representing the FAI and that regional again staked a claim to a representation that the National Committee had not empowered them with.[6]

---

5 *Memoria el Congreso Extraordinario celebrado en Madrid los dias 11 al 16 de junio de 1931*, Barcelona 1932, pp. 50, 66, 68–69.
6 Ibid., pp. 69, 58.

It seems to me there were two healthy attitudes: a grassroots approach determined not to let themselves be manipulated by politicians, and a rejection of *faísta* pressures. The Congress did not resolve matters. Worse still, from outside the Confederation up popped the *Manifesto of the Thirty* (the thirty signatories including Pestaña, Peiró, Juan López and other prominent militants)[7] in August 1931, which belittled the *faístas*.

> The situation being one of far-reaching collective tragedy; the people being eager to break free of the pain by which it is tormented and there being but a single option, revolution, how is this to be gone about? [Some minority groups] trust entirely to chance, with high expectations of the unforeseen, and there is a belief in the miracle-working powers of the blessed revolution, as if the revolution were some sort of a cure-all rather than a painful, heartless act that has to mold man through physical suffering and mental pain. [...] Contrary to this simplistic, classical and somewhat movie-ish notion of the revolution—which at the present time would land us with a republican fascism wearing the disguise of a Phrygian cap, but fascism for all that—there is another notion, the real one, the only one with any sense of practicality and understanding that might bring us—that will inevitably bring us to accomplishment of our ultimate aim [...]: An overwhelming revolt by the people en masse, by the working class on the march towards its final liberation, of its trade unions and of the

---

[7] The group was actually a very motley crew. Many of them went on to take part in the revolution; Cortada switched loyalty to the PSUC and was murdered in April 1937. After the war, in 1940–1941, Fornells and Clará defected to the Falange; in 1965, Alfarache, Cortés and López, purporting to be the CNT, had contacts with the CNS, the top-down single Francoist syndicates. See *Movimiento Libertario Español*, 1974, p. 302.

Confederation, determining the fact, mode and precise timing of the revolution.

Within weeks, an answer came from Durruti's pen:

We of the FAI are not what many people believe. Far from it. A sort of undeserved aura has grown up around us that we must banish, and the sooner the better. [...] Of course, the manifesto published recently by Pestaña, Peiró, Arín, Clará, Alfarache and others has greatly pleased the ruling bourgeois and the syndicalists of Catalonia. [...] We should have gone a lot further than we did [in April 1931] and now we workers are paying the price. We anarchists are alone in defending the principles of the Confederation, libertarian principles that others appear to have forgotten. Proof of this is [the fact that] the struggle was given up just when it should have been redoubled. It is plain to see that Pestaña and Peiró have been given moral undertakings that hobble their performance as libertarians. [...] The revolution needs made and must be made as soon as possible, since the Republic has not offered the people any assurances, economic or political. [...] If, instead of lining up as [one Catalan leader] has done between capital and labor, it had inclined once and for all towards the worker side, Catalonia's libertarian movement would have spread to the whole of Spain and throughout Europe and indeed, might even have made recruits even in Latin America.[8]

And García Oliver also had his say:

Whilst not specifying a date, we are all for the act of revolution, careless of whether we were or were not prepared to make the revolution and establish libertarian

---

8 Op. cit. pp. 304–306, 2 September 1931, in *La Tierra*.

communism, in that our understanding is that the revolutionary question is not a question of preparation but of determination, of craving it, when the circumstances of social break-up, such as Spain is experiencing, abet every attempt at revolution [...]

In ideological terms, the FAI, which is the promoter of anarchism, aspires to the achievement of libertarian communism. So much so that if, once the revolution has been made in Spain and a regime similar to the one in Russia put in place or the sort of dictatorial syndicalism advocated by Peiró, Arín and Piñón, the FAI would immediately lock horns with any such sort of society, not in order to sink them for the benefit of the reaction but rather to give them the additional shove they need in the direction of the establishment of libertarian communism.[9]

Paradoxically, those militants regarded as FAI representatives were not even members of it.[10] But this never stopped Durruti, Ascaso and García Oliver continuing to lobby in its name for immediate revolution. Plainly the 'Los Solidarios' group made up of Ascaso, Durruti, etc., brought pressure to bear to ensure that the CNT and FAI stood up to capitalism. This was out and out implementation of a platformist approach whereby the FAI sat at the heart of the CNT and was itself under the guiding hand of a select group.

---

9 Ibidem, pp. 312–313, 2 October 1931, *La Tierra*.
10 Writing in *Presencia* (Paris), No 7, p. 45 (1967), José Peirats recalled: "Somebody at the Barcelona Local Federation of Anarchist Groups called for an explanation (of the January 1933 attempted uprising). The answer came that Ascaso, Durruti and García Oliver were not under FAI discipline. I myself had confirmation of this bewildering response when in 1934, which is to say, a year later, I served as general secretary of said Federation. In actual fact, the comrades in question were not members of any of the FAI-controlled groups in Catalonia. Yet it was they who did most of the speaking from public platforms on behalf of the FAI".

It is evident that Makhno (whom a number of CNT members in exile had met) and Malatesta, locked up in fascist Italy but well versed in matters concerning Spain and the CNT before of this controversy, espoused a similar line to the FAI's:

> There must be no slowing down of the revolutionary action of the masses. Help must be funnelled more quickly to the popular masses so as to compel the republican Government by force (if no other ways or means are available) to desist in its role of taming the revolution with nonsensical decrees [...] The workers have to be helped so that they can then, in their places of work, set about building their local, self-managing social economy or free soviets, as well as regiments armed to defend such revolutionary social measures, which the workers, their eyes opened and having cast aside their slavish chains, will, when the moment comes, make a reality [...] They should have no fears about taking the organisational and strategic revolutionary direction of the popular movement into their own hands. Naturally, they should sidestep any alliance with political parties generally and with the Bolshevik communists in particular, because, by my reckoning, the Spanish bolshevik communists are the same as or similar to their Russian comrades.[11]

As I see it, the very first moment the government is weak and in disarray should be seized upon so as to wrestle away as much as possible from the State and Capital. Later, the constituent assembly and executive authority will

---

11 See "Letter to the Spanish Anarchists" (addressed to Carbó and Pestaña), 29 April 1931, first published by Nestor Ivanovitch Makhno in the review *Probuzdeniye*, No. 23–27, June–October 1932. See Makhno, *The Struggle Against the State and Other Writings* (AK Press, 1996, pp. 88–90).

try to wrest the advantages gained back from the people and will only respect those gains of the people that they may find it too dangerous to counteract.[12]

Impartial eye-witness, Russian anarchist Alexander Schapiro, passed judgment on the overall position of the CNT in 1933, in the immediate aftermath of the attempted revolution of January 1933. But first he noted this same organisational confusion between CNT members and *faístas*, as in 1929–1930:

> The secretary of its CNT N[ational] C[ommittee], who also served as the secretary of the N[ational] Defense C[ommittee], told him that, as a representative of the CNT, he was against such a precipitate revolt but that, as a militant and an anarchist, he was entirely in agreement with them [...] Believing that the Regional Defense Committee's decision had been taken with the full agreement of the CNT regional committee—which was not the case—the secretary of the CNT N[ational] C[ommittee], acting in his capacity as secretary of the N[ational]

---

[12] Errico Malatesta, letter of 9 June 1931, reprinted in *Articles Politiques* (Paris, 1975, p. 418). Malatesta was also scathing about the anarchist historian Max Nettlau's endorsement of "collaboration between the [Spanish] anarchists and any government, for the purpose of preserving a relatively free State allowing revolutionary forces freedom of propaganda and organisation. He has forgotten the fact that, being an historian, he should know better than anybody else that others, meaning the lordlings in power—even our revisionists—do their damnedest to minimise and constrain all freedoms and that the only brake upon this, the only thing that can stop it in its freedom-killing endeavours is the fear or the fact of a popular uprising". Malatesta, op. cit., 7 March 1932. Nettlau's document stated "Not least for the sake of the general human interest, neither complete national successes nor syndicalist ones, nor indeed an overly firm seizure of the land by its cultivators, are to be wished for". Letter to Federica Montseny, 30 August 1931. See Frank Mintz, *La Autogestión...*, op. cit., pp. 256–257.

Defense C[ommittee] sent out a telegram to several regionals, notifying them that Catalonia was in revolt [...]

A number of anarchist comrades whose courage and integrity none may impugn, but who are utterly oblivious to what a revolutionary uprising signifies, let themselves get carried away by their plainly subjective impatience. They wanted a coup d'état, they wanted "to make social revolution", while paying absolutely no heed to whether the attendant conditions were or were not favorable, and, above all, without paying any heed at all to the interests of the National Confederation of Labor [CNT] [...]

Furthermore, there can be no doubt but that the spirit of rebellion is so powerful in the breasts of the proletarian masses, and especially in the peasant masses, that the enthusiasm and fervor in the broad masses of the CNT membership survive, undiminished even by a defeat such as the one suffered on 8 January. Nowhere is there the slightest sign of discouragement. Only among the militants in Barcelona was there some fleeting disorientation created by the unexpected turn of events [...]

It has to be said that there has been no serious discussion of the issues of the Revolution, not even within the Confederation. The only attempt to move in the direction of practical preparation for the post-revolutionary period was the decision taken by the national plenum back in December 1931 to compile national figures for worker organisation across the country, as well as for agricultural and industrial output [...]

Among FAI members these things have been explored even less. There is a two-pronged trend there: the FAI leads the CNT, and for the FAI to offer good leadership, the CNT needs to be wholly taken over by FAI personnel. This ideology, reminiscent of the famous quasi-bolshevik 'platformism', is in decline right now. It has been realised that it is for the CNT only to lead the rising, and the CNT that should direct it [...]

The comrades from the *'Treinta'* [Thirty] should pause for a moment and apprize themselves of the danger they are running and that they are having the CNT run. Their ranks include a number of bad shepherds whose purpose, whilst not blatantly schismatic, nevertheless has a tendency to 'funnel' the CNT along an evolutionary path [...]

It should not be forgotten that all FAI members are CNT members too. So, as I see it, it was enough for all the anarchists affiliated with the CNT to mount propaganda, as violent as they might wish it, inside their respective union, and reformist infiltration was resisted. No one could have raised the slightest objection. But our FAI comrades did not see it like that. Their view was that the FAI, being the FAI, had a right and a duty formally and organisationally to meddle in the multifarious activities of the Confederation and its national, regional and local bodies.

The entire succession of strife and all of the intestinal dissent that have racked the CNT since the extra-ordinary congress back in 1931 can be traced to this interference.

Let it be said straight way that the second mistake was made by Pestaña and his friends who, during their time as 'leaders' of the CNT, published their notorious manifesto, the so-called *Manifesto of the Thirty*, at a psychologically inappropriate point, with only one possible outcome: merely adding to the bitterness between the factions, forcing the FAI to speak out more than ever to rail against the reformist danger [...]

The FAI sought to impose its ideal. It failed to appreciate that, no matter how fine a day it may be, this anarchy of theirs would lose any value if they set about shoving it down people's throats. The FAI thought that all it had to do was to proclaim the social revolution for it actually to come about.

This bullying mentality has done awful damage. The Confederation had thrust upon it mixed bodies made up of CNT members and FAI members and since, in virtually a majority of instances, the CNT members were themselves FAI members or fans of the FAI but not actual members of it, the CNT wound up having mixed bodies that were nothing more and nothing less than FAI committees.[13]

Since the Schapiro Report was kept confidential and was not translated into Spanish, it made no impact in Spain.

The group made up of García Oliver, Durruti, etc., had turned into a pressure group. If it got no further than it did, it was because the FAI was dominated by a group (Abad de Santillán et al.) that was a lot closer to political contacts, as were the *treintistas*, and because, on the other hand, there were differences of opinion between Durruti and García Oliver. The period from July 1936 to November 1936 perfectly illustrated this situation. Not once did Durruti ever speak in support of a government containing CNT ministers.

Objectively speaking, most young CNT militants and of course the CNT itself subscribed whole-heartedly to the case for immediate social revolution.

It took a number of set-backs (1932, January and December 1933 and 1934) and the new context created in the wake of the February 1936 elections to bring about a rapprochement between *treintistas, faístas* and Durruti's group! But the poison had run deep: they had all looked for support to the upper echelons of the unions. Manipulation had become second nature.

The violent crises that led up to and away from May 1937 could be traced back to those very same practices.

---

13 Alexander Schapiro, author of *AIT. Rapport sur l'activité de la Confédération Nationale du Travail d'Espagne 16 décembre 1932— 26 février 1933. Strictement Confidentiel. Aucune partie de ce rapport ne doit être rendue publique. Exemplaire num. 24.* [*IWA. Report on the activity of Spain's National Confederation of Labour, 16 December 1932–26 February 1933. Strictly confidentiel. No part of this report is intended for public disclosure. Copy No. 24*].

Appendix V
The Two Libertarian Communisms, or, the Libertarian Party versus Anarcho-Syndicalism (revised 2005)

The approach to the destruction of capitalist rule and the immediate introduction of a different society by and on behalf of the workers themselves can be traced to Bakunin, and was first outlined in Bakuninist James Guillaume's pamphlet, "Ideas on Social Organisation" (1876) (worldwide revolution, references to collectives freely federated at county, regional, provincial, national and international levels, statistics, the example of anarchist farming collectives increasingly and gradually winning over the peasants, etc.). Kropotkin's *The Conquest of Bread* (cf. the quotations from that text contained in the Introduction above) was one glittering exposition of this.

In Spain, by as early as 1872, in a resolution carried by the Zaragoza congress that same year, as quoted by Anselmo Lorenzo in his *El proletariado* militante,[1] we can read a foretaste of this:

> All of the major instruments of labor currently in a few idle hands might, overnight, be transformed by a revolutionary force and the usufruct of them immediately handed

---

1 Anselmo Lorenzo, *El proletariado miltante* (Madrid 2005), pp. 295–296. This link between Lorenzo and more recent times is something spotted by the Bulgarian anarchist Pano Vasílev in his *Ideiata na savetite* [The Soviet Idea] (Sofia, 1933), pp. 33 et seq. Vasílev who had been active for a number of years in Argentina, was gunned down in 1933 by the bosses' gunmen as he was leaving a printshop with May Day leaflets.

to the workers who presently operate them. Merely by organising themselves into an Association, if they were not before, and by offering the requisite assurances to local Councils, those workers would then have access to the unfettered enjoyment of the instruments of labor. [...] Our local Councils, which would then be legitimate representatives of all producers, becoming administrative Councils, would be answerable to comarcal Councils for everything relating to the collective; and these to the regional ones and the regional ones to the International [...]

There are tiny garment-making and shoe-making workshops [...] where the work is scattered and where workers are obliged to spend most of their time without light or ventilation and in the most unhygienic conditions and which could be properly inventoried and temporarily relocated to the churches and princely mansions.[2]

Ever since Anselmo Lorenzo's day, the Spanish militant has striven to anticipate what the anarchist society would look like. In the bibliography compiled by the historian and anarchist militant Renée Lamberet,[3] leafing through the books dealing with this topic, I found nine books written between 1882 and 1900; one between 1901 and 1910; two between 1911 and 1920; three for the 1921 to 1930 period; twenty-seven between 1931 and 1936. The upsurge between 1933 and 1936, after the stagnation of 1911 to 1930, is telling. These books are translations dealing with the Russian revolution or, broadly speaking, popularisations or adaptations of Guillaume and, after him, Pierre Besnard.

In 1930, Pierre Besnard published *Les syndicats ouvriers et la révolution sociale* [The Labor Unions and Social Revolution], a book that came to be the ideological handbook of Spanish anarcho-syndicalism and of which the

---

2 For what was achieved in Aragon, see Chapter Three, note 17 above.
3 Lamberet, op. cit. (Paris 1953).

CNT's National Committee commissioned a translation.[4] Besnard's vision was as follows:

> In regards to industry: "Workshop committees, factory councils, industrial labor unions, local and regional unions; national and international industrial federations; a labor economic council with each body liable to recall at any time by such assemblies or congresses".
>
> Agriculture (farmers and share-croppers): "Efforts will have to be made to get them to understand the need for common and collective endeavor. [...] Thus there will be only two forms of farming activities left: collective ventures and artisan ventures.[...] The abolition of inheritance rights will entirely eradicate the latter category after a generation".
>
> International trade: "Barter and cash payments.[...] Gold will be nothing more than a measure, an instrument of evaluation and just that. [Distribution will be carried out] through the presentation of the work booklet or on a per capita basis. [Prices will be standardised and assessed in old money and there will be no actual payment] swapping bills of exchange".
>
> Conclusion: "Above all, let no one ever again argue, due to ineptitude or expertise, the way it has been done to date, that improvisation will sort everything out and that forward planning is pointless".

Besnard's book sparked great interest, as did anything published on the topic, but his book never reached most of the membership. The role of the pamphlet was crucial, which is why, in two essential texts, Isaac Puente ("El comunismo libertario" ["Libertarian Communism"] (1933) and Horacio M. Prieto ("Anarco-sindicalismo—Cómo afianzaremos la

---

4 *Memoria del IV Congreso mundial de la AIT 1931*, p. 9. The translation into Spanish was by Felipe Aláiz with a foreword by Peiró and was published in 1931 as a CNT publication.

revolución" ["Anarcho-syndicalism: How We Shall Secure the Revolution"] (1932)) spelled out their viewpoint on revolutionary change in that format.

Isaac Puente's libertarian communism is defined in these terms:

> *LIBERTARIAN COMMUNISM* is the organisation of society without the State and without private ownership. There is no need to invent anything nor create any new agency in order to achieve this. The building blocks of organisation around which economic life in the future will be erected are already with us in today's society: namely, the Union and the Free Municipality[5] [...] THE FREE MUNICIPALITY, a gathering of ancient vintage [...] provides a channel for the resolution of all the problems of coexistence in the countryside.

And, dealing with the economy, he insisted: "Economic coercion is the cement of society. But it is and ought to be also the only pressure that the collective should bring to bear on the individual. All other cultural, artistic and scientific activities should be beyond the remit of the collective, and left to those groups that are enthusiasts of their pursuit and promotion".

In eight points, Puente rebutted the prejudices against libertarian communism, and it strikes me that it might be useful to summarise these.

Prejudice No. 1 [*Writing crises off as passing phenomena*]: Capital and the State are two elderly institutions beset by a worldwide, progressive and incurable crisis.

Prejudice No. 2 [*The assumption that libertarian communism is a by-product of ignorance*]: Because they see it being put forward by folk who are reputedly ignoramuses and uneducated,

---

5   Isaac Puente, *El comunismo libertario*, p. 6 (reprinted by the MLE in Toulouse in 1947).

by folk with no university qualifications, it is supposed that Libertarian Communism is a simplistic solution that is blind to the complexity of life and the inherent difficulties of change of that magnitude. Inherent in this prejudice is the one we shall spell out below.

Collectively, the proletariat has more knowledge of sociology than the intelligentsia and therefore has a broader view of solutions. For instance, it does not occur to doctors or lawyers or pharmacists that there may be other ways of resolving the glut of professionals by means other than restricting university admission figures. [...]

The workers, on the other hand dare to advance, in accordance with their dabbling in sociology, solutions that are not confined to a single class or to a generation of one class, but rather to every class in society.

Prejudice No. 3 [*The intellectual aristocracy*]: The people are deemed to be incapable of a life of freedom and they thus require tutelage. Intellectuals wish to claim aristocratic privileges over them, the sort hitherto enjoyed by the nobility. They would be the people's leaders and tutors. [...] What we term common sense, insight, intuitive ability, initiative and originality are neither bought nor sold in the universities, and are as likely a feature of intellectuals as of illiterates.

Prejudice No. 4 [*Crediting us with a contempt for art, science or culture*]: What we cannot fathom is why, in order to excel in these three activities, they have to be founded upon poverty or human slavery. In our eyes, they ought to be incompatible with such avoidable pain. If, in order to excel, they require contrast with ugliness, ignorance and uncouthness, then we can, right now, announce that we are incompatible with them, without needing to utter any heresy.

Art, science or culture cannot be bought with money nor won with power. [...] They sprout up spontaneously everywhere, and what they require is an absence of obstacles in their path. They are the fruits of what is human, and the belief that a contribution can be made to them by establishing, through the government, some inventor's bureau or some cultural award is a simplistic view. [...]

Prejudice No. 5 [*The inability to give structure to the new life*]: The new organisation of the economy requires expert collaboration just as it needs the skilled worker and the ordinary laborer. Just as today, even revolutionary forces do their bit for production, so tomorrow everyone will have to. That is, that the new life should not be judged by the abilities we revolutionaries can call upon, as if we were some redemptive political party, but rather on the basis of the abilities to be found in the entire collectivity. What impels the technician to work is economic coercion, and not any love he bears for the bourgeoisie. Tomorrow what will impel everyone to do his bit for production will also be the economic coercion brought to bear on every able-bodied citizen. We do not trust solely to those who do so out of devotion or virtue. [...]

Prejudice No. 6 [*Belief in the need for a social architect*]: This belief, that society needs some overseer authority or that the masses would kick over the traces if there were no police to stop them is a prejudice encouraged by politics. What sustains human society is not coercion nor the clever foresight of its rulers but the instinct of sociability and the need for mutual aid. [...]

Prejudice No. 7 [*Giving learning priority over experience*]: This is tantamount to wanting dexterity to come before training, expertise before practice or calluses before toil.

From the word go they ask of us a perfect arrangement and assurances that things will be done in such and such a manner rather than in some other way, with no hard knocks or trial and error. [...]

Living under libertarian communism will be like learning to live. Its shortcomings and its mistaken aspects will become plain once we institute it. Were we politicians, we would plan a paradise filled with perfection. But being men and knowing what it is to be human, we place our trust in man's learning how to shift for himself in the only way of learning that there is: one step at a time.

Prejudice No 8 [*Mediation by politicians*]: The worst prejudice of all is the belief that an ideal is attainable through the mediation of a handful of men, even though the latter might not wish to be called politicians. [...]

Rather than political action, which is distracting and deceitful, we offer direct action. Direct Action is nothing other than the immediate realisation of the ideal and its being made tangible and real, and not some written, unattainable fiction or distant promise. It is the implementation of a collective agreement by the collectivity itself, rather than its being left to some Messiah or entrusted to some intermediary.

Libertarian communism will be achievable to the extent that direct action is employed and to the extent that intermediaries keep out of it.

In addition to the above, Besnard offered an eleven-point comparative portrait of political and trade union organisation. Its clarity and rationality doubtless made a great impact on his readers, even though this was only a pamphlet.

The big advantage of this theory is that, in rationalising society as it stood and in winning others over by example, libertarian communism could be introduced without unwarranted obstacles.

Horacio Prieto's pamphlet was published in January 1932, even as CNT personnel in Figols were spontaneously proclaiming libertarian communism.

> All power to the people, we anarcho-syndicalists say. This strikes us as the fairest formula and we shall strive to enact it with the utmost loyalty of conscience, in the manner

we deem most effective for a speedy and benign introduction of libertarian communism in the near future [...]

Individualists, bourgeois and anarchist alike—the former on deviationist grounds so as to be able to preserve privilege and the latter out of a lack of belief in humanity—spare themselves effort and struggle. Both attitudes are in error, but the latter, the anarcho-individualists more so. With their Olympian scorn for the masses, they play unwittingly into the hands of the tyrants. Rather than such ideological absolutism, we enjoin revolutionaries and offer the people, crying out for new social justice, a quite logical arrangement for replacement of the bourgeoisie, one that suits the psychology of the Spanish people but that is wide open to modification [...]

Once the proletariat has achieved mastery of the situation and having eliminated the bourgeoisie and its chief supporters to the extent that it may; once the authoritarian system has been liquidated and the revolutionary strike now without purpose, all producers, across the board, must return to their posts. So restoring the situation predating the revolution until such time as statistics, a level-headed evaluation of circumstance, comes up with feasible rules for a start to be made on freeing the producers from useless goods and coercion, in order to redeploy them to meet the new demands of social labor [...]

The entire populace will be required to be worker and law-maker, producer and guardian of social order. Even revolutionary groups will have to disband themselves and direct their energies into the speedy construction of the social crucible wherein the old order will be melted down and recast by us, thoroughly imbued with a libertarian ethic [...]

It will be for the workers themselves to appoint their agents in the factories, workshops, sites and countryside, in their autonomous branches, just as we do today and they will be empowered to regulate work: set their own hours, set up their factory committees, impose disciplinary sanctions on laziness and sabotage and immoral conduct and to boost and reward diligence and study. They will sponsor propaganda, organise shock squads and activist groups and will fill the atmosphere with a wholesome morality, seeking at all times to meet the most pressing needs of production and live up to the precepts of the new revolutionary ethic.

In the countryside there will be the same underlying organisational principle in politics as well as in economic affairs; work activities will have to become specialised or be swallowed up by superior industries. At the same time, farm and livestock ventures that will be connected through the same arrangement of autonomy and federalism to the generality of workers at local, county and national levels, with their specialist production federations and statistic committees in partnership with distribution cooperatives will be set up.

Needless to say, each locality will primarily look to its own particular needs, and the revolutionary ethic will ensure that they will do so with as much commitment as they would be done by, striving insofar as it lies within their power and surplus assets to meet the needs of other communes and of the country at large.

Within this federalist arrangement, there can be no hint of authoritarianism; everything will be tailored to the common welfare, that being the ultimate authority. In accordance with the nature of our libertarian sentiments, all committees and representative bodies are liaison bodies, and symbolise the simplification of tasks and will be re-staffed as the will of the people chooses. But, since such accountable bodies are to be invested with some stature and strong moral commitment in the performance of its duties, they will be afforded the most profound respect [...]

In their sexual relations, human beings will be accorded a completely free hand; all unions are to be recognised as licit by public morals, that is, unions contracted as a result of mutual attraction of the sexes and whose origins and ends reflect the purest natural morality. Pleasures that are against nature are to be punished as degrading and will, properly, be repressed through the psychological backlash from the people [...]

At the same time [the wage-earner] will have a producer's identity booklet that will be a standard requirement across the country in acquiring anything that the producer may need to meet his personal and family needs in terms of sustenance and comfort. That booklet will record details of individuals and their respective trades, the number of family members not capable of work, etc. and there will be special inserts on which cooperatives will record the transfers made to the bearer and that will be issued to the applicant as the need arises. In one special section of the record booklet, the factory and workshop committees will note the owner's work capacity, morals, etc., so that in their assemblies and gatherings workers may practise a system of mutual reprimand and wholesome moral pressures, which may inspire the work-shy to redouble their efforts and avoid the disgrace of being labeled as saboteurs.[6]

This last quotation spells out the multi-faceted pattern imposed upon society; the economic equality, the potential sanctions, the omnipresent ethic. Very oddly, Horacio did not consider that workers might have wanted to hold on to the revolutionary strike or introduce laziness or indeed "immorality", and that they change the capitalist economy on that basis.

His conclusion leads to a top-down *dirigisme* that makes the head spin: "The important point is that we get away from the 'empirical notion of improvisation in times of revolt' and that we rid ourselves, promptly and properly, of the undue trust vested in the people's initiative, something our heads

---

6 Horacio M. Prieto, *Anarco-sindicalismo: Cómo afianzaremos la revolución* (Bilbao 1932), pp. 6, 7, 13, 19–21, 28–29 and 34–35.

have been filled with by the most prestigious propagandists of traditional anarchism".[7]

There are two striking mainstays underpinning Horacio Prieto's entire thought processes: 1. Libertarian communism is something for the future and not the short term, and on the day after the revolution it will be run from the top by the upper echelons of the CNT; and 2. Morality is essential, and majority opinion (which seems to be the same thing as the National Committee) is crucial; deviants are to be punished. This is a startling and unmistakable plea for *dirigisme*, discipline and centralisation, in contrast to "the most prestigious propagandists of traditional anarchism".

Plainly the approaches adopted by Puente and Prieto share nothing in common. By 1932–1933, the CNT was a juxtaposition of two mutually exclusive notions of popular revolution: the spontaneous and horizontal versus the rigid and vertical. One of them had to go; otherwise they were going to have to fight it out, as they did in 1936–1937.

Puente's outlook was bolstered by the collectivism found in Joaquín Costa's writings, and Costa was soon claimed as a theoretical ancestor—even though his thoughts were based on bourgeois reformist thinkers and never at any time made any reference to anarchists.[8] In Aragon, Alejandro Díez Torre has shown how the Costaists and their (Aragonese) party acted in concert with CNT personnel from 1930 onwards.

On the basis of that reassurance, a fictitious and concocted history was even devised, albeit one with a firm grasp of reality:

> Agrarian collectivism is traditional in the Iberian Peninsula and in Berber lands as it is also in Russia where the origins of the imperishable *mir* date back to distant times. Costa and [Gonzalo de] Reparaz have cited lots and lots of examples

---

7 Op. cit., p. 36.
8 He simply cites Fourier and Abreu's *Colectivismo agrario* (Madrid 1915), pp. 246–247.

of Iberian agrarian collectivism [...] History teaches us that, prior to the Roman invasion, there was a communism of the libertarian variety in the Peninsula [...] That was back in the days of the Catholic Kings when the whole of Spain began to feel the burden of State and Church power once and for all [...] But even then, even after five centuries of rule that flies in the face of nature, economics and indeed, geography, the spontaneous disposition towards the free municipality and libertarian collectivism has not been eradicated from Spain [...][9]

On the other hand, Horacio Prieto's centralistic and platformist approach was championed by many notable figures and influential thinkers.

Gaston Leval, an inspiration to many Spanish comrades, wrote:

Neither economically, nor in human terms, nor politically, nor morally can what is advanced in [Kropotkin's] *Fields, Factories and Workshops* with regard to the economy be seen as a boost to federalism; any more than what he depicts as the encouraging trends in contemporary society. [On the basis of freedom of experimentation] we would have the most multi-colored mosaic imaginable. Hence, on the basis of a demand that seems very reasonable in the realm of abstract theory we end up with utopia the moment we look at the reality of it.[10]

Plainly there was an underlying craving for centralism and a rebuttal of the entire analyses of Bakunin and Kropotkin, in the name of some phoney trade union efficiency.

---

9   *Campo libre*, p. 1, 25 January 1936. See also, in the same paper, the articles "Possibilities of Libertarian Communism in Spain" (January to July 1936).

10 Gaston Leval, *Estructura y funcionamiento de la Sociedad comunista libertaria* (Barcelona 1936, prior to July), p. 20.

In *La revolución social y el comunismo libertario* (articles written in April 1933), Joan Peiró explained that, from the outset of the revolution, the unions had to overhaul production and the defenses of the country by sealing the borders to prevent the flight of technicians, as happened in the USSR. The support of these technicians had to be gained before the revolution arrived. Peiró underlined the importance of a bottom-up discipline as far as economic productivity went. And he put his finger on an essential point, the implementation of which he himself did not call for come July 1936: "And in the carrying out of a social revolution of the libertarian variety, it is unthinkable that the people should respect the property of foreign capitalists". Other ideas of his that went to waste were the need to anticipate an armed fight-back against the onslaught of international capitalism, as well as the training of 'guerrilla bands'. Peiró reckoned that the free organisation of "local communes will not merely replace the local federations [i.e. trade unions] as we were saying before. They will also take the place of the existing municipalities, which, in a communist society, will be tied into the entire system of socialisation!" Finally, he insisted that the abolition of money from trade was simply impossible.[11]

Peiró was less emphatic than Horacio Prieto and allowed the grassroots collectives quite a bit of autonomy. But the problem, which Peiró never grappled with, was the potential for trade-union leaderships to ride roughshod over on that autonomy. Hence the two possible interpretations: real power vested in the grassroots, or the trade union leadership with over-arching power.

Pestaña dealt indirectly with libertarian communism when he quit the CNT to found his Syndicalist Party (Horacio Prieto was later to follow suit). His description of the January 1933 revolution attempt is unequivocal:

---

11 Gabriel Pere, *Joan Peiró, escrits 1917–1939* (Barcelona 1975), p. 406, 417.

These men fell in action and, had they done so in a different realm, public opinion might well have dubbed them heroes, but they made a tremendous mistake, a mistake that, no matter how one may look at it, makes them deserving of commiseration [...] men driven to these extremes by the burning flame of fanatical commitment to an ideal. Proof of this is their simplistic vision of revolution, it being, at bottom, the same vision the early Christians had of the triumph of their beliefs [...] revolutions are not made like that. Those who think along such lines are sick. Sick in the head or in the heart. Minds mesmerised by simplistic notions. Deep down Christians, fervent believers in the sacrificial model. Let me sacrifice myself, they say, and others will follow suit.[12]

We find the same authoritarian tendency in a writer who is over-estimated by Daniel Guérin[13] and Noam Chomsky—Diego Abad de Santillán (real name, Baudilio Sinesio García Fernández). In *El organismo económico de la revolución*[14] (published in April 1936, but partly familiar due to extracts published in *Tiempos Nuevos*) Santillán rejects

---

12 Ángel Pestaña, *Trayectoria sindicalista* [24 January 1933] (Madrid 1974), pp. 678–679. The reductionism to simplicity and primitivism—prejudice No 2 as set out by Puente—is entirely polemical and speaks of the man, a would-be politician. There was no social analysis, no denunciation of poverty, no linkage with the many social disturbances [See Appendix II].

13 See our discussion in the review *Autogestion* (Paris) in 1971.

14 "Since this book first saw the light back in April 1936, was account taken of its instructions come the Revolution? By my reckoning the Unions did not pay them much heed when the longed for moment came to make a practical reality of the author's various suggestions. The Revolution went ahead without an economic plan—or a political one—with everyone dancing to whatever flamenco tune took his fancy, some dancing a seguidilla, others soleares". Jacinto Toryho, reviewing the book in *Timón*, No. 311 (1 July 1938), p. 204. *Timón's* director was none other than Santillán himself.

"Economic parochialism [...] whimsical production [...] 'happy Arcadias'".[15]

> Modern industry is a mechanism with a rhythm all its own. The human rhythm is not the one by which the machine abides; rather, it is the machine that sets the human one. Through revolution, private ownership of factories is abolished: but since the factory has to exist and, as we see it, undergo improvements, we must acknowledge the conditions under which it operates [...] But the factory carries on with its work at its own pace [...] The characteristic of modern economic life is cohesion regardless of borders [...] We do not look to the factory for affinity like we do to marriage or friendship and to social interaction; our primary interest in the factory is the workmate who knows his job and performs it without complicating matters with inexperience or lack of expertise.[16]

This is the language and distance of the entrepreneur addressing his operatives, and hints, bluntly, at management— trade union management!—from above.

> And those familiar with union life and workers' bodies know the range of means of coercion available to a union, without its needing to resort to police, court of military mechanisms. We do not mean to say that under the new economic organism we advocate coercion, and authoritarianism will be precluded: such a deviation is an option, *should the need arise.*[17]

Santillán identified important problems such as Spain's coming under a blockade from the capitalist nations in the

---

15 Abad de Santillán, *El organismo económico de la revolución* (Madrid 1978), pp. 92, 95, 210, 212.
16 Op. cit., pp. 210, 212.
17 Ibid., p. 191.

event of revolution. But he displayed a scientific optimism that implied a level of education that was definitely not to be found in the Spain then.

> There is no technical difficulty that cannot be overcome. All of these contingencies have been overcome by modern science [...] with five years' hard work [in agriculture] Spain would turn into an orchard.[18]

In May 1936, the Zaragoza Congress passed a resolution on "The Confederation's Conception of Libertarian Communism", which was a far cry from being a summary or synthesis of earlier publications. It said that money—the root of capital accumulation—would be replaced by the producer's record book. But this supposed, at international level (assuming that other schools of thought would play ball), a plentiful stock of gold or a chance to amass one, plus marketable goods (that is, the technical possibility of continuing to exploit mineral deposits without capitalist or foreign help).[19]

The Zaragoza Congress (May 1936) is hard to untangle from the FAI's peninsular plenum held on 30 January and 1 February 1936, at which it not only re-organised its resources but reaffirmed its understanding of social re-organisation

---

18 Ibid., pp. 75, 69.
19 Antonio Elorza, *Diego Abad de Santillán. El anarquismo y la revolución en España (Escritos 1930–1938)* (Madrid 1976), p. 291. See also *Tiempos Nuevos*, 1 June 1936. Santillán was critical of this sort of resolution on libertarian communism. "Where does that leave us? Is it to be the producers' organisations or is to be the communes that administer society's wealth? Both are feasible, but the resolution tells us nothing concrete [...] This thesis that the communes can enjoy economic autarchy is indicative of a pitiful ignorance of the demands made by the levels of culture and civilisation that we have achieved". As we can see this was an outlook contemptuous of initiatives emanating from the rank and file.

and forecast "an inevitable civil war of a duration that cannot possibly be predicted". Given that, and given the absence of an arsenal of weapons, it set itself the task of looking into "ways of converting certain strategic sectors into peace industries and chemical plants, metalworking establishments, etc., or into industries supplying war materials for the revolution". Propaganda material was also being drafted in Arabic;[20] plainly this did not come to pass.

Such claims are very significant in the sense that they account for the Barcelona proletariat's emphatic response and, as well, they point to the dithering by the CNT leaders who allowed propaganda to be spread about a swift victory rather than confronting people with their responsibilities, that is, rejecting economic contradictions (the absence of banking controls, a degree of squandering of raw materials, etc.), the better to grapple with the possibility of a prolonged war.

The revolution was meant for everyone, including former supporters of exploitation, as Kropotkin spelled it out in *The Conquest of Bread*: "It seems to us that the people, which have always been magnanimous and have nothing of vindictiveness in their disposition, will be ready to share their bread with all who remain with them, conquered and conquerors alike. It will be no loss to the Revolution to be inspired by such an idea and, when work is set going again, the antagonists of yesterday will stand side by side in the same workshops".[21]

Thus, harking back to the attempt made over some hours in one Aragonese village to establish libertarian communism in December 1933, Macario Royo described how revolutionaries had served coffee to Civil Guard detainees: "The Guards went to pay and were told that money had been done away with, so there was no charge to them nor to anybody else.

---

20 *Memoria*, published in February 1936, pp, 20–21, 29.
21 Kropotkin, *The Conquest of Bread* (Elephant Editions, 1985), p. 79.

Then—the corporal exclaimed—let's hope that the regime you have introduced here today succeeds right across Spain! [...] A lot has been written about the feasibility or otherwise of introducing libertarian communism. It is nonsense to deny the possibility of that arrangement's being put in place. In every one of the revolts since the installation of the petite bourgeoisie's republic, the villages involved have introduced libertarian communism. So all that is needed is determination and coordination in the revolts".[22]

---

22 Macario Royo, *Cómo implantamos el comunismo libertario en Mas de las Matas (Bajo Aragón)* (Barcelona 1934), pp. 17, 28.

Appendix VI
Notes on Governmental Collaboration

The influence of the Arshinov Platform, the mirage of hobnobbing with politicians,[1] anarchists' blindspot in detecting authority in everything,[2] the syndicalism of libertarian

---

1   "Thus, especially after the events of 8 January [1933] and the injuries inflicted on García Oliver, I noted an appeal issuing once again from the same comrade [Federica Montseny] and carried in *La Tierra* in Madrid; its hysterical character ought to have been censured immediately by our movement. Take this passage: 'I appeal to the humanity and generosity of all of Madrid's journalists and intellectuals; to the generosity — why not? — of Messieurs Casares Quiroga [minister of the Interior] Esplá [under-secretary of state at the Interior ministry] and Azaña himself [prime minister]... For the sake of the honour of all Spaniards, for the sake of the prestige of the entire Spanish nation in the eyes of the civilised world; for the sake of the prestige of the authorities; the drama going on in Police Headquarters in Barcelona must not go without severe sanction'. The anarchist Federica Montseny trying to salvage the prestige of the authorities is the highpoint of a state of mind, the spread of which would be unduly dangerous for our movement. Happily, all the comrades to whom I have spoken were frankly outraged by this unspeakable insolence". Taken from Alexander Schapiro, op. cit.

2   "Thus, in Valencia there was an advertised talk to be given at the Construction Union by Federica Montseny on 'Syndicalism — the final and most dangerous refuge of authority'" (sic), Schapiro, op. cit. Another example would be a letter from Toryho (a fervent pro-collaborationist and future bullying director of *Solidaridad Obrera*) to Federica Montseny, dated 5 June 1936. "Let me take this opportunity to tell you that I think your fears concerning the beginnings of some sort of liquidation of anarchist ideas within the CNT are

communism from the top down; there was a range of things indicating an involvement in politics.

The CNT's congress in Zaragoza in May 1936 drew a line under the split without going into tactical differences or highlighting doctrinal errors:

> Circumstances merely formal in nature tipped the balance in a split that cannot be traced to fundamental disagreement with the CNT's basic principles. The revolutionary process from that point on and in today's revolutionary circumstances have led to the evaporation of those differing interpretations and formal agreement on the position at present.[3]

It was such reluctance to delve into the reasons underlying differences of opinion—lest this lead to splits in the trade union Organisation—that led to the breakdown of organisation during the civil war years. The CNT leaders responded to the swirl of events with a constant refrain: the membership was bombarded with the message of a policy of fait accompli, their press increasingly cowed and pro-Bolshevik in their reporting of and approach to the USSR.

The upshot was that the workers felt left out of the loop, and struck one of two attitudes. They either let themselves be strung along by whoever was 'shepherd of the day' (reaping some benefit directly or indirectly) or they lashed out and bridled at it.

A number of notables blithely contradicted their own previous records and statements. In July 1936, one of the

---

exaggerated. Because that liquidation is not of recent date but has been under way from a long time ago. The anarchist decline within the unions is a result of there having been very few anarchists in Barcelona engaged with the class struggle organs. Many may call themselves such, but they are more Marxist and authoritarian than those who are known as such". *Salamanca Archives*, B809.

3 *El Congreso confederal de Zaragoza*, op. cit., pp. 92–93.

architects of the CNT-FAI's entry into the Generalitat and Madrid governments, Mariano R. Vázquez—the secretary of the CNT national committee from late September 1936 until the moment of defeat—penned an article entitled: "Let Us Be Clear: State Intervention is Tantamount to Fascism".[4]

An article titled, "The Uselessness of Government"[5] made it into print, and a National Defense Council was mooted, but on 27 September 1936 the CNT-FAI agreed to join the Generalitat government and the Militias Committee was wound up. Abad de Santillán, who made a specialty of doing his worst, only to beat his breast afterwards, characterised this blatant aberration thus:

> We indicated a readiness to wind up the Militias Committee, that is, to back down from a revolutionary position that the Spanish people had never held before then. All just to secure weapons and financial aid in order to prosecute our war successfully. We knew that there was no way for the revolution to succeed unless we first succeeded in the war and for the sake of the war we sacrificed everything. We sacrificed the very revolution, not realising that this sacrifice implied sacrificing the aims of the war.[6]

Aragon received no benefits in terms of equipment and armaments, but the notables stuck to their guns. On the day it was announced that the CNT was joining the Madrid government, when *Solidaridad Obrera* was reporting this as "one of the most transcendental events in the recorded history of

---

[4] *Solidaridad Obrera*, 11 July 1936, p. 8 (back page).

[5] This was a translation of a text by André Prudhommeaux based on Bakunin's *Letter to a Frenchman* and carried in *L'Espagne Nouvelle*, as Prudhommeaux himself explained in *volontá*, Year VIII, No 11, 15 March 1955, p. 612.

[6] Abad de Santillan, *Por qué ... ?*, p. 116.

our nation",[7] the Iron Column mouthpiece, *Línea de Fuego* observed, in an article titled, "The CNT in government":

> The wire service brings us the news, which we duly insert, that the CNT is to become part of the government. That is, that what was always attacked is now to be embraced and the very foundations of our beliefs torn up. From now on there is to be no more talk of freedom, but of obedience to "our" government instead, the only body equipped to direct the war and the life of the economy. The confederal organisation has been guaranteed four ministries, none of which meets the specifications cited as arguments for the establishment of a National Defense council. Four junior ministries, occupied by four individuals with no background in the matters, now are to be entrusted to their care. We are to see a member of the Weaving and Textile Union, greatly adept in warfare, at the Justice Ministry; a female orator and author of love stories and social tales at the Ministry of Justice; and a professional propagandist at Trade [...][8]

And the same newspaper complained:

> There is talk and tedious repetition coming from the very people who do nothing, about all of us making sacrifices and production being stockpiled and stepped up [...]
>
> The same negative outcome flows and is flowing from what might be described, to use a technical term, as an epidemic of "Committee-ocracy", a new bourgeoisie forged in the heat of these upheavals.
>
> Fascism, in the broad and full sense of the term, does not consist of the paraphernalia and modus operandi of regimes that style themselves such, but operates and

---

7   S.O., 4 November 1936, p. 1 (editorial); and Peirats, Vol. I, p. 231.
8   4 November 1936, p. 1.

is practised across territories much broader and vaster than those marked out by the likes of Hitler, Mussolini and Franco. It is authority in all its various forms and guises that lies at the source of and spawns fascism.[9]

In fact, the only dialogue between a segment of the rank and file (the CNT volunteers on the front, which is to say, the soundest, most committed members) and the upper echelons, despite the latter's top-down penchant, came in February 1937 during the plenum of confederal militias and columns (see Appendix VII below) and proved fruitless.

The only good thing to come out of collaboration was the Catalan law permitting abortion, secured through the CNT's minister of Health, Pedro Herrera.[10] That was quite groundbreaking if we compare it to the Argentinean or Spanish abortion legislation of 2008–2009, but, as far as I can tell, it was never implemented by the Republic's minister of Health, Federica Montseny.[11]

Historian and friend César M. Lorenzo takes a different view, to the effect that intervention in government, whereby quite a number of CNT personnel served in various administrations, supposedly curtailed the economic crackdown on self-management. The likelihood is that in some instances it did.

But the underlying problem is still the question of dual power—bourgeois top-down power on the one hand and horizontal, workers' power on the other. And, between 1936

---

9   Ibidem, 6 November 1936, p. 2.
10 For the decree of 13 January 1937, see Peirats, Vol. II, "abortion may be carried out on therapeutic, eugenic, birth control or ethical grounds". Editorial in *S.O.*
11 In her ministerial review *Mi experiencia en el ministerio de Sanidad y Asistencia Social. Conferencia pronunciada el 6 de junio de 1937 en el teatro Apolo, Valencia*, no mention is made of this. Later on, as a émigré, she claimed the credit without ever offering any overall figures for the hospitals, clinics or areas where it might have been implemented.

and 1939, there was allegedly power at the grassroots, which was forever caving in to the pressures brought to bear by republican capitalism.

Emma Goldman offers one conclusion:

> I am profoundly convinced and most certain that had the CNT-FAI, with everything in its hands and under its control, frozen the banks and disbanded and done away with the Assault Guards and Civil Guards, put a padlock on the Generalitat instead of joining it as partners, dealt a fatal blow to all the old bureaucracy, swept aside its adversaries near and far, then, rest assured we today would not be suffering the situation, which degrades and wounds us, because the revolution would have had to be carried through in order to consolidate itself. That said, I am not saying that the comrades could have achieved anarchy, but they could have set out on that road and got as close as possible to the libertarian communism that is all the talk hereabouts.[12]

---

12 Manuel Azaretto *Las pendientes resbaladizas (los anarquistas en España)* (Montevideo 1939), p. 246: taken from an interview in *Il Risveglio Anarchico* (Geneva) on 23 October 1937 (set alongside the Italian original, the translation seems correct: I have amended "anarchist communism" to "libertarian communism" as it appears in the Italian and as was the usage of the day.

Appendix VII
Making Sense of the Plenum of Confederal Militias and Columns

Interesting though it may be, this text[1] was never mentioned by Pierre Besnard in critical articles published in *Universo* (Toulouse) in 1946–47, nor by José Peirats in his *Historia de la CNT*, published between 1951 and 1953. Nor was it cited by Vernon Richards in his analysis, dating from 1953. The official history of the Spanish libertarian movement pays no heed to it at all, which may be because it is in pamphlet format and has an inherent fragility, as well as because of the ultra-critical tenor of the contents.

Another extraordinary aspect of this document is that it represents the only open, direct and blunt debate—a horizontal gathering in a body that embraced bottom-up communication, but which was in the process of adopting the top-down practices favored by the UGT and other left-wing political parties. (Yes, there may be a difference between verticalism and leftward- or rightward-leaning democracy, but it doesn't strike me as a difference of much significance.)

As a result, all of the burning issues are transparently broached, whether it is the CNT national committee's inability to find a solution to the armaments question (outside or inside the government), the fragility of alliances within the republican camp or the drift away from social revolution...

---

1 *Pleno de Columnas Confederales y Anarquistas celebrado en Valencia el día 5 de febrero de 1937* [...] It can be found at http://www.fondation-besnard.org/article.php3?id_article=428. The text was presented in 2006 to a "Congress on the Civil War" held in Madrid that November.

That the Plenum happened at all is evidence of the failure of the Catalan CNT's tactics in July 1936, which then spread to the whole of Spain, with the exception of Aragon. To wit, the impossibility of lasting alliances with the socialist and communist leaderships.

The approach taken is neither military nor tactical in that it presupposed a lengthy and painstaking analysis of every single one of the fronts and how these had evolved between July 1936 and the date of the Plenum.

Let me dwell on the considered and underlying stances adopted, vis à vis the authorities, by the CNT militia and column leaders up to their necks in the battle-fronts. These positions played a major part in the events of May 1937 in Barcelona, in that the "Friends of Durruti"—a CNT grouping that had marginalised itself and become a significant actor—had their backgrounds in the Durruti Column and a number of them took part in the plenum. Cipriano Mera, who wielded a lot of clout at it, was the real military chief of the Casado Junta in March 1939.

Another feature of the Plenum is that the participants had an idea of its importance and made a point of having its proceedings placed on record.[2] Afterwards, they all seemed to appreciate that their brief presence there, far away from the fighting fronts, was exceptional, and not just in order to clarify enigmas and lobby for concrete equipment and backing.[3]

---

[2] "A prior consideration arises: whether the minutes are properly recorded and put to the Columns so that they may inform themselves as fully as possible about this plenum. This was later taken under advisement and passed". (p. 32)

[3] It is notable that the note-taking was monitored and used as a testimony for posterity: "It was agreed that the minutes of the first and second sessions be read and these were passed unanimously, after some minor clarification". (p. 45) "*Tierra y Libertad* asked that the record show its emphatic statement that the Iron Column has performed admirably and with menace towards none and this was carried". (p. 61)

> There was an insistence that the previous day's minutes be read out and when it turned out that none of the copies run off was available at the time, the decision was made to go fetch them. The Iron Column made a number of remarks, its opinion being that the meagre representation sent by the Plenum of Regionals to discuss a matter of such over-arching importance at a gathering that might be described as HISTORIC and upon which the future survival of the anarchist columns hinges was out of order.[4] (p. 33)

There are, then, many reasons why we should dwell upon this document.

I. The Rationale behind the Plenum

The social revolution and the raising of CNT volunteer columns who had a real job to do in the defense of the fronts, as well as the lightning-quick changes in a CNT that was now in cahoots with the government, may account for the CNT fighters' wish to compare their situations, experiences and expectations at a point when the war was stagnating or re-organising due to the apparent dearth and poor distribution of armaments.

A short text introducing the need to hold a Plenum of CNT fighters offered the following reasons:

> Ideas, realities, revolutionary events and partisan interest, everything noble and squalid to be found in men has bounced back urgently and with unprecedented strength

---

[4] Comrade Jover from the Ascaso Division stated: "This gathering will assuredly be, as some comrade has stated, historic". (p. 35). "[Iron Column delegate] I am now gladder than ever that fulsome notes be made of this gathering which I hope will be more practical than historic, because the historic is of relative significance and the practical a potential significance". (p. 38)

and, by melting into one strange but understandable muddle, has brought about a false situation that it falls to every one of us to dispel. (p. 6)

Far from an attempt to set a moral tone, as the hypocrisy of past and current religious and political bigwigs might do, this was a plain-speaking denunciation of unconscionable pro-alliance compromises (supporters of Soviet Russia might stand alongside libertarians and republican servicemen, champions of private property and so on and so on) such as the stockpiling of arms in the rearguard to the detriment of the front lines...

In the rearguard a huge number of decisions—decisions that might well have been taken with an eye to investing themselves with some sort of revolutionary effectiveness—have been made by all manner of organisations and parties, but these have all been afflicted by one major shortcoming: it never occurred to anybody to seek the OPINION OF THE FIGHTING PERSONNEL. (pp. 6–7)

Here we had the divorce between the grassroots and the top echelons, the refusal by those who were laying their lives on the line to be used as cannon fodder in pursuit of ideals to which they did not subscribe and for upstarts whom they despised.

This is unforgivable. Especially since we, the ones who are defending the soil of Iberia, do so with the intention, pretty much well-defined in each and every COLUMN, of creating a new way of life. (p. 7)

They were volunteers pursuing a far and egalitarian society and a very different future.

Obviously, we belong to organisations that have seconded countless delegates to every conceivable committee. But there is one overwhelming and incontrovertible fact: AT THE MOMENT THE REARGUARD SEEMS TO HAVE FORGOTTEN ALL SENSE OF REVOLUTION. (p. 7)

During the soviet revolution (the revolution of the *free* soviets, rather than the Bolshevik revolution) there was a denunciation of rule by committee. This same phenomenon was now repeated, with the aggravating circumstance that two factors were now at work—dereliction (due perhaps to the belief that the defeat of the rebels was imminent) and the feathering of their own nests by cowards and parasites.

On all these points, persuaded that for the fighting personnel of our columns the notion of revolution cannot be dissevered from the notion of the war, we believe, as do other columns from Levante and Andalusia, that as a matter of urgency, a national plenum of Anarchist and CNT columns must be called so as to determine policy or conclude agreements.

In a timely manner we dispatched delegations to visit every single front and their impressions have confirmed us in our views. (p. 7)

So among the CNT's fighting personnel, an awakening of consciences led to a realisation that they needed to organise themselves horizontally in order as to operate accordingly.[5]

---

[5] Yet another assertion by the Iron Column's delegate: "We should point an accusing finger at responsible bodies and at ourselves; since we have been guilty of keeping our best personnel in front line service, leaving the organisations' committees to upstarts who, once ensconced in some comfortable post, worked contrary to the smooth operation of them. We have said all this time and again to the Organisation, which did nothing, so much so that we are all but persuaded that we are on our own, but when the comrades from other columns responded that they found

The agenda and invitation to the plenum could scarcely have been briefer or blunter:[6]

1) Where the columns stand vis à vis the militarization decree and 2) Our dealings with one another. (p. 7)

Both items put their finger on core issues: the opportunity for the volunteers themselves to oppose a decree endorsed by the government and by their own organisation and, therefore, the breakdown of communications and dialogue with the CNT, its top-down approach now starkly at odds with its past record. The invitation hinted at the formation of a quite new social entity or grouping, the volunteer fighters affiliated to the CNT, and at their ability to gather together and spell out their demands. This was horizontal organisation.

II. Underlying Factors Lingering in February 1937

Over and above the dearth of weaponry and military equipment, the core issue was the matter of fictitious alliances. Why fictitious?

Up until 18 July 1936, CNT personnel across the nation had distrusted socialists, POUMists and communists, and the feeling was mutual, with the communists at daggers drawn with everybody. In Catalonia, CNT personnel were at loggerheads with the Catalanists and the POUMists. Despite the government's being reduced to a power vacuum, as far as the CNT was concerned, the victory of the workers in concert

---

themselves in the same boat, we nurtured a hope that the sensibility that was the norm in our actions might yet be restored to the CNT and FAI and the norms of freedom imposed on one and all".(p.9)

6 Note that the militias from Asturias did not attend; as their front was cut off by the rebels; and whereas the Maroto Column was party to the preparations for the Plenum, no delegate from it attended, nor was any comment passed on this fact.

with the class enemy—part of the Assault Guard and Civil Guard corps—merely complicated the strategic considerations even further.

The Catalan model[7] of alliance at the top and restricted libertarian communism at ground level was being imitated in other regions. This was a gamble by the CNT leadership,[8] in that it was agreed without any consultation with the rank and file membership due to the urgency of the situation and the requirements imposed by the war. The whole arrangement was a fragile house of cards because there was no attempt to seek the endorsement of the grassroots members with wide-ranging debate and extra-ordinary meetings.

In Aragon, with Durruti setting the pace, the creation of a Council of Aragon represented a departure from the Catalan approach. But this had no impact beyond Aragon.

The CNT's entry into the Catalan government and then into the republican government was the logical outworking of a stance from which many saw no turning back.[9]

---

7 Escofet, the Catalan police chief, recounts in his memoirs how President Companys contacted him within just hours of the people's forces having routed the rebel military, in order to gauge the chances of eliminating the CNT. To which Escofet replied that, given the weaponry in the hands of the CNT personnel and the recent fraternisation on the barricades between the Mossos de Escuadra and CNT personnel, an attack on the CNT did not appear feasible to him.

8 In keeping with Horacio Prieto's approach dating back to 1932. See Appendix V of this book.

9 "It is the workers, the toilers with a fresh outlook on life and a fresh approach to righteousness, who have rebelled against the old style politics of capitalism and who have answered the call. I am a labourer, I am a builder and it should be me that administers and directs everything that I have created. (Loud applause) And this is the most basic, the most historical, the most defining, the most important point about the CNT's joining the government and the involvement of the CNT in the business of government. Now, once this idea has been floated, once this fact has been demonstrated, once this truth has become an irrefutable, proven fact borne out by events, do you really think there

It is important to note that the delegates attending the Plenum did not waste time with idle chatter about what ought to have been done or the reasons why what was done was done. They knew how little time they had for debate before they were due back on the front lines, hence the feeling that what they had to say was 'historic'. The tendency, therefore, was to get to grips with the tangible and the short-term—armaments and supervision of orders—because they knew that this was a life or death matter as far as the future was concerned.

> [Ascaso Column delegate:] Once we finish we will have an opportunity to impose our thinking on the rearguard [...] If any other ideas prevail, then we will suffer. We must build up our strength on the front lines and never quit them". (pp. 16–17)

> [Collado, from the Durruti Column:] Today the enemy is fascism. Tomorrow, who knows? (p. 28)

In its convening and its description, the Plenum anarchism as a social ideal after the fashion of Bakunin or Kropotkin, an ideal that had nothing to do with pacifism:

> [The National Committee:] We believe it is appropriate to agree to organisation into Brigades. This is our view, even though such militarisation rides roughshod over our anarchist outlook, as does our participation in this war, because taking up arms to kill one's neighbour is not an anarchist principle.

---

is any possibility, any feasibility of governing now through political parties and discounting the workers' organisations sharing in government responsibility, and collaborating in the government—today that is, for tomorrow we shall see? It is no longer a possibility. Nothing can be done in defiance of us or without us". Taken from *Mi experiencia en el Ministerio de Sanidad y Asistencia Social. Conferencia pronunciada por Federica Montseny? El 6 de junio de 1937 en el teatro Apolo, Valencia*, p. 30.

The Iron Column interjected to object to this last remark, mentioning that gun-play at the appropriate time was very much anarchist. (p. 58)

III "Relations between us"

"Between us" was of course a reference to the CNT overall and to the CNT volunteers serving in the front lines.

The internal organisation of the CNT's upper echelons looked unstable, makeshift and lacking in continuity: "The National Committee replied that it took office on 20 November last and has no knowledge of the two communiqués referred to by the previous comrade, though the communiqués will surely have reached the previous Committee. They stressed that they had taken over a Committee in utter disarray, with no archives and absolutely nothing else". (p. 48)

One interesting and typically bureaucratic response, seemingly alien to what the pre-18 July 1936 CNT had been like, took the form of belittling the Plenum itself:

> The representative from the Plenum of Regionals states that it had been taken for granted that he was the one empowered to pass resolutions and take a hand in the matter offered for debate, this being an irregular gathering. (p. 33)

> [National Committee:] This meeting, being utterly 'out of order' and 'irregular' ought never to have taken place and wants noted this description of the gathering. (p. 38)

The most vehement response was as follows:

> Comrade Mera, from the Confederal Militias delegation, says that when the delegations from the Centre received their invitations, it was represented to them as a plenum called by the Iron Column.[...] But now comrade Mera,

speaking in a personal capacity, asks the Committee whether thought had been given, as it ought to have been, to consulting the comrades in the front lines according to confederal practice and not just with regard to this grave issue of militarisation, but when ministers of theirs entered the Government and with regard to other matters.

Given that no consideration had been given to them on any count at all, the National Committee has no right to describe this gathering as out of order or irregular. If what has been left undone thus far has gone undone, it needs doing now. The Committee had conducted itself in an anti-confederal manner by not putting matters out for consultation in the unions and by forcing its decisions—without consultation—on the front line comrades in a dictatorial fashion. These were decisions that it had worked out internally, like keeping them in the family, so to speak. If the younger son, as a minor, has the right to meet up with his brother without his father's permission, then the father really should have spared some thought for how his sons were getting on in the trenches.

The National Committee and Regional Committees are thinking along lines that are strangling the life out of the revolution and this should not be concealed from the fighting men.

We can accept what we might term 'BOLDNESS' and can countenance militarization, but we take exception to the Organisation's forcing something down our throats just because some minister wants it. And let me speak plainly: I don't care about the Organisation in that respect. And I am speaking as Mera here. (pp. 40–41)

After the National Committee and the CNT's volunteer fighters had thus disowned each other, the National Committee spoke with complete sincerity.

Comrade Raquel Castro asks if the Committee could guarantee that if we were to embrace militarisation, arms would be delivered to us rather than us facing the same fate as in some sectors where, after accepting militarisation, none were forthcoming.

To which the National Committee replies: Our duty is to our Organisation and we can guarantee nothing, but let us assure you that we would make it our business to make sure that is how things go. (p. 58)

No one commented on that admission alone representing a complete condemnation of partnership in the government. Without a doubt, the important issue for everyone just then was to get hold of weapons and, after having done that, to galvanise the Organisation for revolution. But in doing so they were lurching in the direction of runaway rule-by-committee. And so, since nothing could be changed, along came May 1937, and the CNT was powerless to stop it over five days. At the end of it, an underground CNT press emerged.

[Pellicer, Iron Column:] We are not speaking out against the Organisation, which we cherish as much as anybody else. We are speaking out against the committees who are bringing it into disrepute. (p. 12)

[National Committee:] The Organisation takes precedence over all and we have to bow to this fact and ensure that nobody puts obstacles in its way. (p. 42)

Among the CNT fighters there was no set stance on the war and the revolution; some could see both being waged simultaneously while others made the war a priority:

[Pellicer, Iron Column:] Our purpose was always to clear the filth out of the rearguard. (p. 11)

[Ascaso Column delegate:] We have absolutely no misgivings about the comrades in the rearguard. (p. 16)

IV. "Where the Columns stand on Militarisation"

Delegates, so critical of the National Committee, made no bones about their intention of "forcing our *moros* [Moors] into front line service" [Iberia Column delegate, p. 20). Plainly this boiled down to picking out one's cannon-fodder, just like the rebel fascist side did. The Moroccan *tabors* were crack assault troops, seemingly ruthless in that their cultural background was different, and most of them were unable to understand Spanish. They were easily replaced, coming as they did from colonised territory. It amounted to embracing the top-down military approach with a real and tragic outcome for recruits prone to being used and abused by their officers. As the invitation stated, this was "everything noble and sordid about men bouncing back". (p. 6)

The problem was that "we are guilty of having kept our best people in the front lines" (as the Iron Column delegate stated, p. 9). They needed some relief, which came in the form of mandatory conscription, thereby eliminating volunteer service. Benito, from the Centre region, referred to "what happened in the Russian revolution with Makhno's Army" (p. 25) and, it seems, failed to point out that volunteer service was the only sort in the Makhnovist army. The value judgment implicit in the use of the term *"moro"* came from just one person.[10]

Their assessment of the situation was blunt:

---

10 The delegate from the Militias of the Centre stated: "Let me tell you that we should not be referring to a segment of our people as MOROS and have no right to do so. That we ourselves would have taken exception to that had it not come from the lips of a CNT minister, for which reason we have all taken it up. But I say again that calling our brethren *moros* flies in the face of our principles". (pp. 23–24)

Despite the government's promises, we are sure that we won't be given the tools to win the war. They mean to sabotage us. The Ascaso Division is finding this out today and things are the same as ever: lots of meddling by Russian military commanders who interfere in the direction of the conduct of the war. More than this though, I have to repeat something I said not many days ago: "Russians galore, but gear from Russia, damned little". (p. 15)

However there was Marxist-leninist dialectics with financial overtones:

[Delegates from the 'Temple y Rebeldía' Column:] The fact is that from our militias' pay they deduct three pesetas a day, for education, so they say, but actually for communist propaganda. This is the case with the pay of lieutenants, 30 percent of whose earnings are deducted; and in the case of captains, the figure is 49 percent and so on. (pp. 18–19)

And there were complaints about weapons pilfering:

[Pellicer, Iron Column:] We learned from some comrades who had been down to Cartagena (on a timely visit) of the huge quantities of weapons being unloaded in that port. Whereas, in Andalusia, only months later, there are still columns doing their fighting with shotguns. (p. 9)

But the Iron Column came up with a suggestion for procuring arms:

We have to see if we can resist the scheming of the Marxists who are cashing in on their current supremacy. Let us put the issue to the government and tell it that the confederation troops we have in service are to withdraw

> to the rearguard. In the face of that threat and on the basis of our incontrovertible strength, we will be given what actually belongs to us. That is our position. (p. 31)

The fact that nobody followed through with this plan says much about the CNT's overall feeling of inferiority generally.[11]

There was one issue that loomed larger than militarization and this was the matter of officers and discipline:

> [Pellicer, Iron Column:] Of course we haven't lost sight of the fact that there are cases of servicemen comrades whose more or less liberal education drew them to us in the early stages of the fighting, and we are not denying that there were a number of them in our own column. But do you know what the High Command does with them? Whenever it sees that they are unduly sympathetic to certain comrades it relieves them and assigns them to desk duties, as has been our own fate. (p. 10)

> [The delegate from Column CNT 13 takes the floor.] Our Column has withdrawn in order to reorganise and militarise, because we've learned from experience that on the battlefront one cannot play at warfare. We've seen (and it

---

[11] "[Jover from the Ascaso Column:] We were refused what we wanted; we wanted it but we held our tongues since the time has come for words to give way to deeds and if we abide by this way of going about things, I for my part will do all in my power to have my forces sever conections with the confederal and specific organisations and then we will wage this war because the war should not be abandoned and, here I would ask the Iron Column not to quit the front nor allow its forces to be relieved". (pp. 35–36). "[Benito, from the Centre:] The cutting of ties, as one comrade had urged with shocking irresponsibility, should not be countenanced since it would abet our defeat at the hands of our present day enemy, fascism, and our potential enemy of tomorrow, Marxism". (p. 48). Note that no one made any reference to the possibility of raiding the Bank of Spain. See Abel Paz, *Durruti*; and Abad de Santillan's *Por qué perdimos la Guerra*.

pains me to admit this) that when it comes to coming under fire, a hundred odd cowards have cried off sick, with a thousand excuses for withdrawing to the rear, and no ideological argument has availed against this.

In light of this behavior, I personally issued them with passes, scribbling in large letters STRICKEN WITH PANIC and they have not been embarrassed to display these on their journey into the rear. So we have to find some way of ensuring that nobody turns back on any pretext. Volunteer service has had its day. Either we wage war or we let war overpower us. (pp. 17–18)

Comrade Mera says: Everything that was stated yesterday is being reiterated today.

What I say is that if those in Aragon were in Madrid, they would have a different opinion. We can see that discipline is needed if we are to bring this war to a happy conclusion. Discipline is need so that the individual serving is compelled to stand by his post rather than abandon it at a given point due to his instinct of self-preservation. None of us here can point to a disciplined allocation of his men. If we are to wage war we have to do it through military discipline. You do not bandy words with an officer, but there is no need to bandy words when he does not perform well either. You should put a couple of bullets into him. War is the very opposite of the man of sentiment. (p. 55)

Another stratagem for countering the Marxist outlook was the political commissar:[12]

Comrade Mera protests that the political delegate must not overrule the military commander. And only inspect

---

12 Be it said that this institution reflected the prioritisation of political purity over military expertise inherited from the monarchy (in 1789) or from tsarist rule (1917–1922) and later, in the USSR, the Cheka was set up in December 1917 on Lenin's decision.

operations once they have been mounted. And in actuality he is only a cipher on the left flank. (p. 52)

[Ascaso Column:] We can see that the commissar serves absolutely no purpose. (p. 55)

A level-headed view was taken of militarisation, and rules were passed:

Comrade Mera says: On point one, militarisation, we have agreement, but we should be militarised along unmistakably confederal lines. Let our own Organisation militarise us into homogeneous confederated militias. One battalion of our people surrounded by Marxists and it will be the death knell for the CNT if the commander is a Marxist. Likewise two battalions of ours plus two Marxist ones under the same commander will be the death knell for the CNT, as we see in practice. (p. 50)

Confederated Militias of the Centre tables a proposal that is read out by the comrade chairman and given due consideration. It states:
1. Militarisation is accepted as a necessity thrust upon us by the war.
2. Militarization is to be carried out on the basis of commands, whether company commands battalion, brigade or divisional. Commands, should be in the charge of comrades answerable to the Organisation.
3. Our divisions ought to be homogeneous, and only when there is no other option are they to be constituted on the basis of two battalions of ours and two other battalions. But again, the commands should be allocated to comrades. (p. 60)

The National Committee and its sham allies turned a completely blind eye as may be inferred from this CNT

National Committee account and what it has to say about the social prime minister-cum-UGT leader.

> I ought to point out that Poblador paid a visit to the War Minister to lobby for weapons. We have done all in our power to get these and Largo Caballero has plainly asked HOW CAN HE GIVE US MACHINE-GUNS WHEN, ONCE WE HAVE THEM, WE WOULD NEVER GIVE THEM UP?
>
> The confederal organisation has no weapons other than the ones it initially snatched from the barracks. García Oliver himself tendered his resignation from the War Council because he disagreed with Largo Caballero's sabotage of our forces, most especially in Catalonia. But the government chooses to ignore this or is simply incapable of supplying the weapons. Militarisation has been decided by a Plenum of Regionals.
>
> We have seen columns—those commanded by communists—showered with military equipment, whereas we are getting shabbier and shabbier.
>
> I myself asked Largo Caballero why this was and he answered: Because the confederal forces refused to organise into brigades and the government had lost confidence in the militias.
>
> "State arms are for state forces"—he told me—"and if they refuse to join in, let their own organisations equip them".
>
> That left us with no option but to raid the depots where the arms were being held. But just think about the implications of this. Just consider the impact it might have: it could have brought about a situation where the frictions between us might provide fascism with a heaven-sent chance of finding us weakened and of pulling off a victory.
>
> We are embracing militarisation, whilst making no bones about the fact that we will not have communists

and socialists in positions of command and that those positions must go to our own militants.

What we need are MOROS (Moors): they should be made to go and not quibble about whether we should or should not countenance this format or that [...]

Another National Committee delegate speaks up to counter the criticisms coming from the Iron Column in particular.

He also mentions that Largo Caballero told him: PUT YOURSELF IN MY PLACE AND SEE WHETHER YOU WOULD ISSUE WEAPONS THAT MIGHT LATER BE TURNED ON YOU.

We have no means of getting hold of them; if you can think of any, let us know and we will be delighted to have you present us with a solution. (p. 21–22)

This lengthy quotation demonstrates the doubly paradoxical ingenuity of losers—justifying Largo Caballero's refusal!—and shows the presence of the USSR and its Communist-Party lackeys.

On the one hand, the CNT's entry into the government changed nothing—despite Largo Caballero's empty promises—and it was a nonsense for the CNT national committee to seek to hang on in there in those circumstances.

On the other hand, as Largo Caballero himself sensed, it was madness to feign control of weapons that ultimately were in the possession of the USSR.[13]

---

[13] "I gave instructions for the acting air force chief (the planes, pilots and commanders being Soviet) to be asked to draft a written memo on the number of planes that could be deployed, and his response was that we could count on ten planes. Ten planes deployable alongside an offensive involving an army of forty-thousand men. I construed this as retaliation for my having failed to make commanding positions available to communists". Largo Caballero, *Correspondencia secreta* (Madrid 1961), p. 275. Written in 1946, and cited in Mintz, op. cit.

V. Matters Outstanding

The notes of this Plenum are the only documentary record of a confrontation between the critical rank and file and the CNT's upper echelons. And it is worth emphasising that, in this instance, the rank and file was made up of militants like Cipriano Mera, Pellicer and delegates from the CNT's own columns who were present at an extraordinary gathering. Equally extraordinary were the harshness and honesty of the dialogue.

Besides their inability to come up with a solution to the supplying of arms to the militias or to extract any reward for embracing militarisation, there was also a notable lack of solutions to the spares problem, a lack of long term analysis from either the National Committee or the men who would shortly be behind the Casado Junta's coup, but all of the negative and dangerous features in political and military affairs were strikingly obvious (by 1938 the signs of a Second World War in the offing were plain in *Solidaridad Obrera*).[14]

They were seemingly oblivious of the approach adopted by their Russian anarchist comrades, as set out in Spanish in the pamphlet *Nabat*, published in Buenos Aires in 1922. Nor were they aware of Makhno's tactics, which were widely known in Spain.[15] Worse still, they were oblivious of the

---

14 The Junta in question, headed by Colonel Segismundo Casado, its troops under the command of Cipriano Mera, foiled plans for a communist coup within the army of the Republic and suied, unsuccessfully, for an honourable peace—Translator's note.

15 "The pace of the masses' revolutionary action should not be slowed. Help to the masses of people should be sped up so as to compel the acting republican government by force (if there are no other ways or means available) to desist in its efforts to bridle the revolution with nonsensical decrees [...] The toilers should be helped to man their work posts right away in an effort to create their local, social, self-managed economy or free soviets, as well as armed regiments for defending such revolutionary social measures as the toilers, eyes opened and having shrugged off the fetters of their slavish status, will turn into a reality when the time comes [...] They should not be afraid to take organisational and

revolutionary tactical and practical outlook of the French anarcho-syndicalist Pierre Besnard.[16] A mountain of mistakes made by the leadership had brought them to the edge of the abyss.

---

strategic revolutionary leadership of the popular revolt into their own hands* Of course they should fight shy of any alliance with political parties in general and in particular with the Bolshevik communists because I reckon that the Spanish Bolshevik communists are the same as or similar to their Russian comrades". Makhno's *Letter to the Spanish Anarchists* (addressed to Carbó and Pestaña, 29 April 1931). (*This view fits in with the earlier quotations from Bakunin: a horizontal popular organisation should not allow the construction of an authority higher than the people, and it is the people who represent power. There was another, less determined, libertarian view during the Soviet revolution, promoted by the Nabat group. See http://www.fondation-pierre-besnard.org/article.php3?id_articles=380.)

16 In 1930, Pierre Besnard was talking in these terms: "It is a matter, therefore, of the forces [of labour, expertise and science] acting in close concert to expel those who hold power and prevent anyone else from taking it or taking over the means of production and exchange and, following a very short period of idleness, indicative of the falling out between the employer and the wage-earner, setting the whole machinery of society in motion once again". See *Les syndicats ouvriers et la Révolution Sociale* (republished 1978), p. 224.

Appendix VIII
Evidence about the Collectives of Ascó and Flix (Tarragona), and the Barcelona Barbers' Collective[1]

I spent the first few months on the front lines until I was wounded and had to drop back into the rearguard. I had occasion to live in three collectives: first there was the Barcelona barbers' collective (I was a member of that union and, to some extent, a pioneer of the collective), and before rejoining the front I had to spend some time on rest and recreation in Ascó in Tarragona. There I lived in a collective founded on the principle of libertarian communism. Initially this collective encompassed the whole village but later a fair fraction—let us say about half of them—broke away from the collective because they didn't share its thinking and because they reckoned that a man making his own way in the world was freer, or else they were hostile to the revolution...

We lived there up until the central government dispatched troops to Barcelona on account of the May events, and from Barcelona troops spread throughout the whole province of Tarragona, with Líster's division doing the same in Aragon. Meaning that it held out in that village, Ascó, for seven or eight months. I was born there but for ten or twelve

---

1 Interview with José Llop in Vauhallan in 1964–65, unpublished in Spanish and partly published in French in *Noir et Rouge* No.s 30, 31–32 in 1965–66. José Llop was a participant in the meeting that founded the FAI in 1927 and his testimony—part of the interview regarding the collectives—was published in *El Movimiento Libertario Española* (Paris 1974), pp. 288–290 and Gómez Casas used it in his book on the FAI.

or fifteen years I had been living in Barcelona, but when I returned from the front, looking to recuperate from my illness—which had more to do with my nerves than anything else—in peace and quiet, I went there. There they were living out libertarian communism and everybody who was able worked but was paid no wage. Each would go to the collective's stores to collect whatever he and his family needed. I don't know but I have my doubts as to whether that would have lasted had it had to change; because the people—and I do not mean just the vast majority carried along by their sympathies, but the actual militants themselves—were not up to the mark. I am not saying that "we were" because I am ruling myself out as I was an outsider in all this, which is why I speak about "they". The comrades were not equal to the demands of living out libertarian communism.

You mean to say there was, shall we say, selfishness, with some of them envious of the others...?

No, it was just, as you say, there was a degree of selfishness. One man can look his neighbour in the eye and make promises but then there's the practical side and it is harder to turn those promises into realities. Very much harder [...] whenever there was a chance to go and get something everybody was in a rush, above all the women. Do you understand me? Meaning that the economy just wouldn't have been able to hold out to them. For the first few months it worked fine and that went on for seven or ten months, but in the longer run perhaps? I'm sure they'd have had to change tack. Meaning that what we were saying at the outset about from everyone according to his ability and to each according to his needs would have had to be amended because the economy just couldn't have held out to every human need.

The collective there was broken up as a result of the May events.

Was that on the orders of the central government or was imposed by any particular party? How exactly did it happen?

It went precisely as follows. Troops from the Center region, central government troops arrived in Catalonia, and Líster and his troops were posted to Aragon. There were collectives of this sort in Aragon. And Ascó sits on the border between Aragon and Catalonia, which is to say that the ideological drive in Ascó came from Aragon. So it was one of the first collectives broken up by the troops. The troops' purpose was to demolish the collectives that were revolutionary in character.

On the other hand, other collectives, such as the industrial ones in Barcelona or the collective in Flix (I was there later), one six kilometers away, were left alone because they did not have the ideological implications that the Ascó one had.

They pounced on the ones that had adopted the features that the Organisation had made a prerequisite for introducing libertarian communism.

Which is to say, they were CNT collectives. Because the Flix collective...

Yes. They were all CNT collectives.

But it was more or less run as a cooperative, which was not that avant garde at the time.

The difference between the two adjacent villages was that, compared to Flix, Ascó was overshadowed in terms of numbers of comrades as well as men of ideas. But in Flix they had an approach better suited to the facts: that is, they set up a farming collective alongside the collective at the chemical plant, which is still there to this day. All in all, there were two collectives: one an industrial collective and another farming collective.

In Flix, unlike in Ascó, a comrade belonging to the collective was paid a weekly wage in accordance to what was laid down by the industrial workers. Come the weekend, the comrade would lift his week's pay, his wage and spend it however he chose.

You will have spotted the difference between these collectives; the wage was the essential point and it was this that made the Ascó collective that much more avant garde in that the Flix collective was more in line with what the Organisation had laid down.

Barcelona's industrial collectives were also run along those lines. Each factory, or at any rate an entire sector, such as the barbers in Barcelona, was collectivised. There had been something like 1,000-odd barbershops, which were consolidated into 200 or 250, amalgamating—and this was general practice. But there were other industries such as, say, the dye industry or solvent industry where the collectives operated only on a factory-by-factory scale. There were collectives in the factories and later they all liaised with one another and had the chance to help one another out with the appropriate agencies.

Which means that the nature of the industrial collectives varied greatly from that of the farming collectives, especially the ones in Aragon, and Ascó was right on the border with Aragon. As to Valencia, I know nothing beyond what I have read about it. So I can offer no opinion, but to all appearances they were less revolutionary in nature there.

Meaning, looking at it with the benefit of hindsight, they may well have had some form of self-management but it was restricted to work: leaving out relations outside of the workplace completely?

Quite. Back then what distinguished a collective and distinguished one collective from another was the wage paid. Ideologically driven collectives, which had ventured into libertarian communism, had their foundations in the willing contribution made by the individual, with no coercion at work, and after that the individual or family could draw everything it needed from the common stores.

What set some collectives apart from the rest, in terms of the day to day reality, was this: in some of them there was no money in use but there was a central fund, so that anybody needing, say, to make a trip to Barcelona, had to go before the committee, which would then issue him with whatever he needed for the trip. In others, they had a family wage arrangement with a fixed sum paid per week and a standardised wage.

In the farming collective in Flix, which was, in that respect, the same as the industrial collective, each comrade received a weekly wage that was, if not quite the same, well, it made no difference whether he was a skilled or unskilled worker.

Later, though, there was an overall set wage for everybody. When everything the collective had ran low—milk, say (there was a sixty-cow byre and milk aplenty), olive oil, vegetables, whatever—everything the collective had was shared with everyone, not in equal measure so much as in accordance with the requirements of each family. So if there was a couple, the couple would get one litre of olive oil, but a couple with two children got two litres. I cannot be entirely precise as to how it worked but it was something along those lines.

As for the Ascó collective, I would maintain that had outsiders not broken it up, it would certainly have been broken up by the comrades within it and it would have been up to us (I joined the collective in the end) to make enforced changes.

Because some people were misusing the facilities?

That's it.

So, Líster's troops swept through and ended the collectives in Ascó and Flix?

In Flix they touched nothing. I was with the Ascó collective as a poultry-breeder (we had set up a barn there). The troops overran the barn, and some people left them, but I stayed on and was told that I could carry on if I liked, but I didn't have the heart to do it.

So the family and I left for Flix. There was another farmstead in Flix and I joined that it.

That's where I was when the retreat from Aragon forced us to move on in '38. We spent something like a year with the collective there. And the set-up in the Flix collective was completely different from the Ascó collective.

So, once Líster had swept through Ascó, were there no attempts to get back to the way things had been before?

Yes, there was one attempt made in which I was involved, but the results were very short-lived. After Líster's troops moved out, the collective was refloated, but instead of 300 heads of family, only about 35 to 40 got involved.

And who were these thirty-five to forty?

Most of them comrades; the ones that sympathised with us the most. But it wasn't the same. The original collective was founded on the individual holdings of each person. There had been scarcely anyone there who didn't have some parcel of land. There is, or was, a procedure they carried out: Anybody with a small-holding that didn't occupy all his time and effort would come to an arrangement with a landowner and, taking a half share, would take a plot, work it and then the produce would be split, half-and-half, between the owner of the land and the person working it.

Later, when the first collective came along, such lands were the property of persons regarded in the village as fascists. So these lands were worked by the collective. Meaning that the collective got the best lands. Later, however, those lands passed not to the owners but to the person who had previously worked them on a share-cropping basis, which is to say, the collective retained a few plots but most people turned their backs on the collective. There was a considerable change to the underlying economic foundations of the collective.

Besides the land area's being reduced, the available equipment also shrank, because all of the work tools, draught teams, etc., were dispersed. This meant that the second collective, which survived up until the retreat from Aragon, was only a shadow of what the first Ascó collective—run along libertarian communist lines—had been.

As to the Barcelona barbers' collective, prior to the war [the sector] had only workers—I myself belonged to it—and our earnings we were far below the other workers in industries such as construction, metalworking and weaving. Whenever the Barcelona barbers collectivised the industry, not only did wages improve until they matched the earnings of other comrades, but working hours were cut.

Prior to 18 July, barbers worked an average of eight hours a day, and that was only because of the demands that they'd already won. And when the industry in Barcelona was collectivised, work days were slashed to six hours and this is something to remember.

What I mean to say is that, in terms of the constructive, collectivisation was welcomed, because under the previous existing small-business arrangement it was left to each person to sort things out himself. In reality, the bosses and the employees were both exploited because their hours were very long and their earnings very low.

When the whole city was collectivised, not only did the workers belonging to the collective see their wages grow, but the employers did as well. In the old days, a barber employer in Barcelona was like another worker in that he had to work. Come collectivisation, all of the employers also decided to join the collective—they became just another comrade member of the collective. The collective pulled this off and placed themselves on equal footing with the workers in Barcelona, and reduced the working day from eight to six hours. And more work came to the collective because of good organisation. The bosses had not been able to do this because of their own interests, troubles and personal interests, but that the collective managed.

For instance, shifts were changed. Where before, the owners had insisted on opening up for business at 8.00 a.m. and work continuing until 8.00 p.m., under the collectives and depending on the location of the barbershop, it might open earlier or later. This meant that over this longer span when the shop was open, workers could put in their six hours of work when it was more convenient for the public to drop in. And so a barbershop in the El Borne [central market] district might open at 6.00 a.m., rather than wait until 8.00 a.m., because the local clientele favoured the morning trade. And they could shut earlier in the evenings. But these were busy hours. It was simply a case of bringing organisation to the collective effort, something that the employers had not previously managed to pull off.

You said there were thousands of salons before and these shrank to 200–250?

I can't be precise as to the exact figures but there had been about 1,200 and these were cut back to 300–350.

How did the reduction take place? Was the number cut back to basics in a district that previously might have had ten or twelve shops?

Centralisation. The shops were cut back and the equipment went to shops located in choicer locations and all the workers used them.

I missed all this myself because in early August 1936 I set off for the front. I was wounded in October and had to withdraw into the rearguard, but I saw everything I am telling you about with my own eyes on visits and during my stays in Barcelona.

Appendices

And was there a change after May 1937?

No. Things carried on because the Barcelona collectives were not affected in the least by the incursions of the central government and Generalidad of Catalonia... The ones affected were the farming collectives, which were founded upon a sort of a compact with the Aragon collectives.

The collectives in Ascó included all the families of those who had been convicted as fascists. They were subject to the same rules as any other comrade, and enjoyed exactly the same rights. They were expected to do their bit when it came to working, and after that they had free access to whatever they needed, like the family of any other comrade.

It was the same story there as it was all around Spain and in Barcelona where I was living at the time, and things happened that some people regarded as criminal.

You mean in terms of force being used to put the new regime in place?

Violence had to be used, yes, although once it was up and running some took the view that a halt had to be called to the violence, whereas others—who also claimed to be revolutionaries—carried on with the violence. That, as I see it, was deplorable, because according to comrades of that sort, who were in favor of violence, the object was to get our enemy before they got us with violence. But that was not my view, then or since, and I know that human criminality, which has nothing to do with revolutionary zeal, evaporated. In this regard human morality was boosted. There was no reason for the violence, and I could not see why anyone should go out and rob anyone else; what little he had was enough for him. At the time, though disparities in terms of clothes and recreation had not been abolished, they had been greatly reduced.

I remember that in Barcelona, an industrial city, and a fashion-conscious city, men used to go about casually dressed. There was vehicle traffic but the cars belonged to the agencies that had been set up and were not privately owned. That being the situation, there was no reason to collect money to buy a car. Which is to say that what drives a man in normal times, making him hungry for the cash to buy one was greatly dulled, and there was a big fall in all of the unnecessary expenditure a man might indulge in.

Also, I'm not aware of any act of expropriation having been carried out or any man's life having been attempted just for the sake of money.

So there was no thievery at all in Ascó by the time you got back there to live in the collective in 1936?

No. During the five to seven months I spent in Ascó there was nothing of that sort. But there were cases, as I have said, where the motive was an excess of revolutionary zeal.

By fascists, you mean?

By people who, without being such and without professing to be fascists, were against the CNT, which was in the majority in Ascó. To begin with, all the malcontents supported the collective, but they then set up this group to lock horns with the Organisation. There was the odd clash between the two sides and no mistake. But this cannot be regarded as an individual matter like robbing one's neighbor or trying to take somebody's life just to get hold of his possessions. There was nothing of that sort.

And that goes for Flix too?

No, not quite. Not so much in Flix because in Ascó those who sided against the CNT saw to it that a certain enmity grew between CNT personnel and the opposition.

Appendices

An enmity that existed from before?

No, an enmity conjured up by their different outlook on things. Whereas some wanted to introduce revolutionary ideas into economic life, one step at a time, others were supportive of the status quo. Meaning that they had come, say, to distribute the great estates okay but they meant to share them out among the small-time workers. They had a different outlook and that wasn't the time to measure these two attitudes against each other and debate them. Though, with hindsight I reckon that would have been the wisest course. And the different outlook they had was outright opposition, counter-revolutionary opposition in the sense of wanting to restore the old ways [...]

In Flix, before the war, the bulk of antifascists had been in the CNT. I'm not even sure that there was a UGT union branch at the chemical plant that was central to the economic life of the town. What I can say is that later, during my time in Flix, there was a good understanding between the various antifascist parties and the CNT [...]

[In Ascó,] when the army revolt came, the CNT comrades went for wholesale collectivisation of the village. We couldn't say by force because force was not used. It was with everybody's agreement. But there was a faction that joined the collective but did not feel itself to be collectivist. With encouragement from the political parties in Catalonia, the PSUC and so on, that faction rallied and on the heals of the Generalidad government's determination that belonging to the collective should be a matter of free choice, they pulled out [...]

And did the same happen in Flix?

Nothing happened in Flix. The plant was collectivised, meaning that there was industrial collectivisation such as they had in Barcelona where the industries had been collectivised, workforce and all. A worker did not have the option of quitting the collective because that was his job. It would have been tantamount to walking away from one's job. On the other hand the farming collective in Flix was characterised by freedom from start to finish.

And some land was left precisely as it had been before?

Right up to the very end, the collective held on to the land formerly owned by fascists, just as it did to the sixty-cow byre that were the property of a fellow who had been regarded as a fascist. The workers employed there belonged to the collective.

Yes, but did anyone with an average-sized holding suffer any interference?

No. I well remember being at one meeting of the Flix agricultural union, and the chairman was a comrade who had some land, a smallholder. He was the president of the farming union to which the collective was affiliated and he put in his produce, his olives, his olive oil and his every need satisfied...

Appendix IX
The Madrid Peasants' Collective[1]

(*This collective dated back to 9 May 1936 when four market-gardener comrades belonging to the Amalgamated Trades Union were fired by an employer [...] The Union resolved to take over the farm and handed it on to the peasants [...] Within eight days it was found necessary to second as many as twelve comrades to it due to its growth*)[2]

I was a member of the Madrid collective. We numbered about a thousand: half were men, many of them illiterate in that there were many war disabled and elderly among us, but they accomplished admirable work.

We started off with a farm given over to hunting in Elipa (east of Madrid), which was swapped for some uncultivated lands. The collective started up with a 15,000 peseta loan from the Regional Committee of the Centre (region), and by the end of the war there were upwards of 100 million pesetas in the coffers.

The collective had a number of rabbit and hen and chicken runs, with roughly the same number of livestock, which were classified according to breed.

These food animals were destined for those wounded at the front, for expectant mothers and new mothers. Not a single one of the collectivists ate eggs or chicken. Before one could enjoy supplementary rations, one had to have permission from a doctor, approved by the rationing agency's

---

1 Summary of a discussion with Manuel Armario in San Lucar de Barrameda, 18 July 1971.
2 *Colectividades de Castilla* (CNT-AIT, Madrid, undated, 1937?), p. 75.

medical inspection board. And, on occasion, from a second inspection agency. This was to avoid collectivists being able to favor or act on behalf of relations or friends.

Roque Provencio, a Murcian from Mula, was the founder and driving force behind the collective, due to his enterprise and amazing efforts, though he was illiterate. After twelve or fourteen hours' work he would fall asleep with his shotgun between his legs, ready to protect the produce from the forces of destruction.

This collective of a thousand workers operated with just three paid officers: the secretary, Roque Provencio; the bookkeeper (Salomón Vázquez?) and a typist who was essential, setting down whatever Roque Provencio dictated before the latter signed it off with a stamp.

The many foreign delegations that visited us marveled Roque Provencio's appearance and his rough and ready language, a world away from those of political leaders or businessmen. He was a rough diamond born of the revolution.

Work was done without any overseer since that post was abolished at the request of one of the collectivists.[3] Whenever the collective needed something, a money value was put on it and we bartered with another collective such as the one in Ocaña.

What became of the assets of the collective after Madrid fell to the Nationalists, I cannot say.

Thirty years on from the events of the time, it seems far-fetched that an illiterate could have accomplished such things. And even today all and sundry go on about the Spanish people's not being grown up enough for democracy. Look at me: crippled and all as I am, I would never have survived had I not had this urge to push myself.

---

3   Manuel Armario himself.

Appendix X
The Adra Fishermen's Collective[1]

In the monthly newspapers (*Nervio* and *El Rebelde*) published for a time by the Andalusian Regional, I wrote a number of articles dealing with the Adra Fishing Industry and, bereft though they may be of any literary merit, they might help you better understand the life of fisher-folk. So allow me to answer your questionnaire as best I can.

In August 1936, a meeting was held at the Capitol cinema in Adra. The meeting was attended by around 1,000 fishermen and a few ship-owners, and at it, they decided unanimously that all of the 'Traiñas' boats should be impounded and collectivised immediately.

The organisations represented at the meeting were the General Workers' Union/UGT and the National Confederation of Labor/CNT. The former accounted for about 10 percent of the fishing population and the remaining 90 percent belonged to the CNT, but it is worth noting that there was no difference or disagreement between the two trade union groupings as far as the launch of the collective and its *modus operandi* were concerned. Everyone was at liberty to quit the collectivised vessels or to join them, depending on demand—meaning that if a boat had need of twenty-five crew members and had only twenty-four, the first-comer could fill the vacancy.

Was there money? Yes, there was no way we could do without money, and both the Union and the Fishing Industry Committee, which had oversight of the industry as a whole, had to work cleverly to ensure that this revolutionary

---

1 A condensation of a conversation with Antonio Vargas in London, November 1970.

venture set in motion by the fishermen themselves did not prove a failure.

Each boat's catch was shared between the crewmembers after a small portion had been set aside for the Committee; the proceeds from the latter were used to replace worn or broken equipment. And another portion, with the fishermen's approval, made its way to the boat's former owner.

I don't remember any noteworthy problem cropping up between fishermen, and the only obstacles we ran into were that, on account of the war, we were short of the materials we needed to go fishing—the fishing was good at that time.

There were considerable improvements made across the board. The fisherman began to rediscover his dignity, as he was no longer a slave. Before the war, the skipper or boat-owner claimed 50 percent of the catch but three-fifths of the remainder. One of the greatest specters was the "seller", a man who, once the catch has been landed, auctions it off, for which "service" he claimed 12.5 percent of the overall sale price. We did away with all that sort of unfair practice. While the collective was in operation, the "seller" was paid 2.5 percent and that was more than enough for him. The collective was a great success in every regard, and this success was down to the dynamism and enthusiasm of all the young libertarians inspired by the ideas of anarcho-syndicalism. The times were upbeat and full of promise.

The collective only lasted until March 1937. The pro-communist Gabriel Morón Díaz, Almería's civil governor, was a socialist back then, but in Mexico he dropped the disguise and defected to the communists; he sent a note to the Assault Guard company stationed in Adra (capitalising on the fact that in the wake of the fall of Málaga most of the village had been evacuated) stating that the Adra Fishing Industry Union had been "wound up" and instructing that the boats should be immediately handed back to their former owners.

At the time, the 6th Mixed Brigade (made up of communists and commanded by a Major Luigi Gallo, today secretary of the Italian Communist Party) was in Adra. The most prominent of us comrades had to run out of there because they wanted to shoot us.

Later, as the situation returned somewhat to normal, we were able to rebuild the influence that the CNT had enjoyed, but most of the fishermen had by then been called up and sent to the front lines, and it proved impossible for us to get that great revolutionary and humane venture up and running again.

Appendix XI
The Artesa de Lérida Collective[1]

You are right in what you say: "To date we have not had in our circles an exposition and concrete presentation of how far self-management got in Spain". As an economic movement operating within a socialist economic arrangement we were breaking new ground in which we meant to lay the foundations of the structure we meant to erect. So there was no collectivist system, just experiments in collectivisation.

Here we (and not least myself) are going to have to acknowledge that when it comes to the facts that we try to recount, it should be remembered, as with everything that is handed down to posterity, that time draws a veil over it and increasingly erases a lot of interesting detail from our memories. If we could rehearse them with utter objectivity... We have to defer to the self-evident.

Take your first question concerning "the Artesa de Lérida Collective" and with regard to the Revolutionary Committee: it needs to made clear—so that there will be no confusion of any sort—that the Committee that took over from the Municipal Committee was the very first one formed in the earliest moments of the rebel uprising. The Municipal Council it replaced stood for the republican regime that was lawfully constituted in accordance with the outcome of the February 1936 elections. I say "Council" because in Catalonia the Municipal Council was the equivalent of what was referred to in other regions as the *Ayuntamiento*.

Let it be said in passing also, just to be clear about this, that in the very beginning of the people's victory over the

---

1   R. Oriol, interviewed in Roanne (France), 10 December 1966.

rebel onslaught, the people were on their own, in that they were on the streets, master of their own fate and without any representative authority, the government having abdicated the leadership. With no political, social or economic formation to assume the leadership, the people were master of themselves until Defense Committees and all manner of things began to be formed, incorporating representatives from all of the agencies that stood up to the uprising. So in Artesa, as in every other rural village, the first committee was made up of village people freely appointed by the village, and percentage representation only came in when an attempt was being made to bestow some legality upon the chaos that the rising had triggered.

Were you around when the collective was formed?

No. At the time the collective was set up I was away from the area (and my absence continues). The uprising caught me unawares in Barcelona; I was in discussion with the company I was working for about employment conditions, the workforce then out on strike. On 19 July, thinking that it was my duty to get back to Lérida, I searched for some a way to get back to the place I stayed overnight. I left for Lérida at daybreak the next day and was surprised to find that the fascists were in control. But when they were attacked they held out for only a few moments, then the soldiers handed over their guns and sided with the people.

Were there written statutes or just oral regulations?

The Artesa collective had written statutes, as did every other collective. The statutes were kept as simple as possible and, in many instances, mirrored agreements reached freely between people at meetings—and sometimes they were not all collectivists, those people. This was the case where there were CNT unions, since the confederation was the supervisor and consultant to the handiwork of revolution. The Lérida Provincial Secretary drew up a model statute that we might refer to as a standard document with just the name of the locality to be filled in. If, in the eyes of the interested parties, it fit the bill, supplementary articles in tune with people's expressed wishes could be tacked on.

And what was the ratio of collectivists and their families to the overall population?

Bear in mind that in Catalonia, in this instance Lérida, *minifundismo* (or tiny little smallholdings) were very widespread, so much so that very few farm labourers could get by on their day-to-day wages alone. There was a sizable number of the dispossessed and it is equally true that most worked independently on the family plot, resorting to share-cropping or sundry other arrangements depending on the area.

The collectivist experiment was made possible by the reactionaries' uprising, but that was not the whole story. The people jumped at the chance to implement that system, even though *minifundismo* neither involved nor recruited them to it.

Be that as it may, the percentage of collectivists in the area we are concerned with would have been somewhere between 20 percent and 25 percent, and as for the supporters of that system, in the early days they accounted for 50 percent to 60 percent of the populations; opponents and those who just did not care accounted for another 25 percent. We should add that, as the counter-revolution's tentacles spread, the barometer was falling, but there was still a good percentage who did not lose faith and retained their initial enthusiasm.

And what proportion of the active population locally was made up of the collectivists and their families?

There were about 6,000 people in the area, roughly 400 homesteads, and the proportion of collectivists with regard to the overall population would have been little different from the percentage mentioned in my previous answer.

And was there a retirement facility for the elderly, a school for the children? Was a library set up or, better yet, literacy classes or cultural activities on offer?

As to the first of those, no. There was no retirement. The elderly were completely free and, according to their preferences, threw themselves into secondary activities which, ultimately, were every bit as useful as any others. Their work consisted of picking the olives when the time came, and harvesting all the other fruit-bearing trees. I should point out that an elderly person is an artist at this sort of thing by dint of years of practice, since not only must one be able to cut back branches but one also has to know which ones should not be pruned so that the tree can grow and the productivity and quality of the crop improved. As to the other activities, they took on the easier and lighter tasks.

In regard to education, there was the municipal school just like before and, whilst it could scarcely be described as rationalist, the schoolmaster was required to use a rational teaching method.

Yes, a library was set up: my own private library, which I turned over to the union (the union and the collective were set up at the same time and were driven by the same spirit). Later, a sizable number of books were added as a result of voluntary donations, and these were all there to be used by anybody who was interested in reading.

I have an anecdote about the library that I just have to tell: On one occasion (in March 1937) a reactionary posing as a UGT member and acting at the instigation of the PSUC (Unified Socialist Party of Catalonia) and backed by the "Red Legion" stationed in the village incited the women to attack the CNT union. They burst on to the premises and tossed all of the books from the balcony and burned them. The only ones to survive the fire were *Man and the Earth* and *New World Geography* by Réclus and Zeraceda, respectively. They were the only literacy lessons the children of Artesa de Lérida ever received.

Now, coming to the economic side of things, after rattling off the names of a number of villages adjacent to Artesa de Lérida, you asked me if trade was particularly with these or if produce was sold off to the highest bidder village, whether it had a collective or not... You might suppose that, being connected by a shared outlook, trading relations were immune from any sort of preferential treatment, and on more than one occasion the provincial or county agency took a hand in trade deals. Assessed commercial value wasn't a factor in the pricing of produce exchanged between the collectives either. For instance, the Artesa de Lérida collective fell short in terms of wine production so it got in touch with another collective that had an abundance and they bartered freely with each other. So much wine traded for so much cereal produced as animal feed or for bread-making, and this arrangement was followed through with regard to all produce.

No, the collective was never at any time regarded as a profit-making venture so it was not interested in marketing its produce to the highest bidding villages or collectives. All of their hand-made, manufactured, natural or imported goods were distributed by the Supplies Department of the Home Rule government of Catalonia, which in turn, together with any nationally controlled products it had received from the central government, distributed them to the county Supplies departments (provinces having been done away with in Catalonia) and so on and so on until they reached the consumer. The difference was that non-collectivists carried on as they had in the past, making purchases from the shopkeeper and paying in hard cash, whereas collectivists turned to the cooperative—which was seen as the distribution agency—and simply handed over their collectivist family record book, jotting down the goods they selected or, in the case of foodstuffs, paying with cash or with collective coupons. Within the collective, state cash was done away with and was useless as an exchange currency.

As the fighting on the battlefronts intensified every day, and as fresh contingents of producers were called up for front-line service, output fell and enthusiasm, in the face of rising difficulties, died down. The atmosphere grew tenser, a situation that the opposition—be it Red or Black (and sometimes they were bedfellows)—exploited. Because of the situation, there was a growing need for tighter controls every day, and collectives found themselves obliged to pass their surplus produce on to the regional supplies agency.

And in theory, did trade between collectives have to be conducted by means of vouchers and without the use of money?

As I mentioned earlier collectivism was something of an experiment. In Catalonia there was no standard format based on federalism (a Federation of Farming Collectives was already up and running in other regions). So each collective took the measure of its production, its geographical location, its climate (that being a factor in the choice of an appropriate style of farming, whether tillage or livestock farming), as well as the customs and character of its inhabitants. With no geographical coordinating agency, each collective was an independent body that stuck to the principle of conducting its deals whilst dispensing with money as a means of exchange. Money was used only in those instances where nothing else would do: dealings with the market and so on.

In Artesa de Lérida, as in most of the collectives with which I had the opportunity to have any dealings, the basic precept was abolition of hard currency, to which end most collectives had printed up a special voucher. One could use these at the collective cooperative to buy the collective had not managed to procure through barter. Plainly this wouldn't have been necessary if this trial system had been adopted wholesale, since the value of products would have been measured in terms of labor and production values.

What sort of help was available from and for the Artesa de Lérida collective?

The Artesa de Lérida collective didn't need any help. The decision was made to launch a collective and work the lands that had been abandoned during the revolt, as well as the lands of smallholders who had agreed to work these in common. The collective found itself with its own natural means of sustenance because it was time to bring in the cereal harvest. Next up was the gathering in of other produce: forage plants, the grapes and the olives. The land was being readied for the upcoming crop, which should have outstripped its predecessor. As was the case in '38, even though the youngest and keenest collectivists had been called to battle.

Note that, properly directed and with the land broken up into areas of suitable cultivation in accordance with soil quality, working the land in common is more profitable.

True there were some collectives that needed help. Any help sought was delivered by the Regional Federation's committee rather than by any government agencies. The committee had access to funds handed over by the unions in the industry, which were meant for helping to boost collective farming. Delivery of the sum applied for, once the board of the collective had given its briefing, was made simply by handing over a receipt and no interest was ever levied.

The collectives and the go-it-aloners (*individualistas*) received agricultural fertilisers from the Generalidad Supplies Department rather than as aid, since the collectives and CNT personnel were overcharged by a percentage, which, at times, was in excess of 75 percent.

That sort of abuse, denounced by a number of collectives and CNT personnel, was verified by the Regional Federation during a tour it made of the region. They gathered a sizable number of invoices and receipts from every one of the four provinces, and on a county-by-county basis they authenticated the dirty tricks used against our comrades. After collecting all the data, a report was drafted and handed to the under-secretary for Agriculture of the central government and brought to a cabinet meeting.

The upshot was that once this irregularity had been proven, it was resolved by ministerial agreement—over the opposition coming from the communist ministers—that the Catalan confederation would be released from Generalidad controls, and figures would be compiled establishing how much land was held by the 94,000 CNT members on the land so as to work out how much fertiliser, fodder, seed, etc., they would require.

In Artesa de Lérida, was there (as elsewhere), a supposedly UGT union set up that was actually made up of collectivism's enemies for the specific purpose of combating collectivism?

I answered that question in the answer I gave regarding literacy classes, the library facility, etc. when I mentioned the burning of the union's books. Even those the people who engaged in that wrecking purported to be UGT personnel, within the Artesa de Lérida collective there actually was one UGT family, but they belonged to the Spanish UGT rather than the Catalan version.

And did the Líster Column sweep through there?

No. But we did have a visit from the "red Legion" of such foul memory as far as the residents of Artesa de Lérida are concerned. It's remembered the way the Líster Column was in Aragon, since they were both of the same persuasion.

And even though the collective was targeted by the reactionary element that was able to count on the backing of the Legion and were encouraged by it to destroy the work of the collective, the trade union and the collective carried on with their efforts right up until the arrival of the fascists.

Where did the hydraulic olive oil extraction plant, the thresher and farm tools come from? From seizures, purchases or donations by other collectives?

To be honest they were neither donated, bought nor impounded but were, instead, gathered up, having been abandoned by their owners. In Artesa there were four olive oil plants, about the same number of threshing machines and, by agreement with the majority in the area, the collective operated one hydraulic plant plus another where the olive oil clinging to the olive pulp was extracted using sulphuric acid.

How long did you serve as secretary of the Regional Peasant Federation in Catalonia? Between which dates?

There is no way I can be specific as to the dates. I remember I was appointed to represent the province of Lérida at the first regional congress held in September 1936, but, on account of my obligations in the province, I was not able to join the regional committee until June 1937. Once I had joined, it was agreed at a meeting that I should oversee the region's collectives and their implementation of the congress's accords. So I made it my business to create an index, a listing by order of economic importance, of the ones already up and running, up until November that year when I had to be co-opted on to the regional secretariat to replace the incumbent who had stepped down on account of his not being qualified, or so he said. I held the post of secretary of the Catalan Peasant Regional from November '37 through to November '38, at which point the Regional Federation of Farming, Livestock and Foodstuffs Industries was set up.

Do you happen to know if the statistical survey of May '37 was actually carried out?

Even though I was appointed at the regional plenum held in February '37 to represent the Catalan regional on the National Peasant Federation, I was unable to take up the post entrusted to me, due to regional organisational business and the upsets of the war. For which reason I can't provide an objective answer to your question.

What became of the archives of the collectives and peasant federations? Were they left behind or are they in Amsterdam among the general archives of the CNT and FAI?

I have no idea how the other regionals handled their documentation, whether at regional or national levels. In regards to Catalonia, following the establishment of the Regional Federation of the Sector and because the usual practice was to set up a fresh administration, the entire records of the first phase were separated and "triaged" as a way of reducing their bulk. We had no means of handling all that bulk, and nobody made it their business to safeguard it or to use whatever transport resources we had access to in order to evacuate our personnel lest they fall into fascist hands and to avert potential reprisals. So, within hours of the fascist troops entering the city, the records were completely destroyed.

Are you aware of other collectives in Lérida province besides Albaterreche, Albesa, Alcarraz, Alguaire, Bellpuig de Urgell, Castellsea, Granadella, Guimerá, Isona, Josa de Cadi, Llardecans, Mayals, Omells de Nogaya, Os de Balaguer, Peramola, Poal, Pobla de Ciérvoles, Seros, Tremp, Val'gorra and Verdú?

Yes, you can add these to your list: Lérida, Arbeca, Puigvert de Lérida, La Portella, Liñola, Solerás, Torres de Segre, Cerviá, Cervera, Montoliu de Lérida and Vinaixa.

Appendix XII
The Barbastro Comarcal Federation of Collectives[1]

Come the uprising and once the front lines had been established, collectives were promptly set up, but this was partly to do with the war. Due to the pressures and the climate of warfare, collectives popped up in virtually every village, but much more out of fear than out of conviction. Staunch belief in collectives was felt only by a minority, as in most things, but it is always a minority that is the fertile ground. The remainder is just a mass. And, of course, when the rebellion started collectives were set up everywhere, but many of these had to be dismantled because they failed to live up to the spirit and freely given consent a collective should manifest.

When you say 'many' are you thinking of the Barbastro comarca or are you speaking generally?

Pretty much Barbastro county, although there were other counties, such as Monzón. Huesca we can forget about: it was in the hands of the fascists, but there was the Angüés comarca [...]

Some people exploited the collectives. There were some smallholders who joined the collective, but if they caught on that the wine crop was going to be good that year and that there was money to be made, they pulled whatever little plots [of land] they had out of the collective. Once the wine had been pressed, they would drop back in again.

---

1 Interviews with Eugenio Sopena in Chevry-Cossigny, June and December 1976.

Obviously we caught on to this. As in all things, a collective is a practical thing and only on-the-job learning and practice can dictate what course to take and how to go about things. Improvement comes with practice, like any trade. When you first pick up a tool you have no idea how to handle it, but practice makes perfect. And therein lies our secret; our view is that the world should taste a time of freedom and during this period of freedom there has to be freedom of experimentation in work and in life. Only practice will prove you right. Practice will tell you what works, and what doesn't and should be discarded. It's through living and doing that one discovers the route to a better life.

For instance, we have set ourselves a target: libertarian communism. The CNT is out for libertarian communism, but let's suppose that in Spain we were to say, right, as of today, let's have libertarian communism. You'd have to take everyone by the hand and tell each how to go about things. So it would be an imposed system. Now libertarian communism is freedom exercised through free politics, and communism means that everything in the air, the earth, and the land belongs to everyone and to no one. Nobody has the right to exploit it, but everybody does. That is libertarian communism and that is why we are against politics when politicians say: "Oh, we've got a program, let's go into government". And when they get into government it transpires then that the government can do nothing because, economically, as is the case in Spain, there is a flight of capital [...]

What changes or improvements were there in terms of purchasing or expanding the area under cultivation?

Well, in Barbastro, for instance, there was one tract that was all little market gardens and there was one large tract made up of private allotments. Now 25 percent of the land was going to waste—a path here, a road there, and the collective had the machinery to cultivate it, so they did and turned the whole thing into a field. At which point, they planted sugar beet—as there was a facility to process it up in Monzón. And the comarcal [federation] bought three or four reaping machines for the wheat, and then the wheat was dried out (which was better done on the hillsides rather than on the flat) at intervals of a day or so between one village and another. Obviously, the machinery would be deployed to whichever village in the county had its wheat ready for harvesting and the crop would be gathered in and the machinery would move on to the next village, and the next and so on. Meaning that it served the entire county.

We had a plan to link all of the villages in the county by telephone but we never managed to do it. We were in touch with the comrades from the phone service who drew us up a plan and a budget because we wanted to install phones in every village. One village might, say, run into trouble and, because they didn't have a phone, they'd arrive by bicycle or on foot (there were no cars in those days). And we wanted to introduce this benefit. We never managed to pull it off but we had plans to do so. Obviously account had to be taken of the circumstances in which the collectives were operating. The youngsters were away at the front, and most of the work fell to the elderly. In spite of that output grew—grew across the board.

There was one year, for instance, when Barbastro had a bumper crop of olives. Obviously there is a lot of manual labor involved in picking olives. With no young people around, we rounded up the daughters of the rich folks who didn't work because they had enough money to live on. Outside the collective everything was in short supply because there was no trading, so many turned to the collective because at least that way they could be fed. So, they had money, yet couldn't eat [...]

As I mentioned earlier, trying to transform society in forty-eight hours is laughable, pointless, a pipe-dream. The only way to transform society is to transform it as you go, through trial and error and over time. Not by force, because force achieves nothing. We knew what they had done to us: the more they persecuted us, the more they tossed us into their jails, the more the people sympathised with us and worked with us. There was a great warmth shown towards me in Barbastro. How come? Because I have been thrown in jail five times. Why were they locking me up? People came up with this analysis, this conjecture, this idea: the more an idea is persecuted, the more one harasses somebody, the greater significance and importance you are investing them with. Which is why I contend that we're against all oppression and the use of any force to implement anything at all.

And during your term in charge of the collectives, what problems cropped up between collectives or collectivists?

I remember one village that wound up its collective three or four times. El Grado. (It may be gone now, swallowed up by a dam that has been built. I'm not sure.)

And there in El Grado, what was the root of the problem? Was it down to personalities?

Personal issues, personality clashes. Some people did not feel comfortable in the collective. Others, for example, had a son away at the front and, because he was at the front, got a wage—a source of income. So at best, father and son might join the collective and then the son would leave and naturally the father had to be pulled out of a hole; he received on the son's behalf, the son being at the front and in receipt of his pay. In practice, various shortcomings and minor matters and certain impositions were all brought to light [...] We had been born into an authoritarian arrangement and even though we professed to be libertarians, we retain certain prejudices as a legacy from our surroundings. The real libertarians will be the ones born into freedom, where there is no glimmer of tyranny and no trace of authority, because it is pretty much the case that everyone who is born, even should he claim to be free, carries certain prejudices inherited from the society around him—from the money system and so on.

Just on this point of money, was everything there organised without money or did it become necessary to reintroduce it at some point?

Yes, there was a collective where money was not used inside the village, inside the collective. The committee or council (which amounts to the same thing) did have money and it handled trade with the outside world. Doctors were paid in cash, for example, though if necessary a patient would be taken in at the hospital free of charge. This was the doctor helping the war effort. Meaning that it was all the same whether he was helping a serviceman or a civilian. And if, for example, some collectivist needed to venture outside, to Catalonia, say, or somewhere else (not having a car, he had to travel by train) it was the committee that gave him the cash to pay for whatever it was he needed to do.

There were other collectives where everything was distributed on the basis of the family card. But the old folks were used to toddling along to the café for a cup of coffee or a litre of wine or a game of cards. This was their custom. There was one old guy and if you'd tell him: We're going back to the drawing board. He'd answer: "Well, this is what I'm used to", meaning that he was happy with the way things were. So they were allowed a little cash to indulge their vices.

But this varied from village to village?

Within the same comarca and within the collectives themselves. There was a Federation of collectives, but, within this, the members of the collective had met in a general assembly and had freely chosen their own arrangements.

On the other hand, there were other collectives that even managed to get hold of a truck. Some villages were richer than others; some made a living from wheat, and others that lived off olive oil and wine and they had more assets. For instance, in a wine-growing village, a cold snap might cost them their crop and they had to survive a whole year until the next one. But of course, should anyone lack for anything, the county was there, because the county was a depot and we kept accounts: each collective had an account opened and when it came to provisions we shared things out. For instance, we kept records of how many smokers there were in each collective and we dispensed the tobacco accordingly. And this was applied to everything. If some village's crop had failed and it was not in a position to pay, and could not put in anything for what it had consumed, it could carry on on the basis of whatever the comarca was supplying. And then later, once it had the wherewithal to repay, it did so, though it did not have to, because this did not matter as long as it was part of the greater whole. So in each locality the profits were disposed of by a local federation. But at county (comarcal) level, there was no way that any village would be allowed to go to the wall, unable to eat and unable to work just because it did not have the assets.

Meaning that mutual aid applied as much between one collectivist and another as between one collective and another?

And as I say there were one or two collectives that had trucks—one in the village of Naval. There, the soil produced salt, and because they had a truck, they were able to ship quite a bit of salt to Catalonia. There was a trading, a bartering connection that left that truck free to go out and pick stuff up and make sales. It was linked to other collectives, factories and local federations; that truck served more than just the county. There were two villages that had trucks: Naval and Salas Altas.

At the anecdotal level, Gaston Leval must at some point have passed through. Did you see him? Or maybe Augustín Souchy, who was definitely in Barbastro?

My daughter has a book by Gaston Leval and she maintains that I was the one who gave it to her. He called to the county and was told how many collectives it had, the approximate number of collectivists, everything in short. Prior to the revolution, I knew Leval because he wrote one or two books that caught my interest because he dealt with matters of the economy. So when he came to Barbastro, he passed through the county and I gave him all of the details because I had even drawn up a map, showing the location of each village and everything, even the roads. I had a folder and the very first thing I did after the revolt started was to keep records of everything that each village had—hens, pigs, the necessities of life—things of economic interest. I knew the economic resources available to each village and county [...]

What happened in Barbastro when Líster disbanded the Council of Aragon?

Líster did not pass our way. It was a different unit that arrived in Barbastro. And they set about breaking up the collectives. We had a rich man's home that had been abandoned by the owner and it was in use as CNT offices. They stormed it. [The comrade himself was away in Barcelona at the start of the events of May 1937.]

Luckily we put up no resistance. Had we put up a fight, I don't know what would have happened. Because there were three CNT divisions on the Huesca front and if we had kicked off and if there had been a clash between those of us, the defenders of the building used by the CNT and the government troops attacking it, then the balloon definitely would have gone up the way it did in Catalonia. But as I realised when the ceasefire call and the calls for calm reached us from Madrid and Catalonia, the priority was winning the war. Of course, later, when troops arrived in Barbastro to dismantle the collectives and attack CNT homes, well, I was one of the first to say that we should offer no resistance. We had a lot of young folk, and they all had guns. Some were at the front and they would drop back into Barbastro two or three times for a fortnight's leave with family. So they had guns. We never fired a single shot. Quite the opposite. I went down and there was a doorkeeper and I told him: Open the door. And he did and since I was standing there with the doorkeeper, the first on the scene, one Assault Guard called me a *"sonofabitch"* and gave me a shove.

They rounded us all up and took us to jail. There was no fighting. Now this is a very telling point: I had seen the inside of prison five times during the Republic [...] And I remember this gent, this Assault Guard who had called me a *"sonofa..."*, implying that I was a fascist. Me? A fascist? When I'd stood up in the fight against fascism prior to the revolution? I had to hold my tongue because in the event of any back-chat, revolvers might have come into play and that would have been worse for us than for him. They make their living that way, whereas we don't believe losing a building is worth losing a life over.

So how did it turn out? Because many claim that collectives were formed after that...

They threw us into jail and we spent three months there [...] At the end of those three months they let us all out, having realised that things were not working without us. Barbastro suffered an air raid at around this time, and it was volunteers and carts from our collectives that ventured out to collect most of the dead. After the air raid there was nobody in charge; everybody had gone into hiding and, yet, even though we were still behind bars, it was our comrades who ventured out to collect all the dead. At that point, the UGT personnel and the communists realised that they needed us and that without us nothing could be accomplished.

While you officials were in jail, did the collectives just carry on?

Yes. In some villages they disbanded but they were later resurrected because they could not get equipment. In Barbastro, there was a ploy I used to use: There were one or two villages where the communists were in the ascendancy. In Aragon they weren't, but in a village or two in our county, they were.

Take the village of Estadilla. Whenever we set up the county [federation] we appealed to all and sundry and said: Look, we are all collectivists, not communists nor CNT people. We are all collectivists here and working as a collective. Our only interest is in the collective and there should be free agreement when it comes to barter and trading relations.

And of course this worked in our favor because even those in the communist collective were against our having been jailed.

But the collectives did survive?

They did. Most of them carried on at pretty much the same scale, but survive they did.

And where there were communists, as in Estadilla, did that collective carry on too?

It did. Take it from me, at the time the war was lost in Aragon, the collectives were still—all but two or three of them—up and running.

That's what I was getting at. So far I have only come across six or seven cases and I have always had my doubts as to it's maybe just being 'spin' as to their reforming or whether there were just those seven instances and no more.

What you've just said reminded me of something. Binéfar started to organise its own union the way Barbastro had. It had a strong union, sound militants. But during the time of the collectives they made a certain mistake and there was a number of authoritarian-style impositions carried out by our side. When the communist troops from Catalonia swept through, well the militants, and a number of collectivists as well, were given the boot [...]

So the Binéfar guys escaped and fled to Barbastro. We had to keep them under wraps because they were on the wanted list and they were CNT people like ourselves. This is by way of explanation, because when I found out that the collective in one village was not working smoothly, I had no option but to wind it up and start it up again. If there were one or three or four people who wanted to pull out of it, they could do so. Because, as I said to them, whenever a beetle wants to damage a plant, he does it from the inside out, gnawing at it and gobbling it up. That kills the plant. Anybody on the inside of a collective who does not have a collectivist consciousness is simply doing harm.

Outsiders do not scare us, because whenever people from the political parties were criticising the collectives, I said to them: So why don't you set up a collective of your own? And if yours proves to be an improvement on ours, show me with hard evidence what a collective ought to be. It's all well and good criticising something. Anybody can do that even if he's incapable of doing anything himself.

Let's say at one of these free assemblies within a collective, folks began to criticise some CNT comrade. How did you respond to that?

I did not sit in judgment of individuals. It was for the members of the same collective to pass judgment on persons and their actions. Whenever a problem that upset the balance cropped up or when a collective needed dismantling, then I would intervene in the argument about what this side or the other was saying, and I would make my own argument, about which there was no quibbling because I was not on alone. A committee of us would go, and then there'd be the villagers themselves who were every bit as able as I was, because I was the only one there from the county committee. Transport issues were handled by Celles, agricultural affairs by Ponzán, and Lagunarrota looked after the economic side of things.

At the February 1937 congress in Caspe, the Barbastro county federation was recorded as comprising 31 collectives and 7,963 members, 113 of these in Barbastro itself. Did those figures count only the heads of household or was every single family member also included?

The 113 in Barbastro were heads of household. Heads of household, I am sure of it. But as for Peralta, the figure covers every single family member.

And the clamp-down on prostitution?

That is a fact but it was decided with the agreement of all sides. It was a big problem with the militians returning from the frontlines but they had to look further afield. The prostitutes were reintegrated into everyday life as cooks, seamstresses and so on.

Appendix XIII
UGT CNT CLUEA. Citrus Fruit Exports from Revolutionary Spain, 1936–1937[1]

Why choose the CLUEA [*Comite Levantino Unificado de Exportación de Agríos*/Unified Levante Farm Produce Exports Committee] out of the hundreds of collectives available?

The CLUEA had a remit broader than county level. It was a creature of the CNT and UGT and dealt with a significant segment of the foreign export trade in farm produce. And it had to deal, on a broad scale, with a range of short term economic problems[2] and other issues that I shall outline anon.

Across virtually the entirety of republican Spain, the threat of a coup was over by 20 or 21 July 1936, but in Valencia the threat was not banished until 31 July. Come August, there were glimmers of opportunities for working partnership with other groups. Thus, at a Plenum of County (comarcal) and Local Federations of the Levante Regional Confederation [held for the purpose of drafting a resolution on the Confederation and government for the forthcoming Plenum of Regionals] a number of grounds for misgivings were publicly articulated:

---

1 Published in *Libre Pensamiento*, 2008.
2 In normal circumstances, Palestinian, South African and North African oranges, bought up by England and France respectively, represented a threat to Spain in terms of the Spanish market. For these reasons sales figures gradually shrank and orange production (in thousands of metric quintals) fell in 1930: 11,963; in 1931: 12,042; in 1932: 11,710; in 1933: 9,672; and in 1934: 9,098. Germany took a significant fraction of the crop, with consumers displaying a preference for unripened fruit.

[Alcoy] Urges that we continue to bear in mind the need to maintain unity with the UGT and that, once we have defeated fascism, we set about pursuing our aspirations in concert with the UGT, if it will go along with us, and, if not, plough our own furrow.

[Resolution] There are grounds aplenty showing it's mistaken to believe that our participation in the governance of public affairs should necessarily degenerate into conventional politics [...] States that we should be organising our own forces, since we cannot rely on any other sector, in that they are all bent on undermining our might and effectiveness in every sphere.[3]

Beginning on 3 September, Ezequiel, a correspondent very well briefed on farm exports, published a report on the problems facing those exports, "Realities of the Times. Forging a Trade Union Economy. Facing into the New Harvest". Just ahead of the "Regional Congress of the Peasants of Levante" on 18, 19 and 20 September, Ezequiel published "Know this, Farm-workers. That Only a Concerted Approach Will Resolve the Orange Problem": "In recent years the value of orange production has been reckoned at 180 million pesetas in gold, and since it so happens that 90 percent of that production is sold abroad, this issue raises difficulties that determination or a range of isolated wills can never overcome, and it would be greatly deplored if, as a result of some unwholesome mania for self-sufficiency we were to sound the death knell for the forthcoming orange crop".[4]

The peasant congress grappled with the fourth item on its agenda: "How to organise exports of farm produce". The minutes reflect strong opposition to the Exporters' Union—a striking example of class frictions between

---

3   *Fragua Social*, 15 September 1936, p. 2.
4   *Fragua Social*, 17 September 1936, p. 15.

peasant and technician, even should they both belong to the CNT—with Sueca and Puerto Sagunto [delegations] suggesting that the exports be handled by "External Relations Committees" or by the "County and Regional" village unions. The delegate from Alfara was more incisive: "let the Exporters' Union be wound up and its members join the peasant unions and set up technical branches". [The delegate from] Alcocer argued that such a union would constitute "a bureaucratic body".

Burriana pressed for "the formation of a Peasant Export Branch" and for the Exporters' Union to be "monitored by trusted delegates from the Peasant Union".[5]

On the final day of the peasant congress, the 20 September 1936 edition of *Fragua Social* reported on the item dealing with exports of farm produce, and on the very same page Ezequiel declared: "Be aware, farm workers, of the importance of orange exports at present [...] If we can administer this colossal resource rationally [...] Yes, let's trade surplus goods in one village for what is lacking in another; but the fact is that, chiefly in Valencia and Castellón, oranges are enormously plentiful in every village and there is a surplus far in excess of the villages' consumer demands [...] *Editor's note*: Respectful of the views of contributors, especially when they are prompted by wholesome intentions, the editors welcome the thoughts of the author of this piece, notwithstanding his tendency to regard as pernicious the trading arrangements at issue at the regional peasant plenum currently meeting [...] Even if only as a polemical piece, may it bring ever useful clarity to these matters and we have no hesitation in printing it, in the hope that it will command the approval of all".[6]

At the end of September, the Valencia Regional Council of Economy was launched. In the 7 October 1936 edition

---

5 *Congreso regional de campesinos de Levante, Valencia, septiembre 1936*, pp. 13–15 (with a slicker version repeated on pp. 23–25).

6 *Fragua Social*, 20 September 1936, p. 7.

of *Fragua Social*, Ezequiel was still laboring his point, and on the same page it was stated: "In light of the forthcoming orange harvest, an interesting note from the CNT-AIT *Sindicato Único* in Burriana to which the Valencia Regional *Sindicato Único* of Fruit Export Workers is affiliated, placing it on record that the government representative was lobbied to this same effect and, on Sunday 28 [September], traveled to Valencia to brief the two CNT and UGT unions. This Regional *Sindicato Único*, for almost the past month, has been pressing for amalgamation of the UGT and CNT for the purpose of handling exports of farm produce, particularly oranges, and states that it is most sympathetic to Burriana's position, urging the UGT to let us have, as quickly as it may, a clear response to our overtures".[7]

And in fact, on 7 October the two trade union associations [UGT and CNT] met to lay the groundwork for the future CLUEA. Even as the technical preparations were being made, the government dragged its feet, not publishing notification of the lawful constitution of the CLUEA in its *Gaceta Oficial*.[8] The CLUEA was able to work with and make progress with regard to the export department because each union and village approved shipments at local level. This was a nonsensical state of airs but only to be expected, given the republican politics of the time, whereby the CNT held the Ministry of Trade but the CP held the Ministry of Agriculture, and the frictions between them were hampering the efforts made at grassroots levels.

An expert on Valencian rural affairs, Aurora Bosch, pointed out: "Yet, these were not the only obstacles in the way of the CLUEA during its first year of life. Lukewarm government backing for an export agency under trade union control, and the Communist Party's and Regional Peasant

---

7   *Fragua Social*, 7 October 1936, p. 10.
8   *Fragua Social*, "The formidable efforts CLUEA is making in the rearguard", p. 11.

Federation's[9] determined opposition were overwhelming factors".[10]

Furthermore, the European market was hit by a glut of produce. Pedro García, secretary of the UGT-affiliated FETT (*Federación Española de Trabajadores de la Tierra*/Spanish Farmworkers' Federation) in Valencia set out his perspective in *La Voz del CLUEA*, No 6, 9 February 1937): "As a result of all of this, my view is that it would be appropriate to cut back on the area under plantation and do away with those orchards that are, on the one hand, in decline, and, on the other, acting appropriately with all those naturally irrigated areas susceptible to frost. In this way we would have land to set aside for other crops". (Aurora Bosch, op. cit., p. 67)

All in all it seems that, in terms of foreign currency earnings, the citrus crop brought it somewhere between a half and two-thirds of the preceding crop—"thanks" to republican and communist sabotage efforts.

The CLUEA experiment straddles two historical periods: the peculiar context of 1936–1939 and the subsequent period, which suggests a distancing from and an interest in the venture per se.

Obviously, under revolutionary self-management, lots of difficulties arose, the crucial ones being the torpedoes fired by other republican factions and the glut in the European marketplace. But despite these impediments, the CLUEA spearheaded the export drive in 1936–1937 and part of 1937–1938, with tremendous commitment at the grassroots.

Examining the CLUEA from today's vantage point brings to light the deep-seated nature of its problems, which were down to differing ideological factions, with each trade union central feeling that it could manage without the other. And

---

9   A body launched in October 1936, largely on the basis of affiliation by the Catholic Farming Unions, followers of the right. See Aurora Bosch, *Colectivistas (1936–1939)* (Valencia 1980), p. x.

10 Aurora Bosch, *Colectivistas*, op. cit., p. xix.

within the same trade union central, the frictions between manual laborers and intellectuals played a considerable role. The likelihood is that tensions of that sort might be hard to overcome even today.

More serious, as I see it, is the fact that any practical grasp of economic urgency of the times evaporated in the face of capricious attempts to conjure up grassroots agencies that threatened to proliferate rather than amalgamate. Expertise in self-management is not, by itself, enough: solidarity and analytical ability are also needed. In this regard *Fragua Social* played an essential role. Debate was crucial if they were to keep their heads. And in every local unit there were manifold problems that went unresolved as a result of the uncertainty of the overall climate.[11] In the absence of some external stimulus, a collective endeavor develops by fits and starts in a lack-lustre manner.

---

11 "It is always during such times of spiritual revival—as natural to societies as to individuals—that the spring-tide of enthusiasm sweeps humanity onwards. We do not wish to exaggerate the part played by such noble passions, nor is it upon them that we would found our ideal of society. But we are not asking too much if we expect their aid in riding over the first and most difficult moments. We cannot hope that our daily life will be continuously inspired by such exalted enthusiasms, but we may expect their aid at the first, and that is all we need". Peter Kropotkin, *The Conquest of Bread* (op. cit., London 1985, p. 99).

Appendix XIV
The Establishment, Growth and Operation of the Barcelona and District Locksmiths' and Corrugated Shutters Collective[1]

With the fascist uprising snuffed out in Barcelona, the locksmith comrades[2] agreed at a gathering of militants to found a collective.[3] The locksmiths' branch did not have the money to pay the workers who were to be deployed on the building or revamping of workshops and who would later make up the collective.

---

1   Ramón Safón (senior) interviewed in Massy in December 1975, as published in the review *Cenit* in 2003.
2   The Barcelona and district locksmiths' section was affiliated to the CNT and had 1,400 members. The UGT would have had another twenty (no section appears under that name in the figures for the Zaragoza congress in May 1936). Previously there had been locksmiths' trades unions, which joined the CNT in 1919. *Treintismo* cut no ice with them. There were problems with the communists who had been capturing offices. The resolution was passed that no CNT member with any political affiliation could hold office. Two office-holders among the locksmiths were stood down.
3   Ramón Safón: "I wasn't around when the idea was mooted of collectivising and summoning a meeting. I was working on the armour-plating of cars and trucks. I was working 54 straight hours because there were no replacements available at the Torres Company. It was there that the very first armoured truck, King Kong, was manufactured, with its three machine-gun turrets. The driver was the owner of the truck and they both headed off to the Aragon front".

To this end it was agreed that branch members would pay a weekly levy of two pesetas. On 19 July 1936, the veteran membership of the branch vanished entirely, or at any rate a fair proportion of it. After the rebellion was snuffed out in Barcelona, those members had enlisted either for front-line service or for positions of responsibility on the councils of the arms plants such as the Labora works, which took on many of them,[4] or else they joined the Generalitat of Catalonia's economic councils. As we shall see anon, the part that these comrades played was very important for the collective, because of the positions they held.

One comrade [Ramón Safón], a specialist in the armor-plating of cars and trucks at the Construcciones Torras workshops, in the Pueblo Nuevo district, was commissioned to take charge of the building—or refurbishment—of the collective workshops.

The comrade in question could not walk away from his armor work because there were not enough workers to make up the three eight-hour shifts on the most pressing tasks such as the county's defenses.

As soon as they were able to organise the shifts, the comrade signed up for the 8.00 p.m. to 4.00 a.m. shift so that, together with an engineer, he could direct and oversee the work of the very first collective workshop.

That workshop, known as Workshop No. 1, was at 76 Calle Sepúlveda. It was a huge hangar belonging to a clothing manufacturer with factories in the town of Tarrasa, and offices in the Rondas de la Universidad. The hangar was taken over and we settled in there, the owner having fled the country.

---

4 Ramón Safón: "From my class onwards (class of 1934) everybody was drafted. The only ones left behind were those vital to the continuation of work. Older locksmiths took over the posts in management and in the war workshops. At the Labora workshops, the director was a locksmith. And the metalworkers' secretary, Serra, was a locksmith".

Now we had our hangar, statutes to operate by and an administrative council made up of comrades of good will, but we had no tools. The comrade in charge of the work had a meeting with comrade Bayarra, the delegate-general from the Labora workshops (where all of the tools from the requisitioned equipment stores ended up). This comrade was a militant from the locksmiths' and corrugated shutters branch.

It was spelled out that we didn't have the machinery and the gear to get Workshop No. 1 up and running: "Grab a bit of chalk and come with me", he said. I followed him to a hangar holding all manner of tools. "Mark off anything needed to get Workshop No. 1 running as soon as possible".

Everything I marked off was at the Calle Sepúlveda premises the next day, and set-up was carried out very quickly since there were lots of comrades there as volunteers, coming to lend a hand after working hours in their own shops. And one fine day, at nine o'clock in the morning, the first collective engine started up. This was a matter of great satisfaction to us as it seemed that the whole problem was being sorted out.

Twenty workers, the most skilled workers in the trade, were commandeered and transferred to Workshop No. 1, and the Construction and Woodworkers' Unions, being the ones most closely associated with ours, were briefed.

The raw materials were under state control and the state was only supplying the war industries, but the branch had comrades everywhere and that problem was solved.

What later became the central offices were set up in one of the Workshop No. 1 premises. It was from there that all of the collective's efforts were overseen, and from there that all of the rules to abide by—budgets, plans and blueprints for the various workshops—issued. That decision was made by the board of the union branch, which functioned as a collective administration. The comrade in charge of Workshop No. 1 was drafted in and appointed delegate-general of the entire collective. This comrade's mission? To check out all of the workshops in Barcelona that might be collectivized, those that boasted good hygiene and lighting conditions, and that might, with a little work, be knocked into shape. He was also to supply material to the collectives; to see to it that the workers and employers alike wanted to collectivise; to keep in touch with all the unions so that all tasks might be steered in the way of the collective; to run down collectivised workshops that did not meet the specifications and to expand those workshops with the capacity for expansion.

Lots of employers, looking to the law passed by the Generalitat of Catalonia regarding collectivisation, refused to collectivise: this was sorted out by withholding work from them and forcing them to cough up their workers' wages. Within a few days, all of the workshops had been collectivised. If the collectivised workshop was in good condition and the location good, then the necessary repairs were carried out and the workforce increased if it could accommodate them. The running of this workshop was handed over immediately to the general office and a workshop delegate appointed at a gathering of the entire workshop. On the other hand, if it was not up to scratch, then the workers would go to the workshop nearest their homes to work and the employer was sent to the central office... assuming that he wanted to work and was capable of it! One way or another he was not left to his own devices and he earned the same as the workers. The workshop was stripped and anything useful removed to Workshop No. 21 in the Sants district.

Now to the details of Workshop No. 21: As will be appreciated, between Workshop No. 1 and Workshop No. 21, there were nineteen collectivised workshops in good order, some inherently so, others having been refurbished by the collective.

But before that, I want to highlight one detail, believing it to be of interest: the Barcelona CNT's locksmiths' branch controlled most of the locksmiths, about 95 percent anyway, but as it happens, in one of the workshops due to be collectivised, there were workers affiliated to the UGT, and that body was not keen on collectivisation. A meeting of the boards of both unions was called to sort out this matter. After some regular meetings, it was agreed that, in the workshop where the CNT was in the majority, the UGT would withdraw its members, and vice versa, but each worker was left free to switch organisations.

Back to Workshop No. 21. I cannot, today, be specific as to the size in square metres. All that I can say is that it occupied an entire block, with doors opening on to four streets. It had previously been used as a reinforced concrete factory, but had been out of operation for quite a few years. The only premises it had occupied were the ground floor, the offices and the apartment, occupied by the concierge who was still there and who was still there even after we pulled out. The remainder of the space was open ground. This workshop was initiated up with the idea of starting up a factory making ironmongery and with a capacity for 500 workers.

The factory was launched thanks to the determination and efforts of all the male and female comrades from the branch, and many a Saturday and Sunday morning we didn't know where to post so many staff, none of whom were being paid for the over-time. During the week, the bricklayers set everything up for the Saturday and Sunday, and in next to no time we had four hangars measuring forty metres by twelve. Once it was ready, the machinery was installed and production could begin. By the time we pulled out of the place, there were 125 workers of both sexes working there. There was the presses section, the lathe section, the crucible section, the nickel-plating section, the mounting section, the casting section, the machine repair shop, the shop that made tubing for the corrugated shutters and a warehouse for raw materials.

Workshop No. 21 was equipped with a kitchen, canteen, cloakroom, showers, washhand basins and toilet facilities. Every section had its production delegate, who was appointed at a factory meeting. All the delegates met on a weekly basis after work hours, and these weekly meetings were also attended by the collective's delegate-general, who could speak and vote. A delegate from the collective's administrative section also had to attend. A record was kept in triplicate; one copy for the steering council, one for the factory floor and another for the metalworkers' union. The administration of the factory was handled by central office, from where manufacturing orders emanated, and the factory offices (where just two comrades worked) would pass these on to the delegate from the appropriate section. The task of the two office comrades was to monitor the raw materials coming in and the manufactured goods produced, and to monitor the comings and goings of the workforce.

I cannot remember the statutes governing the collective in every detail, but I can point out that every collectivist was covered against sickness, operations, all orthopedic equipment, eye tests and dental work over the entire week. Pregnant women were entitled to three months' holiday prior to the birth and to three months after it, if a doctor was involved. This was all covered, as were the wages.

Every collectivist worked a forty-four-hour week for 95 pesetas a week and that was the same for women, office workers, delegates, council members and engineers. This was one collective that was never under State control or under any government agency, but following the May Events, life was made difficult for it, since communist control was growing tighter and tighter. But they never shut us down entirely. For that reason, many comrades left to work in the war industries, because such workers had ration books and were mobilised for work.

The Barcelona and district jobbing locksmiths' and corrugated shutter-makers' collective was organised by the locksmiths' branch of the Barcelona CNT's metalworkers' union. The same trade union board, or steering council, represented both the collective's interests and the trade union's interests, since it was the trade union council appointed by the assembled workforce.

The militants of the branch met with the council and, after quite a stormy meeting, it was agreed that the council should make up its mind if it was an administrative council or a trade union council. We advocated for administrative and tabled our resignations from the union council at a general meeting.

Next, that same meeting had to amend the format of the trade union council, for, whilst all the workforce were collectivists, the council was not going to have to handle the same problems as it had when faced with the bosses! There was quite a bit of debate, and in the end the matter was raised before a meeting of the branch's militants, complete with a delegation from the metalworkers' union, since this was a general issue.

At the meeting of militants it was agreed (in principle) to appoint two trade union delegates invested with the powers of the union council until the first trade union plenum, since this was a general organisational matter. The delegate-general of the collectivised workshops was then appointed acting trade union delegate.

Appendix XV
Marx, Engels, the CP, Councilism, Historians and Revolutionary Spain

In recent Spanish history, anarchism has been at the heart of nearly all social agitation, so much so that all leftwing organisations and political parties can trace their roots to it.

Following the breakaway by the Bakuninist Alliance in 1872 and the departure of the Marxists, Pablo Iglesias and his supporters launched the *Partido Socialista Obrero Español*/Spanish Socialist Workers' Party (PSOE) and, after an initial venture into trade union organising, the *Unión General de Trabajadores*/General Workers' Union (UGT).

In Spain, in the wake of the Russian revolution, there were violent disagreements between libertarian trade unionists (the term anarcho-syndicalism only becoming popular towards the end of the 1920s) and Marxist personnel. Nin and Maurín left the CNT to join with some others to form the Communist Party. After they were expelled from the CP, these same militants went on to set up a number of groups that eventually coalesced as the *Partido Obrero de Unificación Marxista*/Workers' Party of Marxist Unification (POUM) in 1935, with an eye to the 1936 elections.

We've already sorted out the phoney problem of the supposed 'difference' of the size and scale of the anarchist presence within the Spanish trade union movement, by highlighting the libertarian presence in the late-nineteenth and early-twentieth centuries in virtually every large industrial nation, and the crackdown on anarchists mounted by capitalists and Leninists.

Most of the current Marxist interpretations base themselves on Spain's being 'different', singular, and so on, and, what with anarchism being an 'extravagant' movement, well, it was only natural that it should have been strong in Spain.

Yet Karl Marx's interpretation back in 1856 was rather different:

> Spain's middle classes are finding themselves obliged to realise that they have only two courses; either to submit to a political authority that they despise and abjure the benefits of modern industry and trade and the social relations founded upon these, or to sacrifice the privileges that modern organisation of society's productive forces, in their initial phase, have afforded to just one class. It is as impressive as it is unexpected that this should be a lesson taught in Spain also.[1]

And there was more to gratify Marx as well:

> The forthcoming European revolution will find Spain ripe for collaborating with it. The years 1854 to 1856 have been a transitional phase through which she had to pass in order to reach such maturity.[2]

The inroads made in 1868—thanks to a relative liberalisation in politics—by the ideas of the First International bore out Marx's view, which was also shared by Bakunin. Furthermore, Spain turned out to be the most powerful section of the International Working Men's Association, with 40,000 members in June 1870; 25,000 in December 1872, in the immediate wake of a period under ban; and 50,000 by 1873.

Now the spectacular growth of the Spanish workers' movement—workers and peasants alike—was achieved almost exclusively as a result of anarchist counsel. There was

---

[1] *La Revolución Española* (Moscow, undated), p. 150.
[2] Ibid., p. 157.

an attempt to organise the Marxists under the supervision of Marx's own son-in-law, Paul Lafargue—who had fled to Spain as a Parisian Communard refugee and who was particularly well equipped for the task, having a grasp of Spanish as he had been born in Cuba. Lafargue's efforts were a real demolition effort in that he published the names of leading militants of the International on the pretext that they were Bakuninists. He actually published them in order to bring them to the notice of the police—in a splendid implementation of his father-in-law's ethical standards!

Despite this treachery, the International's Bakuninist-inclined Spanish section stayed united and grew, growing to a membership of 50,000, whereas the parallel organisation set up by Lafargue had to be wound up in 1873 due to its weakness.

This situation, marxism's failure in Spain, accounts for the tone of Frederick Engels's text, *The Bakuninists in Action* in 1873, a standard in soviet, Chinese and (the manifold versions of) Trotskyist propaganda output. "Spain is, industrially, a very backward country and so there can be no talk as yet of immediate and comprehensive emancipation of her working class [...] an uprising by republicans [or federalist bourgeois against centralist bourgeois] could only have prospered had the Spanish working class actively and politically taken a hand in it".[3]

---

3 Reprinted in Marx, Engels, Lenin *Acerca del anarquismo y el anarcosindicalismo* (Moscow, undated [1973]) pp. 112–113. Actually Engels, like Bakunin, was a believer in the ethnic characteristics of workers. Hence the nonsensical and racist views from both thinkers. "German workers have two basic advantages over workers in the rest of Europe. The first is that they belong to the most theoretical people in Europe [...] The second consists in the fact that the Germans have been virtually the last to join the workers' movement. [So as to avoid the sort of mistakes made by others] the German workers deserve credit for having capitalised upon their advantageous position with a rare shrewdness. For the first time since the workers' movement came into being, the struggle is being prosecuted in a methodical way down three concerted and interconnected paths:

And so there emerged an analysis of the country that linked political development to industrial development, something that Marx had discounted. In any event, Engels's attempt to tie political evolution to the workers' movement is at odds with the very history of the Spanish workers' movement up until 1873: burnings of textile plants in 1835, the first general strike in Catalonia and the Peninsula in 1855, the first big peasant uprising in Andalusia and redistribution of the land between upwards of 10,000 peasants in Loja (Granada) in 1863. What I mean to say is that at no time was an alliance sought with the bourgeoisie and, up until 1873, if there was one thing that Spanish statesmen had made quite clear, it was their own inability to push through reforms:

> The only point of interest to us regarding that ignominious uprising is the still more ignominious feats of the Bakuninist anarchists [...] 5,000 men [Bakuninists] fought for 20 hours against 32 Guardias and a few armed bourgeois: they defeated them after they had run out of ammunition and lost a total of ten men, nothing more. It is known that the [Bakuninist] Alliance drums into its initiates this wise judgment of Falstaff's, that "discretion is the better part of valor" [...] In short, the Spanish Bakuninists have set us an insuperable example of how not to make a revolution.[4]

This was the Bakuninist James Guillaume's retort to Engels:

> It is known that the workers' sole weapons were a motley collection of some thousand rifles of various calibres; they

---

the theoretical, the political and the economico-practical (resisting the capitalists). In this concentric offensive, so to speak, lies the very strength and invincibility of the German movement". 1874 foreword to *The Peasant War in Germany*.

4 Op. cit., pp. 111, 120, 130.

lacked ammunition; their bourgeois opponents, backed by the municipal police, well-armed, well dug in, were occupying the town hall and adjacent houses; in order to dislodge them, a number of houses had to be set alight, and, to cap it all, Engels pokes fun at this [...] Can there be any viler reading than these chilling jokes over corpses? Engels is a wealthy manufacturer retired from business; he is used to looking upon workers as machine-fodder and cannon-fodder; which accounts for his doctrine and his style.[5]

Harsh comment indeed,[6] but in addition to relishing the workers' defeat, Engels resorted to fabrication (or maybe it was ignorance) as political analysis: in Valencia, where there were "genuine Internationalists" [Marxist ones] there was "ferocious fighting".

In fact these workers were every bit as Bakuninist as the ones Engels was criticizing, and he added, even more chillingly: "In Cartagena, the government released the 1,800 inmates from the city's jail, the foulest thieves and murderers in the whole of Spain. That this revolutionary measure was suggested to it by the Bakuninists is something that is beyond doubt in the wake of the revelations of the report on the 'Alliance'. There it is shown how Bakunin waxed lyrical about the 'unleashing of evil passions' and how he

---

5   9 November 1873, quoted by G. Ribeill, *Marx/Bakounine: Socialisme autoritaire ou libertaire* (Paris, 10/18, 1975), pp. 365–366.

6   Engels treated the workers under the sway of libertarian ideas as poor wretches afflicted with an incurable illness. This was a definitive judgment, as if they could never change their thinking. Marxists in general and Leninists in particular improved on Engels's thinking. One by one they classified all the citizens of a country, singling out disaffected persons and petits bourgeois and their relations so as to discriminate against them in education and at work. This system was enforced in the USSR from 1921 onwards and in its colonies from 1946/1948 onwards until the collapse in 1989 and 1991. I imagine that in North Korea, China, etc., it must still be in force.

pointed to the Russian bandit as the very model of a genuine revolutionary".[7]

---

[7] Op. cit., pp. 126–127. Dismissing the social impact of capitalism and poverty on crime, Engels wrote in 1870, in his foreword to *The Peasant War in Germany*: "The lumpenproletariat, the scum made up of demoralised elements from every stratum of society and chiefly concentrated in the major cities, is the worst of possible allies. These trash are utterly venal and as bothersome as can be. When French workers daubed on the walls of houses during each revolution 'Death to thieves!' and actually shot more than one of them, they did not do so in a fit of enthusiasm for property rights, but in full consciousness that above all else they had to rid themselves of this crew. Every workers' leader who employs lumpenproletarians in his bodyguard and relies upon them demonstrates by that very fact that he is a traitor to the movement". I am indebted for this quote to Raúl Zibecchi in *Genealogía de la revuelta. Argentina: la Sociedad en movimiento* (La Plata 2003), p. 128. As for Bakunin, the lumpen was capable of attaining a revolutionary consciousness as was witnessed in the CNT's Iron Column, which was partly made up of former criminals freed in July 1936. One of these made a declaration to *Nosotros* (12–13 and 15–17 March 1937), which moved Bolloten and which he in turn reprints almost in its entirety: "I am an escapee from San Miguel de los Reyes, a sinister penitentiary built by the monarchy as a living burial place for those who, not being cowards, would never bow before the infamous laws that the mighty lay down against the oppressed. I was taken there, like so many others, to pay for an insult, for rebelling against the humiliations visited upon an entire village for finally killing a *cacique*. I was young then and I still am since I entered that prison aged twenty-three and I am out because the anarchist comrades threw open the gates, I being now thirty-four. Eleven years subject to the torture of not being human, of being a thing, of being a number! Many men came out with me, just as long-suffering and just as pained by the ill treatment doled out to them since birth. Some, on reaching the streets, rejoined the world; others of us joined up with our liberators who treated us like friends and cherished us like brothers. Gradually, with the latter we formed the 'Iron Column'; together with them we made haste to storm the barracks and disarm the terrifying guards; with them we pushed the fascists back into the towering sierras they now occupy. No one, or scarcely anyone, ever paid us any heed. The

The only problem with this evidence is the facts: there were no Bakuninists in Cartagena.

As to the views of the Spanish workers themselves, their Federal Commission had this to say: "Some of our brethren in Italy believed that the Cantonalist revolt, that is, the revolt by the die-hard federal republicans was the doing of the International, when it was only a political disturbance created by politicians without prior consultation with the Internationalists. Given the die-hard federalists' lack of generosity and that their program scarcely differed from that of the well-meaning ones [their adversaries] it follows that they only had recourse to arms in order to satisfy their ambitious cravings, their personal designs".[8]

> bourgeois's stupefaction at our quitting the prison continues to be shared by one and all even now, and instead of looking after us and helping us and assisting us, we were treated like outcasts, accused of being uncontrollable just because we do not tailor the lives that we yearned and yearn still to be free to the silly whims of the few who cavalierly or proudly looked upon themselves as the masters of men just because they had a seat in some ministry or on some committee and because, in the villages we passed through, after having dispossessed the fascist, we changed the whole way of life, annihilating the ferocious *caciques* who were a blight upon the peasants' lives, once we had robbed them and turned the wealth over to the only ones capable of wealth creation: the workers [...] I spent time in the barracks and there they taught me to hate. I have spent time in prison and there, in the midst of the weeping and suffering, oddly enough, I learned how to love and to love with intensity. In the barracks I nearly lost my personality, such was the severity with which they handled me, as they sought to shove their brainless discipline down my throat. In prison, after much struggle, I recovered my personality and became increasingly intolerant of any imposition. There I learned to hate all hierarchy, from top to bottom; in prison, amid the most agonising pain, I learned how to cherish the unfortunate, my brothers, even as I retained, pure and undiluted, the hatred of hierarchy on which I had suckled in the barracks [...]

8 *Libro Copiador de la Federación Regional Española*, translated from the French, No 1040, 447–49, and cited by Miklós Molnar in *Anarchici e Anarchia nel mondo contemporaneo* (Turin 1971).

In the light of Engels's concoction, James Guillaume said:

> We can now see plainly that the likes of Marx, Engels and their followers do not constitute a more or less wrong-headed school of socialism, but are quite simply reactionaries like Mazzini, Bismarck, Castelar and Thiers.[9]

In 1878, Engels was still scientifically and dialectically arguing:

> We can predict without fear of error that the moment some political commission offers Spanish workers the chance of playing an active role again, the new struggle will not be launched by these 'anarchist' charlatans but by the little organisation of astute and energetic workers who remained loyal to the International in 1872.[10]

Actually, the anarchist organisation was always in the majority, with 52,000 members as against the UGT's 15,200 in 1900. True, by 1911, the UGT had 80,000 members as against the 30,000 with whom the CNT started up, but by 1919 the UGT had some 200,000 as against the CNT's 755,000. Spanish socialism's slow rate of growth stands out when compared with other countries: "By the end of the century, when co-religionists around the continent were setting the 'tone' of European politics, in Spain they had yet to successfully return a single deputy to Congress".[11]

And this sluggishness also affected the growth of the Moscow-dependent communist Party, as well as of the other equally Marxist but Moscow-opposed party. The communists' justifications relied on Engels's analysis and prophetic

---

9 The workers of the USSR, its satellites, China and so on suffered the lash of the repression for which Marxism-leninism stands.

10 Marx, Engels, Lenin, *Acerca del* [...], p. 150.

11 Fernanda Romeu, op. cit., p. 11.

determinism (overlooking the fact that their Messiah had foretold a Marxist upsurge for the end of the nineteenth century, without noticing the profound similarity between Spain then and the Russia of 1917):

> Spain's economic and social backwardness.[12]
> The country's sluggish industrial growth.[13]
> The fact is that anarchism has only been influential in countries of meager industrial development.[14]
> There is nothing odd about this success in this country where there are so many ties binding the industrial worker to the landless peasant.[15]

Hope surfaced in the late 1920s:

> And anarchism, which has already given all it had to give, and which has demonstrated its essential inability as a vanguard of the revolutionary proletariat, will vanish from one of the few redoubts it still has left.[16]

Councilism, a non-Leninist strand of marxism, also failed to get the measure of the Spanish experience. What few pages its main exponent, Anton Pannekoek, wrote about Spain appeared in *Workers' Councils*, and his view can be summed up by the following quotation:

> [In Barcelona] armed gangs, in control of the streets, oversaw order and supplies and, whilst the main factories

---

12 Dolores Ibarruri, *A los trabajadores anarquistas* (Mexico 1953), p. 5.
13 *Historia del Partido Comunista de España* (Paris 1960), p. 14.
14 Andrés Nin, in Balcells, *El arraigo del anarquismo en Cataluña* (Barcelona 1973), p. 115.
15 Broué and Témime, *La révolution et la guerre d'Espagne* (Paris 1961), p. 41.
16 Andrés Nin, op. cit., p. 120. Plainly, he was unaware of Rosa Luxembourg's forecast back in 1905.

carried on working under trade union direction, they carried the war against the fascist armies into adjacent provinces. In so doing, the leaders entered the government of the democratic republic of Catalonia, made up of petit bourgeois republicans allied to socialist and communist politicians. This meant that the workers, instead of fighting for their own class, had to fight in the common struggle and keep in line with it.[17]

This view utterly ignores the scale of the collectivisation all over republican Spain as well as the violent backlash (Vilanesa, May 1937, etc.) from workers and collectivists against agreements at the top. As is pointed out by Bricianier—author of the Pannekoek anthology from which we are quoting—"Pannekoek does not appear to have had the measure of every aspect of the Spanish civil war".

Paul Mattick made more interesting observations:

The notion that the revolution can only be made from below through spontaneous action and autonomous initiative from the workers, is anchored in this organisation, even though it may often have been infringed.[18]

But Helmut Wagner, the author of *Anarchism and the Spanish Revolution*, does make some sort of a distinction between the anti-trade union stance of the bolshevik communists and the councilists. The similarities are many:

Doctrinal assertions: "Anarchism is incapable of solving the problems of revolutionary class struggle [...] We regard it as our duty to show, on the basis of the Spanish example, that the anarchist case against marxism is

---

[17] Bricianier *Pannekoek et les conseils ouvriers* (Paris, EDI, 1969), p. 280.

[18] *Expectativas fallidas (España 1934–1939), El movimiento consejista ante la guerra y la revolución Españolas, artículos y reseñas de Korsch, Mattick* (Barcelona, Adrede, 1999), p. 42.

mistaken: that on the contrary, it is the anarchist teaching that has failed".

Historical half-truths: "[...] That the workers of Catalonia did not form a dictatorship of the proletariat is not their fault. The main reason must be sought in the confused international situation [...] Only a small portion of the proletariat is consciously revolutionary".

Ideological reductionism: "[...] the theories of 'free communism' are, when all is said and done, Proudhon's ideas, adapted by Bakunin to modern production methods. The Proudhonist conception of socialism, devised a hundred years ago, is nothing but an idealistic notion of the petite bourgeoisie that looked upon free competition between small firms as the ideal objective of economic development".[19]

The differences are palpable:

Idealisation: "The only organisation to come up with a concrete response was the POUM. It called for the election of a general congress from which a truly proletarian government would emerge".

Siding with anarchism—albeit without mentioning it by name—on the money question: "The fact that everything can be acquired with money and that money is the magical power that opens all doors will pass. One of the first moves of the workers will doubtless be to create a sort of labor card. Only those who carry out useful work will be issued with the card".

Coming up with a novel view (as along as no bolshevik-style control is imposed): "Each worker's consumption is not determined from 'above'; each worker determines it for himself, through his labor, what he may ask of society. [...] It is really simple to work out the average length of time spent on socially necessary work by dividing

---

19 Op. cit., pp. 77–79, 83–84, 96.

the total work time served by the sum of the products obtained".[20]

Actually, councilism has—thus far—shown itself incapable of shrugging off its Leninist clichés when it comes to passing judgment on anarchism.

Karl Korsch is usually bracketed with the councilists, which is a manifest error, as the quotation reprinted below demonstrates.

> [With regard to] socialism's most complicated problem, to wit, collectivisation of farming, the workers had drawn up an utterly realistic program unblemished by urgency, exaggeration or prejudices. The CNT's (June 1931) Madrid congress resolution on collectivisation of land [...] was a practical guide for action in July and August 1936 for farm workers and smallholders who were left a completely free hand, without meddling from any outside authority or oversight [...] Our chief interest in this first stage of Spanish collectivisation is centered upon the important role played by the *peculiar breed of trade unions* most characteristic of the workers of Catalonia and Valencia, which up until shortly before had been assailed and sneered at by the well-to-do British trade unions and the mighty Marxist organisations of central and eastern Europe, as a utopian expression doomed to failure in any compromised situation. Those anti-party and anti-centralist trade union formations were entirely rooted in the unfettered action of the working masses [...] The vigorous anti-state stance adopted by the revolutionary Spanish proletariat, spurred on by organisations of their own creation and free of ideological encumbrances, accounts for their startling success in overcoming all their difficulties.[21]

---

20 Ibid., pp. 87, 91, 100, 99.

21 Ibid., pp. 144–146

All attempts to return the Marxist doctrine entirely to its original function, as a theory of the social revolution of the working class, are reactionary utopianism in this day and age.

The first move that has to be made to resuscitate a theory and a revolutionary practice is to cut all ties to marxism's claim to hold a monopoly on revolutionary initiative and on theoretical and practical leadership.

> These days, Marx is merely one of many precursors, founding fathers and standard-bearers of the working class' socialist movement. No less important are the so-called utopian socialists, from Thomas More through to the present. Also no less important are Marx's great rivals such as Blanqui, and his dyed-in-the-wool enemies, like Proudhon and Bakunin. No less important, in terms of final outcome, are the more recent developments like German revisionism, French syndicalism and Russian Bolshevism.[22]

The POUM was not keen on self-management, although its militants were practitioners in a few cases.[23]

> No way can we run the risk of experiments that might produce a negative outcome; in the context of our farming economy, we must, on the day we want to start to work collectively, have the economic resources and experts to ensure the right outcome.[24]

The official—which is to say, bourgeois—historians adopt a similar approach to the Marxists, their purpose being to conform to the hierarchical norms of the world of academia. In most cases the approach is to deny that there is

---

22 "Ten theses on Marxism" (1950) in *Cuestión*, No. 1, August 1971 (Buenos Aires). The translation has been slightly amended.
23 The most often cited example being the farm collective in Raimat, Lérida.
24 Antoni Ferrer in *Avant* (Figueras), 13 January 1937, p. 7.

any significance to or interest in self-management,[25] and they rely upon two controversial ploys that can be found in the 1936–1939 propaganda of the Spanish CP: dismissing it as a failure and equating it with economic primitivism.

> This anarchist version of agrarian 'politics' had the consequence in Catalonia of a progressive fall in farm output and desertion of the countryside by more than a small segment of the peasantry. A catastrophe in terms of supply was averted thanks to the vigour of the Communist Party of Spain and the PSUC in curtailing excesses, something to which they were successful in bringing to an end by crushing the May 1937 revolt.[26]

Franz Borkenau, a critical Marxist, could blithely argue:

> What really counts is what are the chances of these economic units succeeding and, as a consequence, what prospect they have of winning over the peasant in the reasonably near future. It is my belief that in this instance the Spanish communists' skepticism is quite justified. There is a need for capital to make the big collectivised estates profitable, and not just that, but for technical assistance and capable leadership. And given the civil war context none of this was to hand. The way things were gone about, premature agricultural collectivisations are more or less the last vestiges of the old anarchist belief that sought to found a new society solely on moral enthusiasm and force, discounting practical economic conditions.[27]

---

25 Supporters of cooperatives have nothing to say on the matter. See *Annales de l'économie collective, 1936–1939*. From 1939 onwards, no mention is made of it, Faquet being the sole exception.

26 *Historia del Partido Comunista de España* (Paris-Warsaw (same presses) 1960), pp. 176, 178.

27 Op. cit., p. 204, and especially 162.

This view is unfounded because it focuses on the farming collectives and overlooks the CLUEA, which was an attempt to raise capital. It also pays no heed to the industrial collectives.

Gerald Brenan decribed collectivisation as "a reversion to medieval institutions, not merely in economic terms but also in political".[28] Brenan cites two instances of collectivisation lifted from a book by Langdon Davies, a book that was more of a guide book than a book on politics—Anso (Huesca) and Port de la Selva (Gerona). Rather insubstantial evidence and rather thin research on which to volunteer generalisations. To which medieval tradition are we to link the collectivisation of railways or the CLUEA? On the other hand, Brenan seemed to appreciate that marriage, democracy and court institutions, etc., also predated the middle ages.

In an interesting and well-documented essay, Hugh Thomas conceded that there was some success "in social terms", but he displays the same elitist and Leninist skepticism as to the economic results: "It is hard to conceive of a long-term boost in national output". "They would have fallen apart by themselves". "It is hard to imagine how it could have worked". And "In the long run it seems unlikely".[29]

The proliferation of misgivings when he is dealing with an experiment that was cut short is a nonsense in itself.

"In recent works of history, this essentially anarchist revolution, which led to an important social change, is dealt with as a sort of an aberration, a bothersome accident that prevented the victorious prosecution of the war and the shielding of the bourgeois regime menaced by the Francoist rebellion".[30] And, adopting a maverick approach (as dissected

---

28 *El laberinto Español* (Paris 1962), p. 271.

29 Carr, *Estudios Sobre la republica y la guerra civil*, pp. 318–319.

30 Noam Chomsky in *Movimiento Libertario Español* (Paris 1974), p. 50; and *American Power and the New Mandarins* (Pelican 1969), p. 65.

in such a masterly way by Noam Chomsky), reiterated his assumptions: "I never replied to Chomsky by letter [...] anyone who reads what I actually say about the collectivisations and what Chomsky says can see that I am rather more skepical as to the long term viability of such collectivisations".[31]

And on the 'rebel' or fascist side, collectivisation ought to have provoked responses. The first to surface came from Santiago Montero Díaz,[32] in whose view two stages can be discerned in the situation of workers in the republican camp. The first stage being revolutionary euphoria:

> The underworld, some criminal gangs and a goodly number of political and trade union leaders secured themselves a better life. The workers who held aloof from the criminality and theft saw a minimal improvement in their so-so living standards.

Then economic reality kicked in, in the shape of a number of measures plus the freeze on wages:

> No matter how collectivist it may purport to be, there is no economy capable of weathering months upon months of a concerted pilfering, looting, maladministration, police terror, military levies and the constant surrender of raw materials and gold to two insatiable great powers.[33]

And collectivisation was the chief target of a book by Manuel Roldán:[34]

> The process of destruction of the COLLECTIVISATIONS in Catalonia deserves serious, painstaking examination,

---

[31] In the Spanish magazine *Triunfo*, 8 March 1975.
[32] *La política Social en la zona Marxista* (Bilbao 1938).
[33] Op. cit., pp. 39–41. The reference is to Russia and France.
[34] *Las colectivizaciones en Cataluña (dos años y medio de destruccin de vidas y riqueza)* (Barcelona 1940).

> given what it represented in economic and psychological terms and given its truly catastrophic consequences [...] When the conflict erupted, there was no doubt in the minds of the Jewish bankers and in the Kremlin but that this war would necessarily result in Spain's elimination as a power in the Mediterranean, like the ancient empire of the Maghreb before her. [...] Over the three years of red terror, it could be argued that Catalan industry was non-existent.[35]

The confabulation with some alleged international conspiracy fits in with the usual right-wing mentality, and is joined by a reductionist approach to property, a central value of the Right:

> Each committee tried to devise a formula for making quick money. But their formulas made no difference, since it was pointless offering a factory to people reluctant to work. And, there being no new Lenin to hand, the circumstances that had presented themselves in Russia were not repeated in Catalonia and these would-be millionaires very soon turned into serious stalwarts of private property. But didn't others, such as the people running the monopolies and public services, resort to violence to counter the interference from the Generalidad? What was the May 1937 week-long bloodletting but a stand made in defense of stolen property?[36]

Roldán acknowledges the drive behind collectivisation, albeit that he belittles it as an imitation of the previous arrangement (though he cannot account for why it was accepted when it was just the same as the past):

---

35 Op. cit., pp. 10, 30.
36 Ibidem, pp. 83–84.

The movement towards collectivisation with backing from the outside and from traitors moved on like a steam-roller [...] Let us say it again: class exploitation had not changed direction, as was frequently claimed. It was simply governed, throughout, by the same economic principles as in bourgeois times. All that had changed was the type of wage, the working hours and the cost of living.[37]

And we must not forget to mention the view of the anarchist Horacio M. Prieto, whose anti-self-management views in 1932 we've already seen. In August 1936, on arriving in Barcelona, he was consistent when he stated:

This looks to me to be an impossibility; you have gone too far and we're going to pay a very high price for that; I am utterly convinced that we are going to lose the war because there will be foreign intervention.[38]

By the way, note the absurdity of the view that foreigners—armies from those capitalist nations with an imperialist reach—were going to step in on behalf of good or bad behavior of workers, when they had already done so at the time against the petite bourgeoisie in countries falling within 'backyards', e.g. the USA in Cuba, Nicaragua, Haiti, etc.

Later, in a talk lobbying on behalf of a quasi-anarchist political party, he denied the revolutionary implications of self-management:

The collectivism we are experiencing in Spain is not anarchist collectivism, but the creation of a new capitalism even worse organised than the old capitalism system we have just torn down; and it is a new capitalism complete with all its blemishes and all its immorality, as mirrored in the

---

37 Ibidem, pp. 91, 93.
38 *El anarquismo Español en la lucha política*, p. 6, as cited by C. M. Lorenzo *Les anarchistes espagnols et le pouvoir*, p. 120.

permanent selfishness of the workers running a collective.[39]

And in exile he credited it with a quite negative aspect:

> Hence the emergence, without the opinion being sought of the National Confederation of Labor (CNT)'s leadership bodies, of libertarian collectives that should never have been set up, being unprepared for such extraordinary circumstances; and it was the hasty introduction of collectives that prevented the CNT from being in a position to frame any serious or positive scheme in terms of rebuilding the economy.[40]

These claims were made without any supporting statistics and were worthy of a supporter of libertarian communism from above, whose reductionism proves to have had a close kinship with that of self-management's other opponents.

---

39 6 January 1938, typewritten text, p. 6.
40 *Posibilismo libertario* (France 1966), p. 75.

Appendix XVI
Francoism, Transition to Democracy and Thoughts on Collective Management (written 1997–1998)

Francoism never at any time embraced the notion of collective social labour. However, there were a few officially recognised economic ventures that are of interest: ventures like the cooperative movement across the country, and the cooperatives in Mondragón (Basque Country), which were Catholic-launched and -driven, with supposed grassroots members striking against their top echelons. These were limited alternative solutions, sponsored by a minority faction within the ruling class.

Plainly, the Francoist élites clung to a sullen distrust of collectivism per se, in the wake of the example given of the capability of workers to self-manage the economy.

Certain economic changes were forced through by *Opus Dei* (a happy blend of freemasonry, success and more or less corrupt banking activities) with the acquiescence of Franco, 'Caudillo by the grace of God' to quote the phrase displayed on coins bearing his image (and never queried by any Pope, even though Franco was neither a king nor divine envoy). With *Opus Dei*, Spain emerged simultaneously from a Mussolini-style autarchy (albeit without the Italian fascist successes in terms of *autopistas* and the electrification of the railways) and the economic stagnation inherited from an inquisitorial Catholicism. The country was opened up to foreign capital investment like other developing countries. The same economic model was adopted: tax concessions and guarantees regarding repatriation of much of the profits, plus an obligatory social peace. That policy started in 1956. Oddly enough, that very same year the Communist Party of Spain announced that it was giving up on the armed struggle and lobbying for the democratic route within Francoist Spain.

Some years earlier, the noose of terror had decimated leftist organisations during and in the wake of the civil war. An anti-communist law broadened its definition to include freethinkers, free-masons, socialists, anarchists, anarcho-syndicalists and communists and, since 1938, it had been enforced against individuals and the written word. Divorce was banned with retrospective effect in 1939, and there was a reversion to the situation in 1931 with civil marriage abolished and compulsorily replaced by a religious rite. Of course, revolutionary names were replaced by more 'respectable' ones, Nardo turning into Bernardo and Libertad into Maria Concepción and so on.

The mailed fist crashing down on the reds enforced collective family accountability, sustaining the memories and the anxiety (and sometimes the curse) generated by any such connections. On the other hand, this was precisely what happened in the USSR and its colonies. Ideas connected to the broader left were buried by leftists themselves who chose to keep silent rather than suffer or put their families through suffering. The rare exceptions did nothing to alter this ideological desertification: the legacy of whole generations of workers just vanished. It was replaced by a blend of Catholicism, arriviste individualism and a lack of any sense of civic responsibility, which gave birth to a self-seeking, mutable individual as chameleon-like as the Caudillo himself, and a cavalier attitude to corruption that endures to this very day.

So, confident that it had the wage-earners under control, the regime engaged in peaceful social conflict from 1962 onwards, as Asturias' coal mines were petering out and the employers and workers were mounting joint protests. The conflict spread to virtually the whole of Spain in the form of demands for wage rises, which were, in part, granted. That same year two *Opus Dei* ministers signed Spain's application for membership of the Common Market. Even the monopoly on compulsory union membership, which applied equally to bosses, executives, technicians and workforce alike (in an imitation of the Catholic-Mussolinian corporatist system) was undermined by the vaguely leftist activities of the HOAC (*Hermandades de Obreros de Acción Católica*/Catholic Action Worker Confraternities). However, the martial law regulations governing strikes was retained. Euphemisms about 'labour disputes' and 'lack of work' gained official approval.

From then on a series of tensions came to the surface:

The illegal, but tolerated, Workers' Commissions surfaced: these embraced the opposition in the world of work.

Growing trade with the Marxist-leninist bloc such as during the coalminers' strike of 1962 (when Polish coal was brought in) and the secret signing of the first trade agreement with the USSR (even as the communist leader Julián Grimau, the leader of a faction that the Spanish CP leadership found bothersome, was standing trial and being executed; his death was equally supported by Francoists and communist officialdom).

Critical writings by opposition intellectuals were published in Catalan, and only then in Spanish.

Open controversy between leading Francoist groups—*Opus Dei*, monarchist, Carlist (the rival wing of the official Bourbon dynasty) and Falangist.

The gradual emergence of Basque terrorism and a tentative assertion of Catalan identity.

Every one of these factions turned a blind eye to collective economics. After 1968, Carlists and Falangists began to press for self-management, as a few anarchist groups were doing.

Anarcho-syndicalist militants in exile were unaware of Spain's new economic data. Farming had been transformed by a flight from the land and by emigration from the country and indeed by tourism in a number of areas (the tourist industry being the goose that laid the golden egg). And there was the influx of foreign capital investment.

From 1970–1972 on, the current trend for workers to organise along trade union lines was emerging. Whereas in 1970 there had been a hundred or so UGT militants and about the same number in the CNT and nearly a thousand in the CP, there were profound changes after 1972. The number of UGT members and officials paid for by monies coming from Europe's social democrats outnumbered the CP, whilst the CNT was stagnating.

The Francoist regime picked Franco's successor, in return—naturally—for a cohort of fiery trade union firefighters, self-styled leftists but ready to silence and dampen down disputes in return for a share in power, and bland European-style reforms—democratisation in education, the granting of conscientious objector status, widespread sexual permissiveness, etc.—scandalised a number of Falangists.

One Falangist experiment in pursuing a sub-trade unionist policy was the 1965 compact between the CNT and the CNS (*Confederación Nacional-Sindicalista*/National Syndicalist Confederation), whereby the Francoist syndicates, singular and obligatory, adopted a few quasi-liberal touches. Some Falangists saw this as designed to banish the growing CP influence within the CNS, replacing that with an emasculated anarcho-syndicalism. Certain CNT personnel saw anti-communism as justifying stooping to an alliance with the far right, the object being to capture control of the trade unions. The agreement was denounced by CNT and Falangist personnel together.

In 1975, Francoism awarded the right to strike (albeit after a lengthy and tortuous process) and formally established May Day as a labor holiday and not merely the feast of St. Joseph the Worker.

Next came the transition to democracy (a pleasant euphemism for the leadership turning its coat), during which there were no attempts to mount legal proceedings against murderous police and military figures nor any recovery of the assets unlawfully acquired by rightists. It was obvious that the people who built up those assets had been gunned down. There was a slight expansion in the well-to-do classes and the spread of the black economy provided some ease, economically speaking.

In Argentina and, to some extent, in Chile as well the transition to democracy was largely open to question, albeit without much profit, because the pressures from the growing impoverished sectors has led to an enduring and informed challenge associated with a denunciation of neo-liberalism.

The idea of self-management surfaced only as an option in the administration of a few bankrupted firms. The UGT drew a veil over its own history of revolutionary self-management during 1936–1939, the better to compete with the Workers' Commissions—which resembled the most reformist European trade unionism—by allying itself with the employers and the government. This trend culminated in the Moncloa Pacts of October 1977, with democratic reforms for society, as a whole, traded for workers' agreeing to keep up output with an eye to expediting entry into the Common Market.

It was telling that, in 1976, the year of all the anti-Francoist social stirrings forty years on from the outbreak of civil war, collective management is the great absentee from all disputes and demands and from all the left-wing and far-left movements.

True, lots of self-managed Aragonese, Catalan and Castilian villages from 1936 to 1939 were left almost as hang-overs from the past in the wake of the flight from the land and emigration abroad during the 1950–1970 period. Nevertheless some villages relatively active were left behind in Castile and, especially, along the Mediterranean coastline, but wine production and the tourist industry were the favoured solutions of the day. And when it came to the exportation of farm produce and life in the factories, economic problems were much the same as they had been in 1936 (not so much in the sanitation field as in tillage). On the other hand, the demands voiced and the breaking dawn of consciousness were a lot less outspoken than they had been in 1936.

The CNT had the trump card of direct action in rescuing workers from the snares of uncomplaining productivity drives and blinkered communism. But instead of reverting to its proletarian culture, the better-informed CNT members were caught up in dark factional squabbles in which it is hard to expose the hand of the political police (I have in mind the Scala outrage in Barcelona, orchestrated by a police informer, with hotheaded folk unable to see manipulation when it was happening), instances of unbalanced minds (the witch-hunt against the *cincopuntistas* over the number of articles in a CNT-CNS compact that was never implemented), the masonic politics of a strife-free society (assuredly emanating from Esgleas and Montseny) and the recourse to physical violence against CNT personnel with different preferences.

In addition to this intestinal warfare, the anarcho-syndicalist movement struggled with disagreements over action: there was the issue of active participation in trade union life (taking part in the shop steward elections); the dividing up of the trade union patrimony built up with decades of dues paid in by workers, plus the assets seized in 1936–1939 and doled out in dribs and drabs by those in government (with two factions squabbling over their claims to the initials CNT). In the end, the CNT label was awarded by the courts to the CNT-AIT (the faction with the lesser foothold in struggles), which had referred the matter to the courts (!?); the other CNT was then relaunched as the CGT. At the same time, a 'Solidaridad Obrera' organisation (its foothold primarily among the Madrid metro workforce) was launched as a possible bridge between the other two squabbling factions.

After that, the CNT-AIT split in Catalonia, each faction there publishing its own version of *Solidaridad Obrera* newspaper. Since the late 1990s, there has been an obvious resurgence in CNT-AIT trade unionism. Solidaridad Obrera continues to rise above the CNT-AIT-versus-CGT squabbles. The CGT carried on its way and numbers some 50,000 dues-paying members.

The lack of civic education, a culture of dependency—the result of forty years of Catholic Falangist verticalism that might be compared with some seventy-odd years in the USSR—and fear of repression proved stronger than any craving for social change. This became apparent during Tejero & Co.'s would-be coup on 23 February 1981. That attempt appeared to have succeeded (professional soldiers were awarded pay rises and certain modernisations), in the light of the actual short prison terms handed down (to be served in luxury prisons) and the refusal to look into the hidden instigators. Across the board, militants from the PSOE, the sundry CPs (euro-communist, pro-Moscow and Maoist), the UGT, the CNT, the Marxist-leninist grouplets got the scare of their lives (archives were burnt, homes abandoned, and some arranged outings with non-apolitical friends in order to slip out of the country) and ETA terrorism slumped. Quite a few youngsters had nervous breakdowns at the thought of liquidation and mopping up of leftists and their families. In a short time, the memory of a proletariat in arms of July 1936 was eclipsed by the lingering image of mass graves and firing squads, a mark of the effectiveness of Francoism's Catholic-fascist repression. Worse still, after dithering for a number of hours and with no other initiatives being shown, the king was enabled by the nationwide funk to appear as a saviour.

As it did in the USSR and in the USA, the steamroller of repression banished the militancy that had been a feature of the majority within the anarcho-syndicalist ranks. The transition introduced a 'soft' trade unionism that always agreed with the bosses from 1976 onwards, despite a few localised outbreaks of tough disputes (the shipyards along the Cantabrian coast, the steelworkers in Sagunto, etc.). Only on the basis of a fresh, consistent and serious militancy, complete with the advent of a creative consciousness, can revolutionary collective management make a come-back.

In the absence of such conditions, collective management is simply a ploy by the ruling classes, designed to win the backing of workers so as to silence the critics.[1]

---

1   As is the case with the co-management arrangements in Germany or the early stages, in Yugoslavia, of an imposed self-management wholly confined to the world of work by the Titoist party.

Glossary of Terms and Initials Used in the Text

Terms

Catalanist = person or political party supportive of the idea of at least home rule or, ideally, independence for Catalonia on the basis of her language, literature and historic legacy.

cenetista = CNT member

cincopuntismo = ill-fated overture made to the CNT elements by elements within the Francoist national syndicates in the 1960s.

comarca = area roughly equivalent to a county

faísta = (noun) FAI member or enthusiast, or (adjective) relating to the FAI

Falange = the Spanish fascist party

*Generalidad (*or, in Catalan, *Generalitat)* = Catalonia's home rule government. The word means 'Commonwealth'.

kolkhoz = Soviet state-sponsored collective farm

Mixed Brigade = mode of military organisation widely adopted by the army of the Spanish Republic whereby a brigade would have a range of auxiliary services (gunners, sappers, etc.) normally found only at division level

Mujeres Libres/Free Women = libertarian women's organisation

nomenklatura = the 'inner circle' of the 'more equal pigs' in soviet systems, whose party status entitled them to privileges withheld from the general population.

Opus Dei = Catholic lay order

piqueteros = picketers/road blockaders

requetés = the militia forces of the ultra-Catholic Carlist reactionaries

S.A. (sociedad anonima) = Limited company

sindicato único = in smaller localities where separate trade union were not feasible, the CNT would draw all workers into this single union structure. *Sindicato único* was often used as a synonym for CNT.

treintista = member or supporter of the originally thirty (*treinta*) signatories to the *Manifesto of the Thirty* issued by CNT supporters aggrieved by the Confederation's having to suffer the consequences of revolts into which it had often been 'bounced' by persons following non-CNT agendas.

ugetista = member of the PSOE-linked UGT union federation.

Initials

AIT = *Alianza Internacional de Tabajadores*/International Workers' Association

CEDA = *Confederación Española de Derechas Autónomas/* Spanish Confederation of Non-aligned Rightists). Essentially Catholic political coalition, at best neutral about the Republic.

CGT = *Confédération Générale du Travail*/General Confederation of Labour. Largest French trade union organisation.

Confederación General de Trabajadores/General Confederation of Labour. Post-Transition breakaway from the Spanish CNT.

CLUEA = *Comité Levantino Unificado de Exportación de Agríos*/Unified Farm Produce Export Committee of Levante

CNS = *Confederación Nacional-Sindicalista*/Nationalist-Syndicalist Confederation. Francoism's corporatist syndicates, sometimes also known as Vertical Syndicates, modelled on fascist Italy's syndicates.

CNT = *Confederación Nacional del Trabajo*/National Confederation of Labour

Glossary of Terms and Initials Used in the Text

ETA = *Euzkadi ta Askatasuna*/Basque Homeland and Freedom. Organisation pursuing armed struggle in pursuit of an independent Basque nation on seven Basque provinces presently forming part of the French and Spanish states.

FAI = *Federación Anarquista Ibérica*/Iberian Anarchist Federation

FIJL = *Federación Ibérica de Juventudes Libertarias*/Iberian Libertarian Youth Federation

FNTT = *Federación Nacional de Trabajadores de Tierra*/National Land Workers' Federation. Also known as the FETT (*Federación Española de Trabajadores de Tierra*).

HOAC = *Hermandades de Obreros de Acción Católica*/Workers' Franternities of Catholic Action

IWW = Industrial Workers of the World

JJ.LL = *Juventudes Libertarias*/Libertarian Youth

PCE = *Partido Comunista de España*/Communist Party of Spain

POUM = *Partido Obrero de Unificación Marxista*/Workers' Marxist Unification Party

PSOE = *Partido Socialista Obera Español*/Spanish Workers' Socialist Party

PSUC = *Partido Socialista Unificada de Cataluña*/Unified Socialist Party of Catalonia

UGT = *Unión General de Trabajadores*/Workers' General Union

UHP = *Unión de Hermanos Proletarios*/Union of Proletarian Brothers

Index

82nd Mountain Brigade 121

A

Abad de Santillán, Diego (Baudilio Sinesio García Fernández) 11, 190, 204, 211
Acción 50
Acín, Ramón 80
Ademuz (Valencia) 121
Adra Fishermen's Collective 249–251
Albalate de Cinca (Aragon) 126
Albalate del Luchador (Teruel) 129
Albaterreche (Lérida) 261
Alberola Novarro, José 86
Albesa (Lérida) 261
Alcampel (Huesca) 86
Alcañiz (Teruel) 85
Alcarraz (Lérida) 261
Alcolea (Almería) 85, 92
Alcora (Valencia) 127
Alcorisa (Teruel) 85, 88, 92, 129
Alcoy (Alicante) 95
Alfara (Valencia) 97
Alfarache, Progreso 183, 184
Alfonso XIII (king) 46
Alguaire (Lérida) 261
Alicante (Alicante) 109, 128
La Almalda (Zaragoza) 91
Álvarez, Ramón 50
anarchism in Spain (development of) 21–27

anarcho-syndicalists/anarcho-syndicalism 12, 19, 20
  ideology of 34–35
  international decline 20
  visions of future society. *See* Appendix V
Andalusia 9, 23, 25, 47, 130, 137
Anso (Huesca) 300
anti-semitism 118
Antona, David 47
Aragon 22, 49, 79, 85, 87, 93, 99, 130, 137
  collectives in Huesca 80
  collectives in Teruel 80
  collectives in Zaragoza 81
  municipal election of 1937 89
Aranguren Roldán, José 141
Arbeca (Lérida) 261
Arenys de Lledó (Teruel) 169
Argentina 13
  piqueteros 14
  women 13
  workers' self-management in 14
Arín (*treintista*) 184, 185
Armario, Manuel 247
Arnal, Jesús 157
Arnedo (La Rioja) 164, 165
Arquer, Jordi 143
Arshinov, Peter 51
Arshinov Platform (The Organizational Platform of the Gen-

eral Union of Anarchists) 51, 180, 188, 209
Artesa de Lérida Collective 252–261
Ascaso Division 217, 227, 228
Ascaso, Francisco 47, 52
Ascaso, Joaquín 92, 185
Ascó (Tarragona) 129, 135, 146, 235
Assault Guard 98, 214, 221, 250, 269
Asturian uprising (1934) 170–173
Asturias 47, 49–50, 53, 57, 63, 133, 165, 166
Azaña Díaz, Manuel 163
Azuara (Zaragoza) 91

B

Badajoz 10, 83
Badalona (Barcelona) 106
Bajo Llobregat (Barcelona) 125
Bakuninist/Bakunin's Alliance 42, 179, 286, 289, 290
Bakunin, Mikhail 21, 42, 47, 51, 53, 151, 179, 191, 202, 211, 287, 291, 298
Balsareny (Barcelona) 129, 165
Barbastro 85, 92, 262
Barbastro Federation of Collectives. *See* Appendix XII
Barbieri, Francesco 99
Barcelona 22, 25, 42, 66
Barcelona and District Locksmiths' and Corrugated Shutters Collective. *See* Appendix XIV
Barcelona and Outskirts Wig-maker and Barber Employers' Federation 74
Barcelona barbers' collective 238, 241–244
Barret S.A. 67
La Batalla 98
Beceite (Teruel) 169
Bellpuig de Urgell (Lérida) 261
Berga (Barcelona) 165
Berneri, Camillo 98, 99
Besnard, Pierre 56, 192, 215, 234
Bétera (Levante) 166
Binéfar (Huesca) 85, 271
Blanqui, Louis Auguste 298
Boletín de Información CNT-FAI 66
Bolivia 13
Bolloten, Burnett 11
Borkenau, Franz 299
Bosch, Aurora 276
Brademas, Stephen John 12
Brenan, Gerald 11, 21, 22, 98, 300
Bricianier, Serge 295
Britain 2, 3, 66
Buenacasa, Manuel 47
Bugarra (Valencia) 166
Bujaraloz (Zaragoza) 81, 86, 91
Bukharin, Nikolai 48
Buñuel, Luis 80

C

Caballero, Largo 45, 118, 132, 169, 231, 232
Cádiz 58, 167
Cafiero, Carlo 51
Calanda (Teruel) 80, 85, 92
Campo Leal (Ciudad Real) 128
Campo Libre 127

Index

La Canadiense (power company) 43
  strike 44, 48
Candasnos (Huesca) 90, 91
Cantabria 138, 139
Carabaña (Madrid) 107
Carballeira, Raúl 47
Cardona (Barcelona) 165
Cartagena (Murcia) 227, 292
Casado, Segismundo 233
Casas Viejas (Cádiz) 167
Caspe (Zaragoza) 87
Castejón de Monegros (Huesca) 91
Castellón 22, 130
Castellsea (Lérida) 261
Castelserás (Teruel) 120
Castilblanco (Badajoz) 164
Castile 5, 9, 128, 130, 139
Castro, Raquel 225
Catalonia 22, 47, 63, 93, 138
Catholic Church 85, 157–161
CEDA (Spanish Confederation of Non-Aligned Rightists) 9, 170
CENU (New Standard School Council) 121
Cervera (Lérida) 261
Cerviá (Lérida) 261
CGT (France) 144
Chomsky, Noam 3, 11, 204, 300
Ciliga, Antón 52
Ciudad Real 126
Civil Guard 132, 164, 165, 167, 214, 221
Clará, Sebastián 183, 184
CLUEA (Unified Levante Farm Produce Exports Committee) 300. *See* Appendix XIII
CNT 50
CNT (Confederacíon Nacional del Trabajo) 5, 21, 22, 27, 41, 47, 53, 54, 66, 93
  and colonial exploitation 42
  and electoral politics 57–58
  anticipation of fascist coup 60
  anti-electoral campaign 168
  child labor 38
  CNT Collaboration 7, 53, 76, 209–214
  congresses 33, 38–42, 41, 43, 50, 53, 54, 55, 56, 59, 63, 80, 84, 95, 105, 181, 189, 206, 210, 279, 297
  defense groups 45
  disabled/handicapped workers 39
  introduction of collectivisation 94
  leadership vs. rank and file 150
  membership 42, 44, 46, 95, 162, 293
  National Committee 46, 54, 56, 96, 97, 98, 99, 181, 187, 223, 224, 230, 233
  notions of revolution 201–208
  Regional Committee 54, 97, 182, 187
  Relationship to FAI 187–190. *See* Appendix IV
  women workers 38

collectivisation. *See* Appendix VIII
  chronology of 71–77
  clashes between anarchists and Marxists 134–136
  commerce 69
  communications 69
  company takeovers 71–72
    clothing industry 73
    joint UGT-CNT takeovers 72–73
    metalworking and automobile 72
    printing trades and paper-mills 73
  energy 69
  entertainment 70
  imposed by force 86
  joint CNT-UGT collectives 87
  metalworking 66
  neo-capitalism 115–116, 122, 146
  number of participants 137–139
  opposition to strikes 123–126
  organization of 112–119
  philosophy of 146
  provisions 69
  shortcomings 146
  size of collectivised economy 104, 137–139
  socialization vs. nationalization 113
  statistics 119–120, 125
  technology 120
  transport 68–69
  unemployment 102
Column CNT 13 228

Combina, Pérez 51
Comín Colomer, Eduardo 1
Communist International 2
communist party. *See* PCE
Comorera Solé, Joan 124
Companys, Luís 63, 75, 221
confederal work certificate 117–119
Corral de Almaguer (Toledo) 129
Cortada, Roldán 183
Cortés 183
Costa, Joaquín 201
council communism 294, 295
Council of Aragon 89, 90, 125, 135, 221
Council of Economy 106
Cullera (Valencia) 128
Cullera collective (Valencia) 135

D

Decembrists 47
Díaz del Moral, José 21
Díaz, José 56
Díez, Galo 47
Díez Torre, Alejandro 201
Di Giovanni, Severino 99
El Diluvio 66
direct action 48
Durruti, Buenaventura 47, 52, 81, 132, 143, 157, 184, 185, 190
Durruti Column 82, 216
  executions 82

E

Ecuador 13
education. *See* rationalist schools
Ehrenburg, Ilya 98, 121
Elipa (Madrid) 247

Index

Engels, Frederick 42, 288, 289, 290, 291, 293
Épila (Zaragoza) 164
Escofet, Federico 221
Esgleas, Germinal 310
Esperanto 50
Estadilla (Huesca) 270
Estrugo, J. M. 119
Examination Councils 91
Extremadura 5, 9, 138

F

Fabra, Manuel 50
FAI (Iberian Anarchist Federation) 45, 51, 52, 66, 86, 118
   peninsular plenum 206
   relationship to CNT 187–190. *See* Appendix IV
Falange (Spanish Fascist Party) 9, 24, 59, 308
   massacres during revolution 83
fascism 60, 213
La Fatarella 128, 134
Federalism 49
Ferrer Guàrdia, Francisco 26, 42, 49
FETT (Spanish Farmworkers' Federation) 277
Fígols (Barcelona) 164, 165
First International 42, 46, 104, 146, 151, 179, 287
Flix (Catalonia) 237
Flores Magón, Enrique 150
Flores Magón, Ricardo 150
FNTT-UGT (National Land Workers' Federation) 109, 162
Fornells, Ricardo 183
Fornoles (Teruel) 169
Fortuna (Murcia) 134
Fraga (Huesca) 82, 84, 86
Fragua Social 95, 275, 278
France 2, 20
Franco Bahamonde, Francisco 3, 4, 9, 213, 305
Francoist dictatorship 1, 12, 305
Friends of Durruti Group 216
Fuenmayor (La Rioja) 169

G

Galarza, Ángel 97
Gallo, Major Luigi 250
Gandía (Valencia) 97
García Oliver, Juan 7, 47, 52, 64, 75, 77, 124, 132, 135, 184, 185, 190, 209, 231
García, Pedro 277
Gelsa (Zaragoza) 81, 92
Germany 20, 34
Gerona 124
Gijón (Asturias) 22, 170
Girona Company 67
globalism 49
Goldman, Emma 214
Gomá (Catholic Cardinal) 160, 161
González Morado, Tomás 47
González, Nazario 21
González Pacheco, Rodolfo 70
Gorelik, G. 51
El Grado (Asturias) 265
Granada 22
Granadella (Lérida) 261
Graus (Huesca) 85
Grimau, Julián 307
Gudell, Martín 51
Guérin, Daniel 204

Guerra di Classe 99
Guillaume, James 191, 192, 289, 292
Guimerá (Lérida) 261

H
Hambresin, Émile 126
Haro (La Rioja) 169
Herrera, Pedro 213
Herzen, Alexander 47
Hitler, Adolf 3, 10, 213
HOAC (Catholic Action Worker Confraternities) 307
Hobsbawm, Eric 21
Hospitalet de Llobregat (Barcelona) 64
Huesca 262
La Humanitat 66

I
Ibáñez, Blasco 26
Ibarruri, Dolores 133, 136
Iglesias, Pablo 286
individualist anarchism 21
inflation 103
Institute of Agrarian Reform 90, 94
Iron Column 97, 134, 212, 217, 219, 223, 226, 227, 228, 232, 291
Isona (Lérida) 261
IWA (International Working Men's Association) 42, 287
IWW (Industrial Workers of the World) 20
Izquierda Republicana 89

J
Jackson, Gabriel 11
Joll, James 21, 98
Josa de Cadi (Lérida) 261
Jover, Gregorio 228
Juanel (Juan Manuel Molina Mateo) 64

K
Kaminski, H. E. 121, 127
Klein, Naomi 14
Korobizin, A. 98
Korsch, Karl 297
Kronstadt revolt 149
Kropotkin, Peter 21, 26, 51, 53, 104, 143, 145, 148, 202, 207
Kropotkin, Sophia 118

L
Lafargue, Paul 288
Lagunarrota (Huesca) 85
La Hormiga (Publisher) 17
Lamberet, Renée 21, 192
Lécera (Zaragoza) 81, 91
Lenin, Vladimir 20, 42, 48, 79
Lérida 56, 110, 126, 131
Lerroux government 170
Leval, Gaston (Pierre Robert Piller) 4, 16, 139, 202, 268
Levante 22, 88, 93, 95, 125, 128, 138
Lewis, Avi 14
Liaño, Concha 7
Línea de Fuego 212
Liñola (Lérida) 261
Liria (Valencia) 129
Líster, Forján, Enrique 89, 148
Líster's brigade 88, 89, 135, 235, 240
Llardecans (Lérida) 261

Index

Llop, José 129, 235
Loja (Granada) 289
López, Juan 96, 183
Lorenzo, Anselmo 47, 145, 191
Lorenzo, César M. 213
Luxembourg, Rosa 294

M

Madrid 22
Madrid Peasants' Collective 247–248
Makhaiski, Jan Waclav 48, 104
Makhno, Nestor 51, 186, 233
Makhnovist army 149, 226
Makhnovists 81, 82
Málaga 58
Malatesta, Errico 26, 186, 187
Maquinaria Terrestre y Marítima 67
Marañón, Gregorio 141
María Martínez, José 172
Marianet 64. *See also* Vázquez, Mariano R.
Marín, Dolors 7
Maroto Column 220
Marxist-leninism 17, 44, 51, 146, 290, 293
  objection to collectivization 134
Marx, Karl 42, 179, 287, 289
Mascarate (Toledo) 135
Mas de las Matas (Teruel) 85, 92
Mas, Valerio 96
Mattick, Paul 295
Maurín, Joaquín 44, 286
Mayals (Lérida) 261
May Days (Barcelona 1937) 216, 295, 302

Mazzini, Giuseppe 179, 293
Membrilla (Ciudad Real) 126
Menem, Carlos 13
Mera, Cipriano 47, 216, 223, 229, 230, 233
Ministry of Trade 96
Mintz, Frank 4
Mintz, Jerome 167
Mola Vidal, Emilio 9, 46, 83
Moncada (Valencia) 97
Moncloa Pacts 309
Mondragón cooperatives 305
monetary policy 174–178
Monteagudo del Castillo (Teruel) 91
Monte Aragón (Castile) 131
Montero Díaz, Santiago 301
Montoliu de Lérida (Lérida) 261
Montseny, Federica 7, 48, 64, 75, 76, 135, 147, 172, 209, 213, 310
Monzón (Huesca) 262
Mora de Rubielos (Aragon) 91
Mora (Toledo) 135
More, Thomas 298
Morocco 42, 60
Morón Díaz, Gabriel 250
Mosqueruela (Teruel) 85
Mothers of the Plaza de Mayo (Argentina) 14
Mujeres Libres 7, 121
Mujeres Libres 107
Mussolini, Benito 3, 10, 213

N

narodniks 47
National Federations of Industry 113, 114, 118

National Peasant Federation 123
naturopathic medicine 50
Naval (Huesca) 267
Navarcles (Barcelona) 165
Navarra 9, 87
Negre, José 47
Nervio 249
Nettlau, Max 51, 118, 187
News Chronicle 75
Nin, André 44, 56, 286, 294
Noir et Rouge (France) 16
Nosotros 50, 291
La Novela Ideal 50

O

Oliete (Teruel) 85
Olona, Mariano 90
Omells de Nogaya (Lérida) 261
Oriol, R. 252
Ortiz, Antonio 47
Orto 50
Orwell, George 11
Os de Balaguer (Lérida) 261
Oviedo 58, 170

P

Pannekoek, Anton 294
Paret del Vallé (Barcelona) 107
Paris Commune 9
PCE (Communist Party of Spain) 58, 89, 103, 126, 127, 128, 133, 139, 142, 163, 186, 306
  opposition to collectivization 90
  See also: Stalinism 6
Peciña 131
Pedralba (Valencia) 166
Peirats, José 16, 47, 64, 166, 185, 215

Peiró, Juan 47, 52, 56, 77, 183, 184, 185, 203
Pellicer (Iron Column) 225, 227
Peñalba (Huesca) 86, 91, 92
Peñarroya (Córdoba) 132
Perales de Río (Toledo) 135
Peramola (Lérida) 261
Perdiguera (Zaragoza) 131
Pestaña, Ángel 30, 34, 42, 46, 47, 51, 52, 60, 158, 183, 184, 189, 203
Piller, Pierre Robert (see Leval, Gaston)
Pina (Zaragoza) 91
Piñón, Camilo 185
pistolerismo 44
Plenum of CNT Militias and Columns (Feb. 1937) 215–234
Poal (Lérida) 261
Pobla de Ciérvoles (Lérida) 261
Poblador 231
Popular Front 9, 93
Port de la Selva (Gerona) 300
La Portella (Lérida) 261
Portugal 45
POUM (Workers' Party of Marxist Unification) 6, 23, 44, 59, 63, 83, 84, 296, 298
  origins of 44, 286
Pradas, Garcia 98
Pravda 84, 98
Preston, Paul 162, 163
Prieto, Horacio 51, 60, 63, 64, 117, 118, 180, 193, 197, 201, 202, 203, 221, 303
Prieto, Indalecio 43, 89

Index

Primo de Rivera dictatorship 45, 47, 170
Primo de Rivera, José Antonio 9, 45, 59, 169
professional record book. *See* worker's record book
Proudhon, Pierre Joseph 298
Provencio, Roque 248
Prudhommeaux, André 92, 211
PSOE (Spanish Workers' Socialist Party) 10, 45, 58, 89, 113, 118, 163, 286
PSUC (Catalan communist party) 83, 84, 98, 245, 255, 299
La Publicitat 66
Puebla de Hijar (Teruel) 86
Puente, Isaac 48, 56, 64, 93, 193–196, 201
Puigcerdá (Girona) 135
Puigvert de Lérida (Lérida) 261

R

Raimat (Lérida) 298
rationalist schools 26, 120–122
El Rebelde 249
Réclus, Élisée 51
Redención 50
Regional Federation of Farming, Livestock and Foodstuffs Industries 260
Regional Peasants' Federation 94
Reparaz, Gonzalo de 201
Republican Government 10, 128, 135
La Revista Blanca 50
Ribarroja (Valencia) 166
Richards, Vernon 11, 12, 17, 138, 215
La Rioja 87
Robles, Gil 9, 170
Robuster, José 60
Rocker, Rudolf 51
Roldán, Manuel 301
Ronda (Malaga) 48
Russia 20, 47

S

Sabaté Llopart, Manuel 47
Sabaté Llopart, Quico 47
Safón, Ramón 279
Safor (Valencia) 164
Salas Altas (Huesca) 267
Salazar, Antonio de Oliveira 10, 45
Sallent (Barcelona) 165
Sanjurjo Sacanell, José 9
Santander 128
Sanz, Ricardo 47
Sariñena (Huesca) 83, 84
Sástago (Zaragoza) 91
Schapiro, Alexander 187
Seguí, Salvador 44, 47
Seisdedos (Francisco Cruz Gutiérrez) 167
Seros (Lérida) 261
Seville 22, 56, 83
sex education 50
sindicato único 36, 43, 48, 276
 organizational make-up 37–38
socialist unionism 22
Solerás (Lérida) 261
Solidaridad Obrera 50, 54, 59, 64, 66, 211, 233, 311
Solidaridad Obrera 311
Solidaridad Proletaria 50

Sopena, Eugenio 262
Souchy, Augustín 268
Soviet Union 2, 34, 133, 139, 143, 290
Spanish fascism. *See* Falange
Spanish Republic (1931) 46, 57, 158, 167, 181
Spanish Revolution
  militirization of militias 226–232
  outbreak of 63, 141–145
Spartakists 20, 54
Stalinism 2, 3
Stalin, Joseph 2
Steel and Metalworking Federation of Catalonia 111
Suria (Barcelona) 165
syndicalism 28
  ideology of 28–32
  See also anarcho-syndicalists/ anarcho-syndicalism

T

Tardienta (Huesca) 84
Telefónica, The 69
Tercio (Spanish Foreign Legion) 170
Teresa de Cofrentes (Valencia) 129
Teruel 80, 129
Third International 44
Thomas, Hugh 21, 98, 300
La Tierra 50
Tierra y Libertad 50
Tierra y Libertad 26, 87
Torre del Compte (Teruel) 169
Torre, La (Valencia) 128
Torrens Company 66
Torres de Segre (Lérida) 261
Toryho, Jacinto 204, 209
treintistas 52, 166, 183, 189, 279
Tremp (Lérida) 261
Trotsky, Leon 20, 44, 48

U

UGT (Workers' General Union) 22, 41, 53, 58, 59, 67, 87, 94, 108, 163, 286, 309
  Executive Commission 118
  growth of 42
  membership 44, 45, 46, 162, 293
UHP (Union of Proletarian Brothers) 53, 57, 141, 171
Unión Republicana 89
United States 20
  anarchism in 20
Uprising of December 1933 168
Uprising of January 1933 168
US Bell 69
USSR 306. *See* Soviet Union
Utiel (Valencia) 97
Utrillas (Teruel) 84

V

Valderrobres (Teruel) 87, 168, 169
Valdés, Nelson P. 112
Valencia 22, 93, 95, 97
Val'gorra (Lérida) 261
Vallina, Pedro 48
Vargas, Antonio 249
Vasílev, Pano 191
Vázquez, Mariano R. 47, 64, 75, 87, 96, 117, 118, 211
Vázquez, Salomón 248
vegetarianism 50
Verdú (Lérida) 261

Index

Vilanesa (Valencia) 128, 135, 295
Villacañas (Toledo) 128
Villas Viejas 127
Vinaixa (Lérida) 261
Voline (Eikhenbaum, V. M.) 51
Volunteers in Spanish Civil War 10
La Voz del Campesino 50
Vulcano Company 67

W

wages 103, 104–112, 237, 238–239
  communist 111
  differentials by gender 106–107
  family wage 106, 176, 239
  scale in agriculture 109
  scale in construction industry 109
  UGT wages during collectivisation 110
Wagner, Helmut 295
Weil, Simone 143, 144
women's emancipation 50
Woodworkers' Union 114, 124
worker's record book 116, 200, 206
workers' self-management 5, 6, 12
World War I 43

X

Xena, José 64

Y

Yartchuk, Efim 51

Z

Zalamea de la Serena (Badajoz) 164
Zaragoza 66, 80, 81
Zibecchi, Raúl 291

Support **AK Press!**

AK Press is one of the world's largest and most productive anarchist publishing houses. We're entirely worker-run & democratically managed. We operate without a corporate structure—no boss, no managers, no bullshit. We publish close to twenty books every year, and distribute thousands of other titles published by other like-minded independent presses and projects from around the globe.

The Friends of AK program is a way that you can directly contribute to the continued existence of AK Press, and ensure that we're able to keep publishing great books just like this one! Friends pay $25 a month directly into our publishing account ($30 for Canada, $35 for international), and receive a copy of every book AK Press publishes for the duration of their membership! Friends also receive a discount on anything they order from our website or buy at a table: 50% on AK titles, and 20% on everything else. We've also added a new Friends of AK ebook program: $15 a month gets you an electronic copy of every book we publish for the duration of your membership. Combine it with a print subscription, too!

There's great stuff in the works—so sign up now to become a Friend of AK Press, and let the presses roll!

Won't you be our friend? Email friendsofak@akpress.org for more info, or visit the Friends of AK Press website: www.akpress.org/programs/friendsofak